The Marketing Blueprint

Business Blueprints

This series presents the latest developments and concepts in the key business disciplines in an accessible way. Each title concentrates on the most crucial subjects within its area and presents the critical issues in a format and style that helps managers to develop real business skills. Using short case studies and practical examples the *Business Blueprints* series shows practising managers and students of management how to apply current management theory and best practice.

The *Business Blueprints* series is unique in its merging of the latest developments and concepts in management thinking with actual applications of those concepts.

Published
The Marketing Blueprint
Christine T. Ennew

The Strategic Management Blueprint
Paul Dobson and Ken Starkey

The Business Accounting and Finance Blueprint
Ian R. Davidson and Chris A. Mallin

The Marketing Blueprint

Christine T. Ennew

BLACKWELL
Business

First published 1993
Reprinted 1993, 1996, 1998, 1999

Blackwell Publishers Ltd
108 Cowley Road
Oxford OX4 1JF, UK

Blackwell Publishers Inc
350 Main Street
Malden, Massachusetts 02148, USA

British Library Cataloguing in Publication Data
A CIP catalogue record for this book is available from the British Library

Library of Congress Cataloging in Publication Data
Ennew, Christine
The marketing blueprint/Christine T. Ennew
p. cm.
Includes bibliographical references and index.
ISBN 0–631–18715–4
1. Marketing. T. Title.
HF5415.E675 1993   92–32455
658.8—dc20   –   CIP

Typeset in 11 on 13pt Palatino
by TecSet Ltd, Wallington, Surrey
Printed and bound in Great Britain
by Athenæum Press Ltd, Gateshead, Tyne & Wear

This book is printed on acid-free paper

1 0 06211092

For Graham Wyllie

Contents

List of figures

List of tables

List of exhibits

Preface

Probably the clearest indicator of the growing importance of marketing, both as a business function and as an academic discipline, is the ever-increasing number of books that are published on the subject. Many of these books warn of the dangers associated with product proliferation, but such strategies do not as yet appear to have harmed either publishers or their authors and the market for marketing books is continuing to grow. This book is yet another addition to the market, but one that is (hopefully!) differentiated in a number of respects. The aim of this text is to provide a concise introduction to the broad areas of marketing strategy and marketing management for the reader who wishes to obtain some familiarity with the subject without an intensive investment in time or money. Inevitably, in a book of this size, no one issue can be covered in any great depth; rather, the intention is to offer the reader a flavour of the subject in the hope that he or she will be sufficiently interested to seek out some of the more detailed studies of specific aspects of marketing management and marketing strategy. Like other books in the Business Blueprint series, it is targeted towards those students who are studying the subject either at post-experience or MBA level. It should also provide an accessible and readable introduction to undergraduates who are studying, but not necessarily specializing in, marketing.

The book is organized around fourteen short chapters dealing with the key components of marketing strategy and marketing management. The discussion in the text is supplemented by a variety of illustrations of the marketing activities undertaken by a range of organizations. These illustrations are primarily derived from the experiences of UK and European firms and cover both commercial and non-profit organizations. A number of case studies are included at the end of various chapters to encourage the reader to examine in more detail the ways in which a range of organizations have dealt with their particular marketing problems. For chapters where no case study is presented, the reader is given a number of questions to aid their understanding the material in that chapter. Suggestions for further reading are provided at the end of the book.

In writing this book, I have benefited from the assistance of many of my colleagues in the School of Management and Finance at the University of Nottingham. In particular, Helen Leverton provided invaluable assistance in the preparation of the manuscript during one of the busiest times of the academic year. Sally McKechnie managed to find time to read and comment on various drafts in between marking exam scripts, and her input has significantly improved the quality of the end product. Last, but by no means least, Helen Whalley and Mike Wright both provided useful comments as the book reached its final stages. The responsibility for any remaining errors is entirely theirs!

Christine Ennew
July 1992

1 Marketing: an overview

Introduction

Marketing is increasingly recognized as being central to the success of any organization, irrespective of its size or the sector of the economy in which it operates. This was not always the case. In the past many, manufacturing firms relied simply on the belief that the ability to mass produce products and price them competitively would be sufficient to ensure success because consumers would look favourably on products that were both widely available and affordable. This approach was successful when markets were typified by conditions of excess demand, in which consumers' willingness to purchase goods and services outstripped organizations' production capacities. Indeed, the initial success of Henry Ford was based on just such an approach to business. The original Model T was mass produced to a standard specification and sold as cheaply a possible to an eager public who were so concerned about owning a car that they were more than happy to take *any colour you like as long as it's black!*

However, economic conditions change; productivity increases and the development of new technologies combined with relatively slower rates of growth in income and wealth in Western economies have altered the business environment. The level of competition has increased and many markets are characterized by conditions of excess supply where the capacity to produce goods and services exceeds existing and expected levels of demand. In such a situation, the production orientation described above is not sufficient. On the contrary, with greater competition and with more sophisticated and quality-conscious consumers, business success requires that the firm become marketing orientated, and looks to the markets in which it operates with a view to developing and producing products that will fulfil the needs of consumers in those markets.

This marketing orientation is perhaps most visible, and most commonly associated with fast-moving consumer goods, such as food and drink, and consumer durables such as household goods, electrical goods and so on. In practice of course, marketing is important to all types of businesses, whether they are large or small, whether they produce tangible goods or intangible services or ideas, and whether they sell to final consumers or to other businesses. This chapter examines what is meant by the term *marketing*, how the concept has evolved and explains its relevance in both commercial and non-profit-making organizations. Finally, a brief overview of the processes of marketing management is presented to provide a framework for the rest of the book.

What is marketing?

The term 'marketing' is one that is widely used and misused. To some it has an image of glamorous and exciting careers; to others it concerns the cynical exploitation of consumers using a variety of means of persuasion. Certain marketing activities such as selling and advertising are the most visible and least mysterious parts of marketing expenditure. Consequently, they often form the central components of many people's understanding of the subject. In practice, marketing as a business philosophy encompasses many more activities; it is not always glamorous and rarely does it involve persuading consumers to buy what they do not actually want.

The basis of marketing is the need for exchange. Most economies operate on the principle of specialization in production through the division of labour. This specialization in turn creates a need to exchange goods and services, either for money or for other goods and services. For this exchange to occur, buyers and sellers must be willing participants, they must have something to gain from the exchange process and they must have knowledge of what is available within a market. The purpose of marketing is to manage this buyer–seller interface and facilitate the process of exchange between the two parties. It is perhaps useful to stress that neither of the two parties enters into this exchange for altruistic purposes. Buyers and sellers both enter into exchange relationships in order to achieve their own particular objectives. In the case of a commercial business, the objective may be profit; in the case of the consumer, the objective may be to increase satisfaction. One of the key principles of marketing is that any organization will improve its chances of achieving its own objectives if it helps its consumers to achieve their objectives. This marketing orientation views organizational success as being driven by the provision of long-term consumer satisfaction.

Thus, in broad terms we can see marketing as being concerned with facilitating exchange and improving business performance through the creation of long-term customer satisfaction. However, there is rather more to the marketing philosophy than this basic definition would indicate. There are five key dimensions to marketing, as indicated in figure 1.1.

Consumers

The guiding principle of marketing is that the needs and wants of the consumer should be central to the business approach adopted by an organization. The nature of the goods or services that an organization produces should be guided by these needs and wants rather than by simple criteria of cost and efficiency in production. The organization must therefore concern itself with clearly identifying its consumers. It is not sufficient simply to know who these customers are; the organization must also establish what they expect and what they want. Consumers may be

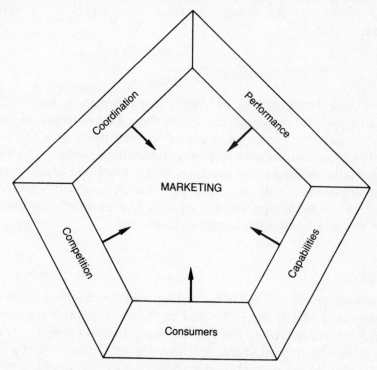

Figure 1.1 The elements of marketing

viewed as a single group or as separate sub-groups (segments) with distinctive needs and wants. The products that are produced should match the needs of the organization's consumers, in terms of the features and benefits offered, their availability and their price.

Organizational capabilities

We should perhaps note at this point that it would be naive to suggest that marketing simply requires that the organization establish consumer needs and supply products that precisely match those needs. If it were to do so, an unnecessary diversity of products may result, because consumer requirements are both highly variable and frequently change. With such a diversity, it is likely that production, inventory and marketing costs will be so high that the organization cannot then operate profitably. Thus, in reality, the marketing approach involves analysing consumer needs and evaluating the organization's capacity to supply those needs and whether it is appropriate to do so given the nature of the business environment. The ultimate aim is to ensure that the organization creates a match between what its consumers want and the type of products it is capable of supplying.

Competitors

Adopting and implementing a marketing orientation also acts as a competitive tool for an organization in that the organization which is most successful at meeting the needs of its consumers in a cost-effective way will be placed in a relatively strong competitive position. In practice, it may not matter whether the products being marketed are a very good match to consumer needs or a very poor match in absolute terms, what does matter is whether the organization is able to meet consumer needs more or less effectively than its competitors.

Coordination

As an element in our concept of marketing, coordination is concerned with the importance of the interrelationships between marketing and other functional activities within the organization. In the current competitive climate, it is often suggested that marketing is far too important a function to be left solely to the marketing department; rather it should be seen as a business philosophy and an orientation towards consumers that must permeate the entire structure of an organization. The marketing-orientated organization will be successful only if the marketing philosophy is adopted, not just at senior management level but by employees at every level. Consequently, marketing is not just external in orientation, it is also internal. Internal marketing concerns itself with ensuring that staff at all levels within an organization are aware of and understand their role in developing and maintaining a marketing orientation. For example, the successful turnaround of SAS (Scandinavian Airline System) by Jan Carlsson owed much to his own commitment to the marketing philosophy and his ability to communicate this philosophy to staff throughout the company.

Coordination is not just about ensuring a common belief in the marketing philosophy at a given point in time, it is also about ensuring that marketing plays a key role in organizational development over time. To develop successfully, an organization must remain aware of its customers and competitors and be responsive to changes in its markets. A failure to do so can potentially have serious consequences. For example, the Hollywood film industry found itself in considerable difficulty in the late 1950s and 1960s because of a failure to recognize the growing importance of television, while the Swiss watch industry suffered a substantial loss of sales in the 1970s because of a failure to appreciate the market potential of the electronic watch. Thus, marketing is not simply a short-term tactical component of business activities; it has a critical role to play in ensuring the long-term survival of an organization.

Performance

Marketing should be viewed as an activity that is concerned with improving organizational performance; certainly it will increase costs but successful marketing will also provide the means to increase sales and profits. Extra costs may be incurred in order to establish the nature of consumer demand and modify products in order to come as close as possible to matching this demand. In turn, this would typically lead to either an increase in the volume of sales or the ability to charge a rather higher price for a product which more closely matches consumer needs, and thus generate a higher revenue.

Central to the concept of marketing is the need for organizations to adopt a proactive approach to their markets. Marketing is not just about identifying consumer needs. It is also about anticipating changes in consumer requirements so as to enable an organization to gain a competitive edge by being first into the market with new products that reflect changing consumer demands. Indeed, some authors suggest that the ability of an organization to develop a truly proactive approach and identify markets that do not yet exist will be the key to future success. Hamel and Prahalad (1991), for example, argue that the organization should see itself as a portfolio of competencies and that it should look to build markets around these competencies. They go on to argue that it is no longer sufficient for an organization to follow its consumers; it needs to lead them. This does not imply that organizations should ignore their consumers; rather it recognizes that it is rarely possible for the consumer to articulate a need for the truly innovative product. It is doubtful whether many consumers could have expressed a need for the microwave oven or the compact disc player before those products existed. Thus, rather than simply focusing on expressed consumer needs, the organization should try to understand consumer lifestyles and aspirations, and lead consumers to where they wish to go through the development of innovative products.

An organization with a marketing orientation is one that places the consumer at the centre of its business and attempts to develop products and services that meet the needs and expectations of those consumers, both now and in the future. To do this effectively, an organization must focus its attention on the nature of consumer needs and wants and not just on the range of products that meet those needs. Focusing attention on the products themselves rather than customer needs can lead a business into what Levitt (1961) calls the 'marketing myopia' trap. One of the often quoted factors behind the decline of the railway companies in America was the belief, on the part of management, that railways were their business; in truth, they were in the transportation business and the recognition that they operated to service these particular needs might have provided them with a sounder base for future development. Thus, for example, the drill manufacturer, Black and Decker, would be mistaken if it defines its business as being the manufacture of drills. The firm's real business is to provide customers with the ability to make holes in solid objects. Similarly, Rank Xerox should be seen not as a manufacturer of photocopiers but rather as providing customers with the means of reproducing documents. For any organization, the essence of successful marketing is to focus attention on providing customers with the means to fulfil specified needs or wants.

The marketing function therefore encompasses a wide variety of techniques and activities. It is concerned with identifying and analysing existing and potential markets; understanding consumer's motivations and behaviour in those markets; and identifying groups of consumers of particular interest to the organization. To build the link between the organization and its consumers requires the development of an appropriate marketing strategy and an appropriate marketing mix. The marketing strategy defines the organization's target markets and identifies the ways in which products are to be presented to those markets. The marketing mix refers to marketing variables that the organization can use and control in presenting products to the target market and it is commonly referred to as the 'four Ps'. The components of this marketing mix are:

- Product
- Price
- Promotion
- Place

and these must be managed to ensure that the right type of product is available at the right price, in the right place and that the right consumer is aware of this. Although these four elements of the marketing mix are of undoubted importance, their simple manipulation will provide little in the way of long-term solutions to an organization's marketing problems. Effective marketing is dependent on the organization taking a strategic view and considering marketing as an integrated and driving force in its long-term strategy and planning.

The development of the marketing concept

The marketing orientation described above is not the only approach to business. The ways in which organizations could conduct their business and face their markets can be described under four general headings.

The production concept

The production concept, which was mentioned briefly in the introduction to this chapter, is perhaps one of the most well-established approaches to business. It is based on the idea that mass production and low cost are the key to business success because consumers are interested primarily in wide availability and low price. This approach can be effective under conditions of excess demand, when the consumer is concerned more with being in a position to purchase the product itself than with the finer points of the product's features and attributes. It may be equally effective for products whose initial costs are high and for which there are substantial economies of scale (falling average costs with increasing levels of output). A good example of this approach is provided by Texas Instruments who, in the 1970s, concentrated their efforts on expanding volume and bringing down the prices of products such as hand-held calculators. Although potentially very effective, such an approach can equally be vulnerable to changes in consumer tastes and changes in technology which affect production process. For example, the development of manufacturing techniques such as CAD, CAM and flexible manufacturing systems has enabled many organizations to produce a considerable variety of products cost effectively (economies of scope). These economies of scope have become more important than economies of scale in many industries; if variety can be supplied at a low cost, there will be little for the organization to gain from mass producing standardized products at a similarly low cost.

The product concept

The product concept is in many respects a research and development driven approach to business, often characterized as the desire, on the part of the organization to *build a better mousetrap*. It is based on the premise that consumers will prefer products with the best range of features, performance or quality. While this approach may be effective in small, specialist niche markets (e.g. Rolls Royce cars), there is the danger that following the product concept may lead organizations into the marketing myopia trap, as discussed earlier. The Swiss watch industry provides a good example of this problem. Despite having invented the electronic watch, Swiss manufacturers, convinced of the superiority of their high-quality mechanical watches, made no real attempt to exploit this innovation and as a consequence, lost a large share of their market to Japanese and other Far Eastern competitors in the 1970s.

The selling concept

The underlying premise of the selling concept is that consumers may be interested in the organization's products but will not actively seek to make a purchase. Business success depends therefore on actively and aggressively selling those products to the consumer. The essence of the selling concept is succinctly described by Kotler (1991) as *selling what you make rather than making what you sell* and it is essentially a 'sales push' approach to business. In the short term, the selling concept can provide the basis for success, but there is the problem that aggressive selling without specific consideration of customer needs will lead to short-term gains at the expense of long-term losses.

The marketing concept

Many of the elements of the marketing concept have been outlined earlier in this chapter. In essence it is an approach to business based on consumer sovereignty and the presumption of 'demand pull' – that is, sales will be generated because consumers will actively seek the product being offered if that product provides a good match to their needs. It would be a mistake to consider the marketing concept as a simple alternative to any of the approaches outlined above. It is not. In many senses, the marketing concept embraces these approaches. Concentrating on low cost, mass production may be appropriate, but only if that is what consumers expect and that is what is appropriate in the chosen market. Similarly, research efforts to *build a better mousetrap* are equally important as a source of product innovations, but will only be successful if developed in conjunction with marketing. Finally, while the importance of personal selling should not be underestimated, it will be more effective and beneficial in the long term if the product is one that consumers require.

Recent years have seen a modification of the marketing concept as an approach to business and this is usually described as the societal marketing concept. Although the societal marketing concept is often treated as distinct from the marketing concept, it is essentially a development of the traditional approach. Societal marketing argues that organizations should try to maintain a balance between the interests of the organization itself, the interests of consumers and the interests of society. It demands that organizations behave in a manner that is socially responsible and suggests that the reward for social responsibility will be in the form of improved long-term profitability. Green marketing is one variant of societal marketing that has become increasingly important in recent years. An example of the application of the societal marketing concept is presented in exhibit 1.1.

> ## Exhibit 1.1 Social responsibility in marketing
>
> ### Tesco
>
> Tesco, one of the United Kingdom's leading supermarket chains, recently announced a £3m promotional campaign – *Computers for Schools* – in conjunction with Acorn, the United Kingdom's largest supplier of computers to schools. The campaign reflects the growing importance of social responsibility in marketing and is part of Tesco's attempts to create a mutually beneficial presence in local communities. Recent market research by MORI indicated that 72 per cent of consumers were more likely to purchase from a company that supports the community, and 62 per cent believed that such companies would not sell poor quality products.
>
> The two aims of this promotional campaign are to improve computer literacy and boost store traffic. Tesco's customers will receive a computer voucher for every £25 spent and these vouchers are then passed on to local schools. Once the school has collected a large enough number of vouchers, they can exchange these vouchers for computer hardware or software. A standard software package requires 200 vouchers – equivalent to £5,000 worth of expenditure in Tescos.
>
> *Source:* Slingsby (1992a).

The scope of marketing

So far, much of our discussion of marketing has implicitly centred around the role of marketing in commercial organizations. But the development of a marketing orientation is not just restricted to businesses. On the contrary, marketing is relevant to any organization, whether it is a non-profit-making body, a public sector organization, a commercial business or an industrial conglomerate. Marketing concerns itself with understanding what customers want and attempting to match these wants to the products or services that the organization is supplying. In the business environment these customers pay directly for goods and services. In other areas, such as health and education, there is no direct purchase, but the users of these

---

Exhibit 1.2   Non-profit marketing

Marketing Britain's universities

Britain's universities are operating in an increasingly competitive environment. Changing legislation has created opportunities for polytechnics to become universities; research and teaching are to be exposed to public scrutiny and institutions are having to compete for students, staff and funding (from both private and public sectors). In response to these changes, Britain's universities are moving out of their ivory towers and embracing the marketing methods more commonly associated with commercial organizations. Having recognized the need to build credibility in a variety of target markets (students, staff, government, industry), a number of universities have turned to design consultancies to help them establish clear corporate identities. The University of Nottingham took this process a stage further, taking out a full-page advertisement in a national newspaper to herald the publication of the annual report. The polytechnics have also been actively involved in marketing their services and Wolverhampton Polytechnic has introduced an innovative new service – the Higher Education Shop. Located in a prime city centre sight, the shop offers help and advice to people who are interested in polytechnic courses but who might otherwise be discouraged by the intimidating atmosphere of the institution itself.

Source: Hall (1992).

---

services are customers nevertheless. Developing a marketing orientation will enable public sector organizations to meet the needs of these 'customers' more effectively and thus improve organizational performance. Exhibit 1.2 explains the growing importance of marketing in Britain's universities.

Marketing management

The previous discussion has focused on the meaning of the term *marketing* and the importance of developing a customer focus in the conduct of business. We now consider how that translates into more practical management activities. In many senses, this is the main purpose of the book and the current chapter will simply attempt to give an overview and a framework within which this aim can be achieved.

Marketing management can perhaps best be thought of as the implementation of marketing concepts to deal with practical problems. A popular, but simplistic, image of marketing managers is that their key objective is to expand the level of demand for the organization's products or services. Certainly, marketing managers will often concentrate on the specific objective of increasing the level of demand, but their more general concern is with regulating the level, timing and character of demand for a product. The nature of the current level of demand compared with what is required in order to achieve corporate objectives will determine exactly how the level of demand should be managed. In principle, according to Kotler, eight different demand situations can be identified. Different marketing tasks are associated with each. These are summarized in table 1.1.

Negative demand
Most or even all important segments in a market dislike the product, even to the extent of being prepared to pay a price to avoid it – e.g. some people have a negative demand for dental care, others have a negative demand for air travel. The task of marketing in this situation is generally to identify the cause of negative demand and attempt to counter it. For example, if the product has a poor reputation or image, or its features or performance are inadequate, then marketing managers will need to consider how to alter

Table 1.1 Possible demand states

Demand state	Marketing task	Formal name
Negative demand	Disabuse demand	Conversional marketing
No demand	Create demand	Stimulational marketing
Latent demand	Develop demand	Developmental marketing
Faltering demand	Revitalize demand	Remarketing
Irregular demand	Synchronize demand	Synchromarketing
Full demand	Maintain demand	Maintenance marketing
Overfull demand	Reduce demand	Demarketing
Unwholesome demand	Destroy demand	Countermarketing

Source: Kotler (1973).

the reputation of the product, whether to change its features and generally determine how to ensure that the correct image is created for that product.

No demand

This usually covers products with no perceived value in a particular market. In relatively crime-free areas, for example, there may be no demand for security systems because consumers may not appreciate the need for such products. The task of marketing then becomes one of stimulating demand for that product. In practice, this often means persuading consumers to buy or use a particular product or service. This element of persuasion means that stimulational marketing is often subject to criticism for being manipulative, but of course we must remember that it may be beneficial in many cases, such as encouraging vaccination and encouraging health screening.

Latent demand

In this case, a large group of consumers share a need for something that does not yet exist in the form of an actual product – e.g. the user-friendly computer system or the good-tasting, nicotine-free cigarette. The task of marketing is then to identify the nature and characteristics of latent demand, establish (often in conjunction with R&D) whether a product can be developed to meet these characteristics and determine how it should be presented to the market.

Faltering demand

In this case, the demand for a product is declining and this decline represents something more serious than a temporary drop in sales. Examples might include rail travel in the United States, vinyl records or mechanical watches. The task of marketing is to identify causes of decline and to reassess the nature of the product, its features, its target market and the marketing campaign with a view to either reviving demand for the product or deleting it. We should perhaps note that attempts to revive a product go beyond simply relying on large-scale advertising and promotional efforts since these often act as an indication to the consumer that the particular product is experiencing difficulties.

Irregular demand

Irregular demand is arguably one of the most common situations facing anyone involved in marketing in the service sector. It involves a situation where the pattern of demand is based on seasonal factors or other sources of volatility, such as short-term economic fluctuations. There are many examples of this type of demand in food markets, holiday markets and travel markets. The task of marketing management in this situation is concerned with attempting to synchronize demand and supply. Marketing may tend to focus primarily on the demand side by discouraging use when demand is at its strongest, encouraging use when demand is at its weakest or finding alternative markets with counter-cyclical patterns of demand. However, there may need to be some consideration of the supply side and the potential to which supply can be increased by the holding of larger stocks, improved distribution or increased output.

Full demand
Demand is currently at a desirable level and one that is consistent with the existing corporate and marketing objectives. The main concern in this situation is to maintain this level of demand by continuously monitoring and adjusting marketing campaigns as and when attitudes change or competitive threats appear.

Overfull demand
Demand exceeds the level of supply on what appears to be a permanent basis – i.e. demand is above supply and there is no desire or ability to increase supply. Such a situation may occur with certain exclusive products such as specialist cars, restaurants or with non-renewable resources such as oil. The marketing task is to reduce but not remove demand – perhaps by making the product less available to less attractive market segments or by making it generally less available by reduced promotions, increased price or limited distribution.

Unwholesome demand
Any positive level of demand is regarded as excessive because of the undesirable qualities of the product. This situation is probably most commonly associated with 'vice' products such as drugs, smoking and other 'social cause' products. However, counter-marketing may also be relevant in the business community when it may be used to phase out firms existing products. This may involve ending promotions, raising price or even, for some products, the implementation of legal restrictions.

These categories of demand demonstrate that the task of marketing management is much broader than simply creating and maintaining demand – rather it involves responding to and managing patterns of demand within the market place. However, it is important to stress that this demand management does not take place in isolation. Marketing must manage demand more effectively than the competition in order to be successful and must be prepared to respond and react to what happens in the marketplace, not only in terms of existing and potential consumers but also in terms of competitors' activities.

How is marketing managed?

Marketing managers could be required to deal with a variety of demand situations as explained above. Each has different characteristics, presents different problems and requires different solutions. Since the demand characteristics of a product or service will change quite considerably over time, forcing managers to deal first with one situation and then another, it is important to develop a systematic approach to deal with a number of different sets of circumstances. Three key components can be identified in the techniques for marketing management:

- The need for planning.
- The management of the marketing mix.
- The need for information.

Planning the marketing effort is important to ensure that the marketing approach to a situation is consistent and coherent with the objectives and capabilities of the organization and the needs of the marketplace. The planning and strategy process is discussed in more detail in the next chapter, but its key function can be summarized as providing a systematic framework for the organization's marketing activities. Planning will establish targets, identify how and when those targets are to be achieved and establish who will take responsibility for the relevant marketing tasks. By stating objectives, procedures, processes and personnel requirements prior to the start of a marketing campaign, the plan also provides a framework for the monitoring and control of marketing activities.

Within the marketing plan, the set of techniques that can be used to influence the buying behaviour of consumers and therefore the overall level of demand is described as the marketing mix. This concept was described earlier in the form of the 'four Ps'. Although there are a number of different components of the marketing mix, it is the interaction of these components and their impact on the consumer that is important. In order to influence the level of demand and the behaviour of consumers, marketing managers must first understand what motivates buyers and how they make their purchase decisions. From this understanding the aim is to develop a marketing mix that will create a particular image for a product and send specific signals to consumers which may increase, maintain or reduce demand levels as appropriate. In order to do this successfully, it is important that the individual components of the marketing mix are consistent with one another; an attempt to create the image of a unique and exclusive product will be ruined if the product is available at a low price and in every high street store.

Effective planning and implementation is impossible without access to pertinent information. The need for information is not unique to the marketing function – any organizational decision-making process depends on a variety of information flows. However, the value of good information is being increasingly recognized, not only to provide the right sort of support for decision-making processes, but also to provide the organization with a competitive edge in its market place. Thus at every stage in the marketing process, whether the organization is trying to understand consumers, or understand, markets or establish levels of profitability for products or determine price, a variety of different types of information will be required. Equally, throughout a marketing campaign, information will also be a key component of any monitoring and control functions. Thus, in order to manage marketing it is necessary to obtain and manage information and this is the role of the marketing information system.

Conclusions

As markets become more and more competitive and customers become more sophisticated and quality conscious, the adoption of a marketing orientation becomes increasingly important in ensuring organizational success. This marketing orientation requires that the consumer be seen as central to the business and that the organization focuses its attention on identifying and responding to consumer needs as they are at present, as well as trying to anticipate future needs. However, the type of products that can be developed will be affected by the organization's own capabilities. The key principle of marketing is to be able to meet consumer needs more effectively than competitors.

If these principles are followed, the organization will be in a position to generate higher sales and/or command higher prices. Thus adopting a marketing orientation will provide the basis for long term survival and enable the commercial organization to improve business performance. Marketing can be equally important to non-profit-making organizations where the process of matching the organizations offering to the needs of its 'consumers' will improve organizational performance.

Self-test questions

1. How do changed economic conditions explain the increased importance of marketing as an approach to business?
2. What are the five important features of a marketing orientation?
3. How does marketing help businesses to out perform their competitors?
4. Why is marketing relevant to non-profit-making organizations?
5. What do you understand by the term 'latent demand'? How should marketing deal with such a situation?
6. What are the key elements in managing marketing?

2 Marketing strategy and planning

Introduction

The traditional view of marketing as a functional activity concerned primarily with managing the different elements of the marketing mix is increasingly being overtaken by the view that marketing needs, and should have, a strategic dimension. In a rapidly changing and increasingly turbulent business environment, it would be unwise for businesses to rely on largely reactive marketing policies. The need to anticipate and, where possible, manage environmental change is becoming the key to successful marketing. Indeed, many would argue that marketing is, almost by definition, a strategic activity. To market a product successfully is not just a matter of developing the right blend of marketing mix variables, it is also a matter of operating in the right markets at the right time. While marketing is becoming more strategic in orientation, it can also be argued that strategy in general is becoming more marketing oriented (Schnaars, 1991). The effectiveness of low costs and efficient production as a basis for competitive advantage has increasingly been replaced with the belief that the ability to create and maintain customer satisfaction is a more effective foundation for long-term business success.

This increasing overlap between marketing and strategy has resulted in some confusion over definitions of and differences between marketing strategy and corporate strategy. Clearly, there is a difference. Corporate strategies and their associated corporate plans deal with the broad issues relating to the way in which an organization competes within its operating environment, while marketing strategies focus more specifically on the nature of the interactions between the organization and its markets. In that sense, marketing strategies are best viewed as a subset of corporate strategies and marketing plans as a subset of corporate plans. The process of planning corporate and marketing activities becomes essential to guide business development in an increasingly unknown and uncertain future.

Developing a planned, strategic approach to marketing will help organizations anticipate changes in their environment and provide them with the means to sustain a competitive position in any given market. This chapter reviews the concept of strategic marketing, its role in the overall strategy process and the methods and techniques associated with the development of strategic marketing plans.

What is strategic marketing?

Precise definitions of the concept of marketing strategy and strategic marketing have proved elusive. As with the term *marketing*, there are perhaps as many definitions of marketing strategy as there are writers on the subject. Furthermore, a survey of UK companies by Greenley (1982) found that while most companies claimed to have a marketing strategy, the definitions put forward by marketing executives varied immensely and often had little in common. The issue is further confused by the tendency to use the term *strategy* in conjunction with a variety of marketing activities. Any marketing text will include discussions of pricing strategies, product strategies, advertising strategies and distribution strategies. The concept of a marketing strategy is, however, much broader than this.

Any strategy is concerned with the selection of the most appropriate course of action to take in the light of specified objectives, available resources and existing and anticipated environmental influences. This course of action is then implemented through the use of the most appropriate tactics. A useful way of conceptualizing the distinction between strategy and tactics is in terms of the distinction between efficiency and effectiveness. While tactics are primarily concerned with implementing courses of action efficiently, strategy is concerned with being effective, i.e. with following the correct course of action at the most appropriate times. Conceptually, an organization may find itself in one of four possible situations as shown in figure 2.1. Being inefficient and ineffective is clearly a recipe for disaster; not so the other positions. The organization that is basically efficient, but largely ineffective may still perform acceptably provided it is operating in a relatively stable and predictable environment. However, in the presence of rapidly changing and turbulent environments, there is a premium attached to effectiveness. In such circumstances, being effective but inefficient will at least provide the basis of survival, but the truly successful organization needs to be both effective and efficient. By emphasizing the importance of understanding the environment in which the organization operates and anticipating

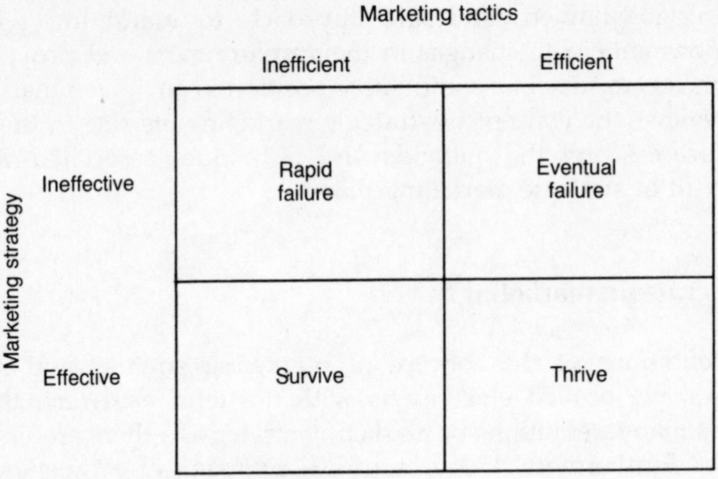

Marketing tactics

	Inefficient	Efficient
Ineffective	Rapid failure	Eventual failure
Effective	Survive	Thrive

Marketing strategy

Figure 2.1 Efficiency and effectiveness
Source: Adapted from Macdonald (1989)

changes in that environment, a marketing strategy will help the organization to be effective as well as efficient. In effect, both corporate and marketing strategies are concerned with finding a *fit* or a *match* between the skills and attributes of the organization and the opportunities offered by the market environment.

Strategy and planning

Strategy is often associated with planning, though as Dobson and Starkey (1993) point out, this need not necessarily be the case. Two common perspectives distinguish deliberate and emergent strategy. Deliberate strategy is the result of consciously planned activity, while emergent strategy is the outcome of patterns of behaviour within an organization that emerge unintentionally and have a degree of consistency (Shiner, 1988). In practice, although most strategies are likely to develop and appear on some continuum between these two extremes, any consideration of strategy requires some explicit treatment of planning.

Formulating a strategic plan has a number of benefits associated with it, including:

- reducing the risk associated with an unknown future;
- coordinating the activities of individuals and departments;
- encouraging management to think ahead and anticipate change;

- improving communications within the organization;
- providing an explicit focus on the product–market interface.

Inevitably, there are also costs associated with the planning process, including:

- direct costs of resources used to formulate the plan;
- opportunities that may be missed because of the time associated with the planning process.

Although it is often suggested that planning can result in organizations experiencing *paralysis by analysis*, it is widely recognized that an appropriate planning process can be beneficial in encouraging organizations to think, not just about how things are being done, but also about what it is being done and why.

We have already mentioned the growing overlap between marketing strategy and corporate strategy. Strategies are formulated at different levels within and organization and so are plans. One common framework for considering strategic planning is based on the notion of a hierarchy of strategies and an associated hierarchy of plans. Both Shiner (1988) and Boyd and Walker (1990) suggest that three levels of strategy can be identified, specifically:

- corporate level strategy;
- business level strategy;
- market level strategy.

This hierarchy is based on the idea of an organization being composed of a portfolio of strategic business units (SBUs). These SBUs are typically independent activities with responsibility for their own profits and control over the variables that determine profitability. They are also typically distinct in terms of the technologies used, the products offered and the markets served. In practice, the identification of distinct SBUs on all these criteria may be difficult, and as a consequence, the factors used to determine SBUs will vary across organizations. For example, the firms in the pharmaceutical industry identify SBUs according to product types such as anti-inflammatory drugs, cancer control drugs, etc. (Corstjens, 1991), while a food manufacturer may define SBUs as frozen foods, tinned foods, dry foods and beverages.

It is the potential existence of SBUs within organizations that underlines this concept of a hierarchy of strategies. Corporate-level strategies deal with all SBUs; business-level strategies focus on individual SBUs; and market-level strategies focus on specific product groups within an SBU.

However, the concept of the organization as a portfolio of SBUs will not apply in all cases. For many businesses, the SBU may be the organization itself, in which case the distinction between different levels in the hierarchy may become blurred. Analytically, however, it is useful to consider each element as a distinct stage:

- *Corporate strategy* Corporate strategy concerns itself with organizational development at the highest level including the definition of overall corporate mission and objectives, the coordination of different SBUs and resource allocation across business functions and across SBUs. It will integrate broad strategies with regard to finance, research and development, human resources, production and marketing.
- *Business strategy* Business level strategies are typically formulated at SBU level and will be concerned with establishing the basis for competitive advantage in relation to products and markets served. While strategy at this level will necessarily incorporate decisions relating to a variety of functional activities, it will also include marketing strategy as a key component. This marketing strategy will concern itself with how the SBU can establish and sustain a long term competitive position in its chosen markets.
- *Market strategy* Market level strategies focus on specific strategies in relation to specific markets. From a marketing perspective, strategy at this level can be thought of as being primarily concerned with the development of appropriate marketing mixes to achieve the organization's desired position in the relevant markets.

While the concept of a hierarchy of strategies and plans suggests a *top-down* approach to planning, this need not and probably should not be the case. The development of effective strategic plans requires inputs from various functional activities in a *bottom-up* process to ensure that what is laid out in the planning process is realistic and achievable at an operational level. This two-way information flow is essential in ensuring commitment to the plan at all levels within the organization. Each level of strategy might be expected to have an appropriate plan associated with it and objectives and strategies laid out at the corporate level should feed though to objectives and strategies at business and market levels.

Developing such a planned, strategic approach ensures that the marketing efforts of any organization are internally coherent, consistent with its goals and tailored to the needs of its target markets. It should also ensure that the resources available within the organization are allocated in

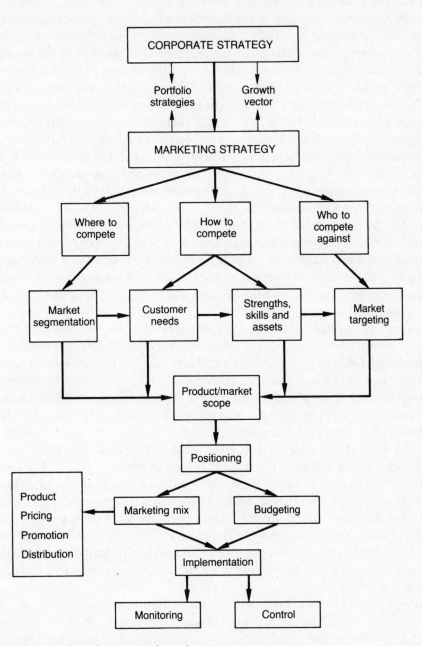

Figure 2.2 The elements of marketing strategy

a systematic manner consistent with specified objectives. Figure 2.2 presents a schematic outline of the key elements in any marketing strategy.

The nature of any marketing strategy will be dependent on overall corporate strategy and decisions regarding the composition of the product portfolio (the range of products offered) and the chosen patterns of growth (growth vectors) of the organization. This is not a one-way process: product portfolio decisions and the chosen pattern of growth will be made through interactions between marketing planners and corporate planners. Furthermore, the entire process will be conditioned by the nature of the operating environment, which is outlined in more detail in chapter 4. The essence of marketing strategy is to provide the organization with a sustainable competitive advantage in the markets in which it operates. This requires that the organization not only understands consumer needs but also identifies how those consumers can be grouped into different market segments. By identifying these segments and selecting target markets, the organization can determine where and against whom it intends to compete. The basis on which the organization will compete is the overall product offering and this should be formulated by matching internal skills and capabilities to customer needs.

Having determined where to compete, who to compete against and the basis of competition, the organization will have effectively determined its product/market scope, i.e. what products are to be offered in which markets. The next stage involves establishing an appropriate position for the organization's products in the target markets. The whole purpose of positioning products in markets is to establish a competitive edge for these products. For example, American Express green and gold cards are positioned as high prestige charge cards with a level of service (and a price) which reflects the status of the holder. Through creating this image for its products, American Express seeks to build and maintain a sustainable competitive advantage. However, the chosen product position must reflect attributes that are valued by the target markets (and not merely by the supplier) and the organization itself must be capable of delivering these attributes. In selecting such a position, the marketing strategy is essentially defining the image that the organization wishes to create for its product in its target markets.

Once a position has been established, that position will guide the formulation of the marketing mix. Product attributes, pricing decisions, methods of distribution and communication should all seek to reflect the chosen position. In effect, the marketing mix represents the tactics employed to implement the chosen strategy. However, the strategy process does not end there, since the decisions made with respect to the marketing mix must be operationalized and the outcomes monitored to check that actual outcomes match what was intended. Should the outcomes begin to deviate from what was planned, then there is scope for corrective action in the form of further modifications to the marketing mix, or even modifications to the overall strategy.

Marketing and corporate strategy

In developing either corporate or marketing strategies, most organizations will have to make decisions about resource allocation. This is likely to be complicated by the fact that most organizations will have a variety of products and many will have a number of different divisions (i.e. for different product groups, or for different geographic markets). Financial and human resources must be allocated between products and divisions in a manner consistent with the achievement of corporate objectives. Some areas will be designated for expansion, others perhaps for contraction. This process of resource allocation is a key component of corporate strategy and it indicates the direction in which specific markets or products are expected develop. It therefore provides direction for the development of market level plans.

A key element in resource allocation is the allocation of funds across SBUs – a process that is often described as managing the product portfolio. In addition to allocating resources to SBUs, there are also decisions to be made regarding the planned pattern of growth for different SBUs. Both these decisions are particularly important from a marketing perspective because they determine the parameters within which the marketing strategy must operate. They are also typically decisions to which marketing staff will have a significant input. While there are a variety of models and analytic frameworks that can be employed in guiding such decisions (see, for example, Dobson and Starkey, 1992), we will review briefly two of the most widely used techniques, namely the Boston Consulting Group growth share matrix for managing the product portfolio and Ansoff's product–market matrix for identifying future growth opportunities.

The Boston Consulting Group (BCG) matrix

The BCG matrix, which is illustrated in figure 2.3, works by classifying SBUs (or in some cases individual products) on the basis of their market share relative to that of their competitors and according to the rate of

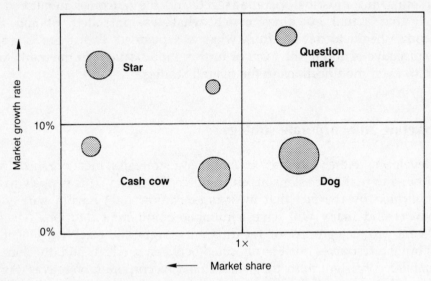

Figure 2.3   The Boston Consulting Group matrix

growth in the market as a whole. The division on the horizontal axis is usually based on a market share identical to that of the firm's nearest competitor, while the precise location of the division on the vertical axis will depend on the rate of growth in the market. In this example, a growth rate of 10 per cent is used to differentiate fast and slow growth markets. Products are positioned in the matrix as circles with a diameter proportional to their sales revenue. The underlying assumption in this matrix is that a larger market share will enable the business to benefit from economies of scale, lower per unit costs and thus higher margins.

Each product can then fall into one of four broad categories and on the basis of this, an appropriate strategy can be identified:

- *The question mark* (or problem child)   An SBU with a small market share in a high growth industry. The generic products offered by this SBU are clearly popular, but customer support for the specific company versions is limited. A small market share implies that competitors are apparently in a strong position and that if the products offered by the SBU are to be successful, the SBU will require a substantial injection of funds, particularly on the marketing side. If future market growth is anticipated and the products are viable, then the organization should consider increasing the resources available to this SBU to permit more active marketing of its products. Otherwise, the possibility of withdrawing the relevant products should be considered.

- *The star* This is an SBU with a high market share in a high growth industry. By implication, the star has the potential to generate significant earnings currently and in the future. However, at this stage it may still require substantial marketing expenditures to maintain this position, but would be regarded as a good investment for the future.
- *The cash cow* An SBU with a high market share but in a comparatively mature and slower growing market. The products offered are typically mature and in a strong position in the market with a high degree of consumer loyalty. Product development costs are typically low and the marketing campaign is well established. The cash cow will normally make a substantial contribution to overall profitability. The appropriate strategy will vary according to the precise position of the cash cow. If market growth is reasonably strong then a holding strategy, which simply seeks to maintain the SBUs position, will be appropriate. If growth and/or share are weakening, then it may be more sensible to pursue a harvesting strategy which requires that the organization cuts back on marketing expenditure and looks to maximize short-term cash flow from the products offered by the SBU.
- *The dog* An SBU characterized by a low market share in a low growth market. As with the cash cow, the products offered by this SBU will typically be well established but are apparently losing consumer support and may have cost disadvantages. The usual strategy would be to consider divestment unless cash flow position is strong, in which case the recommended strategy would be to harvest.

Although this approach is potentially useful, a weakness of growth share analysis is that it focuses only on one aspect of the organization (market share) and one aspect of the market (sales growth). Furthermore, the BCG matrix treats market share as the key objective and assumes that a large market share will mean lower per unit costs and higher profits due to either economies of scale or experience curve effects. Yet, in practice, many businesses may find that all their products are classed as 'dogs' because they have relatively low market shares. Nevertheless, those products can be highly profitable if they are explicitly targeted at the needs of a specific group of customers. Woo and Cooper (1982), for example, found that many organizations with low market shares still performed well by offering higher quality products and lower prices in mature, slow-growth markets. Clearly then, market share is not the only route to successful business performance.

Ansoff's growth vectors

A common framework for the analysis and determination of growth strategies is Ansoff's product–market matrix, which suggests that the strategy decision rests on whether to concentrate attention on new or existing products in new or existing markets. As figure 2.4 shows, this produces four possible options:

- *Market penetration* An organization pursuing a market penetration strategy is aiming to sell more of its existing products in existing markets. There are two basic routes to increasing market penetration: first, expand the total market, and second, expand market share. From a marketing perspective, market share can be increased by either persuading existing users to use more of the product (e.g. two applications of shampoo rather than one) or by attracting consumers from competitors. By contrast, the total market can be expanded by persuading non-users to use the product. It should be noted that market penetration will, in general, only be a viable strategy when demand is not at, or close to, its maximum.
- *Market development* This strategy entails expanding into new markets with existing products. These may be new markets geographically, new market segments or new uses for products. As a strategy, market development depends upon the organization being able to spot new markets, identify cost-effective mechanisms for market entry and formulate imaginative marketing campaigns to establish a competitive position. Exhibit 2.1 presents an example of market development strategies currently being pursued by a number of FMCG (fast moving consumer goods) manufacturers.
- *Product development* This strategy involves the organization operating in its existing markets and developing innovative or modified versions of its existing products to appeal to those markets. For example, many manufacturers of frozen convenience foods have reformulated their products to appeal to the increased concern about healthy eating in their traditional markets. Similarly, McVities and Mars have pursued similar product development strategies with the launch of ice-cream snacks based on Penguin Biscuits and Mars Bars respectively. A strategy of this nature relies on good product design, packaging and promotion, and often plays on company reputation to attract consumers to the new product. The benefits are that by tailoring the products more specifically to the needs of some existing consumers and some new consumers the organization can strengthen its competitive position.

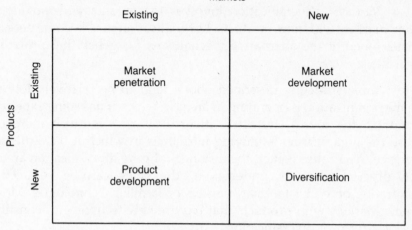

Figure 2.4   Ansoff's product–market matrix

Exhibit 2.1   Market development

Brand building in Eastern Europe

The newly liberalized economies of Eastern Europe are proving to be attractive areas for market development. Despite poor economic performance and low incomes, there appears to be considerable pent-up demand in many former Eastern Bloc countries. Companies such as Procter and Gamble (P&G), Unilever, Nestlé and United Biscuits have gambled on overcoming political and economic chaos in the hope of establishing first-mover advantages in what are expected to become some of the fastest growing markets of the future. Acquisition of local production or distribution facilities has been chosen as the most direct route into these markets. Thus Nestlé have acquired a 97 per cent share in the Hungarian confectionery manufacturer Intercsokolade, and P&G have acquired a share in Rakona, the Czechoslovakian manufacturer of soaps and detergents. Local production facilities should allow the parent company to develop branded products for these markets at affordable prices. However, the long-term success of these strategies is likely to be heavily dependent on the quality of the acquired plant, workforce and management.

Source: de Jonquières (1992).

- *Diversification* Diversification involves the organization moving into new markets with new products. Diversification may become necessary when none of the alternative mechanisms for generating growth are feasible.

The first three strategies described above tend to be relatively low risk, since the organization is operating in areas in which it has some experience. By contrast, the fourth strategy – diversification – is much more risky because the organization is moving into areas in which it has little or no experience. As a consequence, the instances of pure diversification are rare. When diversification is undertaken, the risks can be reduced by concentrating on either familiar markets or familiar technologies. Moving into new markets with products that require new technologies constitutes the riskiest form of diversification.

Both the BCG matrix and Ansoff's product–market matrix are recognized as tools that can be used in formulating overall corporate strategy. However, they may also be used at later stages in the development of a marketing strategy. The BCG matrix can be equally effective when used to analyse individual products rather than SBUs, and Ansoff's growth strategies can be relevant both to the pattern of growth of a product as well as to the pattern of growth of an SBU. As mentioned earlier, there are many other similar techniques for strategy formulation that also have direct relevance to marketing. It is important to stress, however, that none of these techniques can uniquely determine what an organization's strategy should be. Rather they should be viewed as analytical frameworks within which management can organize information and think about directions for future organizational development.

Formulating a strategic marketing plan

The key requirement from any format for a marketing plan is that it should follow a logical structure. Typically, such a plan would begin with a statement of objectives, accompanied by historical and current analyses of the organization and its markets. Following from this analysis, the plan would then identify the most appropriate strategic approaches to the relevant markets, both in general terms and in the form of specific recommendations regarding the marketing mix and levels of marketing expenditure. The final component would usually be an outline of the appropriate methods for implementing and controlling the plan. The issues of implementation often appear briefly at the end of any discussion of marketing plans and yet arguably the process of monitoring and controlling marketing activities is the most crucial factor in determining the extent to which a plan is successful or not.

While the main function of the plan is to offer management a coherent set of clearly defined guidelines, it must, at the same time, remain flexible enough to adapt to changing conditions within the organization or its markets. Each organization will have its own particular process for developing corporate and marketing plans. Rather than consider all the possible variations, a simple, hypothetical example of a marketing plan is presented in figure 2.5. Each element in this hypothetical plan may be explained as follows:

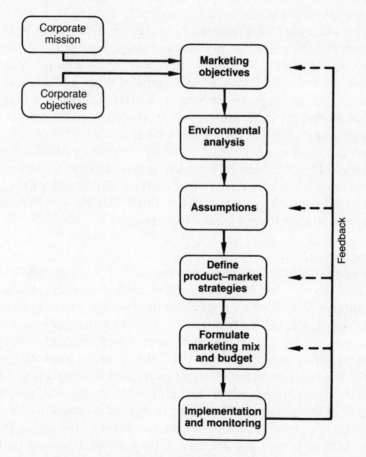

Figure 2.5 Developing a strategic marketing plan

Corporate mission

The corporate mission is simply a statement of what an organization is aiming to achieve through the conduct of its business; it can even be thought of as a statement of the organization's *raison d'être*. The purpose of the mission statement is to provide the organization with focus and direction. The precise nature of the corporate mission depends on a variety of factors, including the organization's history and culture. The commonest approach to determining the corporate mission is to rely on the product – market scope. The mission statement is then essentially based on target customer groups, needs served and technology employed. This approach may be of particular use from the perspective of marketing since it forces managers to think of the customer groups and the particular set of needs/wants that the firm is looking to satisfy. This brings us back to the concept of marketing myopia introduced in chapter 1.

Thus, for example in the case study in chapter 8, Derwent Valley Foods might identify their corporate mission as being concerned with 'the supply of snack foods for a sophisticated adult market'. A mission statement of this nature can offer guidelines to management when considering how the business should develop and in which directions. With the benefits of a clear mission statement, future growth strategies can look to rely on what are regarded as distinctive competencies and aim for synergies by dealing with similar customer groups, similar customer needs or similar technologies. Thus in considering their future direction, Derwent Valley Foods might look to expand into other markets with snack products (using their existing technology) or develop other related products that will appeal to the markets with which they are already familiar.

Statement of objectives

Objectives enter into the planning process both at the corporate level and at the market level. Corporate objectives define specific goals for the organization as a whole over a specified time period and may be expressed in terms of profitability, returns on investment, corporate turnover, earnings per share, etc. These will feed down through the planning process and will be reflected in the stated objectives for marketing and other functional plans. Clearly, the objectives specified for marketing will not be identical to those specified at the corporate level, and an important component of the marketing planning process is the translation of corporate (often financial) objectives into specific marketing objectives. These may take the form of targets for the size of the customer base, growth in the usage of certain products, gains in market share for a particular product type, etc. Whatever the status of a set of objectives, they must conform to four criteria: they must be achievable, they must be consistent and they must be stated clearly and preferably quantitatively.

Environmental analysis

As we have emphasized, an understanding of the environment is a key component in any strategy development since it affects the nature of the organizational mission and the stated objectives, the choice of strategic direction and the formulation of the marketing mix. Although some understanding of the business environment will have provided an input to the mission statement and the identification of objectives, a much more comprehensive analysis is required for the development of both overall and market-specific strategies. Environmental analysis requires a thorough study of the broad social, economic and political trends that may affect the organization, as well as a detailed analysis of markets, consumers and competitors. In particular, it may involve some consideration of the nature and extent of market segmentation. It also requires an understanding of the organization's internal environment and its particular strengths and weaknesses. Market research and external databases provide the main source of such information relating to the external environment, while an audit of the organization's marketing activities provides information on the internal environment. The nature of the business environment is analysed more fully in chapter 4.

Assumptions

Planning is concerned with guiding organizational activities in the face of an uncertain environment. Thus, in specifying any strategy it will be necessary to make some explicit assumptions about how both the organization and the environment will develop. These assumptions provide the basis on which subsequent strategies are formulated. It is important that these assumptions are clearly stated in the marketing plan to ensure those involved in the implementation are aware of the logic behind the chosen strategy. Furthermore, during the monitoring of plan implementation, an awareness of the underlying assumptions is crucial to ensure that planners can establish whether deviations from stated targets are due to implementation failures *per se* or whether they result from incorrect assumptions.

Defining product–market strategies (market targeting)

Given the environmental analysis and stated assumptions about future developments, planners must analyse individual markets or market segments to determine where the marketing effort should be concentrated. In so doing, planners define the organization's product–market scope. For each product–market combination, the strategic plan also requires the identification of a specific competitive position for a product in relation to customers, competitors and the organization's own particular skills and competencies.

The marketing mix
The market-specific variables that are typically under the control of marketing are product, price, promotion and place. The development of this marketing mix is guided by the need to ensure that the product is appropriate to the market in terms of its features, its image, its perceived value and its availability.

Marketing expenditure
The level of marketing expenditure will largely be determined by resource allocation decisions at corporate levels, but nevertheless a statement of the budget required and the way it is to be spent will be an important component of any marketing plan.

Implementation
Implementation requires the identification of specific tasks that need to be performed, the allocation of those tasks to individuals and the establishment of a system for monitoring their implementation – e.g. identifying the nature of any short-term marketing research that needs to be undertaken to determine how appropriate the product is, the nature of customer reactions and so on. The implementation procedure may also include some elements of contingency planning. However well thought out the marketing plan may be, the market environment is always changing. Consequently, certain planned activities may turn out to be inappropriate or ineffective. It is important to be aware of market changes and deviations from planned targets and be in a position to respond and, if appropriate, modify the strategy as new information becomes available.

Any marketing plan must include each of these core elements, though the precise format and description of each stage may vary from company to company.

Conclusions

In developing a marketing strategy, an organization is seeking to find the most appropriate position in its operating environment. This process may involve adjusting the nature of the strategy to fit into the existing market environment, though in some cases it may involve attempting to change the environment to fit with the strategy. The resulting strategy must enable the organization to meet the specific needs of its consumers and do so more effectively than its competitors. A number of techniques can be used in developing a marketing strategy. These tools are not intended to give precise answers; rather their purpose is to guide the thinking of those involved in developing marketing plans.

Self-test questions

1. Why is an understanding of the marketing environment essential to the development of an effective marketing strategy?
2. What are the advantages of a planned approach to strategy development?
3. What is the difference between organizational efficiency and organizational effectiveness?
4. What are the limitations of the BCG matrix?
5. What are the key stages in the development of a strategic marketing plan?

3 Information for marketing decisions

Introduction

Analysing the marketing environment is a continual process, and the information produced is a key input to all aspects of strategy formulation. In addition, the marketing function will collect and generate information that is crucial to activities throughout the organization. The collection, organization and analysis of this information is the responsibility of a marketing information system (MkIS), which in itself is part of the hierarchy of information systems that exist within organizations. This information will typically include details on consumers and markets, sales (past, current and forecast), production and marketing costs, and more general analysis of the operating environment (competitors, suppliers, distributors, etc.). In large organizations, the MkIS may be a complex and sophisticated operation employing a large number of staff, while in the smaller business, it may simply be the part time responsibility of an individual. However the MkIS is organized, it is important that marketing information is gathered, analysed and disseminated in a systematic fashion. This chapter reviews the composition and functioning of a MkIS and examines two specific components in more detail, namely marketing research and the marketing audit.

Marketing information systems

A MkIS is more than just data collection. Data by themselves are often of little use; they are simply a set of facts and figures. To be of use, data must be transformed into information, that is to say, they must be organized into a systematic and meaningful framework. This is the function of a MkIS. It will typically comprise a structure of individuals, procedures and equipment that are organized to collect, sort, analyse, evaluate and distribute up-to-date information required by marketers in the planning, management and control of marketing activities. Traditional marketing research which is often thought to be concerned primarily with consumers and their buying behaviour is only one component of this information system.

Typically a marketing information system will have four interlinked components as shown in figure 3.1.

The internal database

Essentially, the internal database refers to all data generated internally, much of which originates from accounting databases. In a manufacturing company, this database would typically include information on costs, production schedules, orders, sales and may also include some types of financial information relating to customers (such as credit ratings) and possibly also product profitability information. The information produced by an audit of the organization's marketing activities may also constitute a component of this internal database. The elements of such an audit are discussed in more detail at the end of this chapter.

The external database

The external database covers all types of information collected from external sources and such information is commonly referred to as marketing intelligence. An external database may simply take the form of press cuttings from newspapers and trade journals, published government statistics, analyses of sales reports or information gathered from competitors. However, it may also include subscriptions to external databases such as those supplied by Extel, Datastream, and Dun and

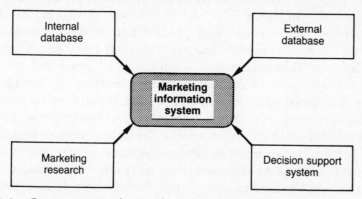

Figure 3.1   Components of a marketing information system

Bradstreet. Some organizations may also subscribe to databases that provide information on consumer demographics and credit ratings. A number of the sources of external information are discussed later in this chapter.

The marketing research system

While the internal and external databases generally focus on marketing intelligence, i.e. information which flows into an organization on a regular basis, marketing research is normally a process of information collection and analysis that is undertaken on an *ad hoc* basis to provide answers to specific questions. Marketing research can provide a variety of information from consumer views of the product or the supplier through to evaluations of the efficiency of distribution systems and the effectiveness of advertising. The marketing research process in discussed in greater detail in the next section.

The decision support system

Essentially this consists of a series of analytical techniques that enable marketing managers to make full use of the information provided by the other three sources. Some of the information available may be used in the form in which it is presented but much requires further analysis. Increasingly, the simple retrieval of information from databases is insufficient to aid decision making and additional analysis is required. This analysis may range from simple financial ratios and summaries of sales patterns to more complex statistical models.

The workings of the marketing information system are shown diagrammatically in figure 3.2. The information system is linked to the various sources of data and will process and analyse information for management use. Information may be collected from either internal or external sources. This information is collected, analysed and transmitted back to management to enable planning decisions to be taken and strategies developed. The information system continues to analyse the environment during the course of plan implementation to enable monitoring and control. In response to management requirements (represented by the dotted lines), the information system will collect and analyse data relevant to the marketing plan; any significant deviations from targets can then be identified and management is in a position to develop tactical responses.

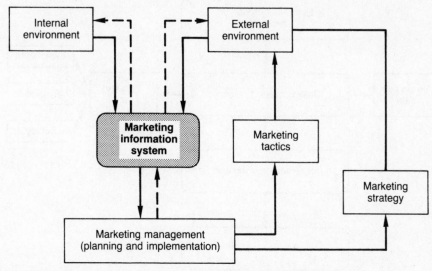

Figure 3.2   The functioning of a marketing information system

Marketing research

Marketing research is probably most commonly associated with the process of interviewing consumers about their product preferences, their buying behaviour, their levels of expenditure and their attitudes. In practice, marketing research is much broader than this, since it covers any form of *ad hoc* information collection required for the development and implementation of marketing plans. Marketing research is distinct from marketing intelligence: the latter is an on-going process of information gathering in relation to specific products and/or markets, while the former refers to the process of collecting information in response to a specific research need.

Although some marketing research can be undertaken 'in house', many organizations lack experience in this area and consequently a large volume of work is handled by specialist marketing research companies. For organizations that lack the relevant expertise, there are clear cost advantages to commissioning external marketing research, as well as the benefits of obtaining an objective view of the market situation and the organization's position in that market. Larger organizations, which more commonly have specialist market research departments, need to make the choice between internal and external providers of research. Given the presence of an in-house research facility, the cost advantages associated with the use of external agencies are less obvious, but may still be relevant

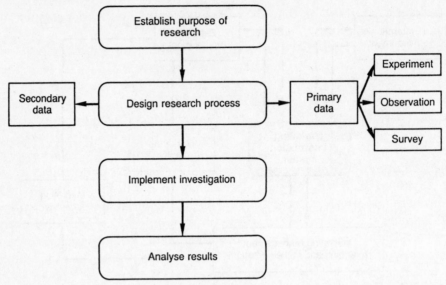

Figure 3.3 The marketing research process

if specialist skills are needed or if workloads are such that the in-house facility cannot provide the research required.

Irrespective of the source of marketing research, we can identify a typical procedure for carrying out this work as is illustrated in figure 3.3.

Establish purpose of research
Marketing research collects information that enables others to generate solutions to particular problems. The first step in any research must therefore be to identify the precise nature of the problem under consideration and establish what information is needed to solve it. Marketing research can be used to provide information for a variety of marketing problems. Although it is most commonly associated with understanding consumer behaviour, it may also be used for assessing advertising effectiveness, monitoring competitors activities, concept testing products, assessing sales promotion, etc. The type of data required for each type of study will vary, but it is essential at this stage to ensure that the data collected is appropriate to the nature of the problem that is under consideration.

Designing research process
The design of the research process requires first that the market researcher determines what type of data are required and what are the most

appropriate sources for that data. Subsequently, mechanisms must be designed for collecting that data.

The data being collected can be defined as either secondary or primary. Secondary data are data that already exist (often in a published form) but were collected for another purpose. Primary data are data that the researcher collects specifically for the project in hand. Secondary data have the obvious advantage of being considerably cheaper to collect and widely available, but the disadvantage is that they may not be entirely appropriate since they will typically have been collected with a different research objective in mind. Primary data, though much more costly to collect, have the advantage of being tailored specifically to the needs of the research programme. In practice, most market research will rely on both secondary and primary data. The research programme would begin with desk work to collect and evaluate available secondary data. Where necessary, desk research would be followed by field work to collect primary data for topics on which no appropriate secondary data is available.

For marketing purposes, a considerable amount of information is available in secondary (published) sources. In addition to government statistics, organizations such as Mintel and Euromonitor publish reports on a variety of consumer markets and there are numerous databases that can supply information on companies and markets. Some of the commercial sources of information are discussed by Norkett (1986), while the Central Statistical Office (CSO, 1990) reviews the available government statistics. Table 3.1 outlines some of the main published secondary sources of market research data.

In addition to the various government and commercial sources of information, useful secondary data can be collected from trade associations and professional associations. Trade associations represent the interests of particular groups of organizations and often have libraries containing information relating to particular markets. Professional organizations such as the Chartered Institute of Marketing and the Market Research Society are also potentially useful sources of market specific information. Finally, universities and colleges may be able to provide information for particular industries or markets based on studies undertaken by their own staff.

If the required information is not available from any of these sources, or is not available in a suitable form, it may be necessary to turn to primary data, which involves the market researcher collecting the data directly. There are three basic methods of data collection, namely experimentation, observation and survey. The characteristics of these different approaches are reviewed briefly below, but are described in greater detail in specialist

Table 3.1 Some sources of secondary data for market research

Source	Comments
(a) Government	
Annual Abstract of Statistics	Annual summary of key economic, social, industrial and demographic variables
Business Monitor	Industry-specific summary information including number of manufacturers, sales and imports
Monthly Digest of Statistics	Monthly data on key economic, social and industrial variables
Social Trends	Annual summary of key social variables, including population, education, health and leisure
Regional Trends	Information on population, income and expenditure by region
Census of Population	Detailed statistics on population and households produced every ten years
Annual Census of Production	Annual data on output, employment, capital expenditure, etc. for UK industries
Family Expenditure Survey	Information on weekly expenditure for a variety of products and services
Business Bulletins	Variety of statistics relating to UK business including orders, stocks, output, international comparisons of profitability, rates of return, etc.
UK National Accounts	Annual summary of key macroeconomic variables
(b) Commercial	
Financial Times Business Information Service	Information on aspects of national and international industry, including brand share, advertising and purchasing patterns
Kompass, Kelly's Guide	Company names and addresses
Extel	Financial and related information for UK and European companies
Datastream	Company accounts, share and bond prices, key economic indicators
Economist Intelligence Unit	Regular reports on specific sectors such as automotive and retail distribution, plus a variety of one-off special reports
Frost and Sullivan	Variety of sector-specific market reports
Jordans	Overviews of specific industrial structures and trends, variety of financial information
Mintel	Profiles of a range of FMCG, consumer durable and consumer service markets including information on customers and competitors
Euromonitor	Similar to Mintel, with European coverage and various special reports
MEAL (Media Expenditure Analysis Ltd)	Information on advertising expenditures for companies and individual brands
Target Group Index	Profiles of a large range of products according to who buys what
Keynotes Reports	Market size, structure and trends for some 200 consumer and industrial markets
Dun and Bradstreet	Supply data on business credit ratings, company accounts and offer a market identification service. Also publish *Key British Enterprises* and *Who Owns Whom*

market research texts (e.g. Parasuraman, 1991; Chisnall 1991; Worcester and Downham, 1986).

Experimentation

Experimentation is widely used when the research programme is concerned with a specific problem relating to the effect of a small number of marketing variables. This approach involves adjusting the levels of the variables that are of interest and monitoring consumer reactions. This monitoring would typically be accompanied by comparisons with a control group who may be located in a different geographic area or may be separated by time. Thus, for example, the researcher who wishes to establish how sensitive consumers are to price might arrange to reduce price at one outlet, increase it at another and leave it unchanged at a third. A comparison between sales across these outlets will give some indication of consumer price sensitivity. While this approach has a number of benefits, including the ability to monitor what consumers actually do rather than what they say they do, the researcher needs to be aware of the potential for uncontrollable factors to distort the outcomes.

Observation

This method of data collection essentially involves observing consumer behaviour in a particular marketing situation. This may involve observing numbers of consumers in a retail outlet, observing purchasing patterns or shopping habits or observing reactions to particular displays or promotional activities. Although relatively simple and inexpensive, this method of data collection suffers from the problem that although it may provide information on what consumers do, it gives no indication of why they follow particular patterns of behaviour.

Surveys

Surveys entail collecting information from the relevant individuals or organizations by directly asking questions on the issues of interest. Surveys can be conducted by mail, telephone or in person and the relative merits of each approach are outlined in table 3.2. Personal interviewing is potentially very valuable because it enables the researcher to use quite specific and complex questions. However, it can also be very time consuming. At the opposite extreme, postal questionnaires are more economical and enable the collection of large amounts of data. However, with a postal questionnaire it is rather more difficult to collect very specific or complex sets of information.

The success of any survey will depend on the construction of the questionnaire, and this is of particular importance in postal surveys where there is no opportunity for the interviewer to explain any aspects of the questionnaire which may be difficult to understand. Questions are typically of three types:

Table 3.2 Advantages and disadvantages of different survey methods

Criteria	Personal interview	Telephone interview	Mail questionnaire
Cost per respondent	High Interviews in respondents home are particularly costly, focus group discussions or interviewing in shopping centres may be less costly	Moderate Includes interviewers' time and telephone bills, but significant savings on travel time and costs	Low Primarily printing and postage costs. Costs will rise if response rates are low
Flexibility	High Interviewer can aid with explanations, rephrase questions, use visual materials, etc.	Moderate Some ability to rephrase questions and tailor them to respondents	Low Usually requires simply standard questions
Potential for interviewer bias	High Personal interaction between interviewer and interviewee can affect outcomes	Moderate Some potential for interaction biasing outcomes	None However, bias can arise from phrasing of questions
Ability to handle complex questions	Good Interviewer can explain and adjust questions to the situation. May encounter some difficulties with personally sensitive questions	Average Some ability to explain and present complex issues	Poor Complex questions are difficult to incorporate, but better chance of responses to sensitive questions
Sample size	Low	Moderate	High
Response rates	High	Moderate	Low
Speed of data collection	Moderate	Fast	Slow
Amount of data collected	Most	Least	Moderate

- *Open ended* Respondents are free to write in their own responses. Although this can generate a lot of useful information, particularly with regard to explaining behaviour, these responses can be difficult to analyse in large samples.
- *Dichotomous* These closed questions offer the choice of two responses only and typically are used to collect very simple factual data.
- *Multiple choice* Again, the question is closed in that the respondent can only answer from the options provided. This type of question is usually used to collect more complex factual data or relatively simple attitudinal data. Depending on the nature of the question, respondents may be restricted to a single answer, allowed to give multiple answers or offer rankings.

Exhibit 3.1   Direct and indirect questions

Instant coffee

In trying to understand why people are motivated to purchase particular products, marketing researchers must recognize that there may be a distinction between a *good* reason and the *real* reason for purchase. Asking consumers directly about their motives for purchase may produce unsatisfactory results because consumers may give *good* reasons for purchase and may be unwilling to reveal, or unable to recognize, their *real* reasons for purchasing a particular product. This problem is clearly illustrated with some market research relating to instant coffee. Women who were questioned directly about their preference for real coffee over instant coffee indicated that the decision was based on the superior taste of real coffee. However, an indirect approach produced rather different results. Two shopping lists were constructed which differed only in the type of coffee (instant or real). Half the sample received lists which included real coffee and the other half received lists which included instant coffee. Each respondent was asked to describe the type of housewife who would have prepared each list. The housewife who buys instant coffee was seen as being rather lazy and less well organized compared with the housewife who buys real coffee. Thus, the *good* reason for buying real coffee appeared to be taste, but the *real* reason appeared to be the desire not to appear lazy or disorganized.

Source: Haire (1950) quoted in Moutinho and Evans (1992).

Type	Example
Dichotomous	1. Are you? (1) Male (2) Female
Multiple choice, multiple response (factual)	2. Which of the following financial products do you own? (1) Bank current account (2) Bank deposit account (3) Building Society account (4) Credit Card (5) Life assurance etc.
Multiple choice, single response (factual)	3. Which is your main bank? (1) Barclays (2) Lloyds (3) Midland (4) National Westminster
Multiple choice, single response direct question (attitude/motives)	4. What was the most important reason for choosing your current bank? (1) Offered best service (2) Convenient location (3) Recommended by parents (4) Friendly staff
Multiple choice, single response indirect question (attitude/motives)	5. How would you describe someone who does not pay off their credit card in full each month? (1) Living beyond their means (2) Unable to manage their money (3) Carefree and enjoying life

Figure 3.4   Some examples of question types

Further distinctions are also drawn between direct questions, which are designed to relate directly to the respondent's own views and behaviour, and indirect questions, which are concerned with indirectly collecting information on the respondent's attitudes. Exhibit 3.1 gives an indication of the usefulness of indirect questions in marketing research. An example of the different types of question is shown in figure 3.4.

Once the survey has been designed, it is necessary to establish the sample to be used for the investigation. Unless the group under consideration is sufficiently small (e.g. specialist manufacturers of industrial products) it will be necessary to focus only on a sample of the respondents who are of interest. The main priority is to ensure that the individuals selected are representative of the group as a whole, and this is normally achieved through some form of random sampling. Alternatively methods of sampling, including stratified sampling, quota sampling and non-probability sampling, may be appropriate in specific situations and these methods are described more fully in standard marketing research texts.

Implementing investigation
This is the process of actually carrying out the research. The better designed the research process, the easier the process of implementation. Of particular importance at this stage is monitoring to avoid the introduction of bias, particularly when undertaking interviews. In survey work, the potential for bias can be minimized by standardizing the interviewing/ data collection process as far as is possible.

Analysing data
This is not the problem-solving stage as such; rather it refers to the organizing and analysing of data such that it can be used for problem solving. The degree of sophistication in data analysis will vary according to the problem under consideration. It is important to remember that interpretation plays a key role at this stage and so may be a possible source of bias in that the analysts may be looking for patterns they expect to see rather than patterns that are actually there. Indeed, as a general principle, two points should be borne in mind. First, market research is only as good as the data on which it is based and second, that data is only as good as the interpretation placed on it by the researcher.

Marketing audit

A marketing audit is an important contribution to any marketing information system. It is a systematic analysis and evaluation of an organization's marketing position and performance. An audit may cover the whole range of marketing activities within an organization, or it may simply focus on particular products or particular activities such as pricing or promotion.

While a marketing audit will focus on all the relevant marketing activities, the following may be singled out as being of particular importance:

Marketing capabilities

It is important to identify strengths and weaknesses in relation to the organization and operation of the marketing function. For example, an organization might focus on the following areas in considering its marketing capabilities:

- How flexible/responsive is the marketing department?
- What is the organization's image/reputation?
- How strong are product lines?
- What is the extent of brand loyalty?
- Is advertising/sales promotion effective?

Analysing these areas will often be dependent on subjective assessments, but their importance should not be underestimated because this information will often form the basis of future marketing campaigns.

Performance evaluation

Performance evaluation is the process of comparing the actual achievements of marketing with what was expected. This process is an important component of the monitoring and control of marketing plans. Particular issues that require attention include:

- Are sales meeting forecasts?
- Is advertising presenting the desired/planned message?
- Is the distribution system getting the product to consumers as anticipated?

This evaluation will identify weaknesses and strengths of current marketing campaigns, which can then be modified when developing future marketing plans. It will also provide the basis of tactical adjustments to marketing campaigns during the course of plan implementation.

Competitive effectiveness

Essentially this focuses on evaluating the source of a organization's competitive advantage. An assessment of competitive effectiveness will require some analysis and understanding of the organization's competitors, the markets they are targeting and the particular features they use to their advantage. For example, it has been suggested by Porter (1980, 1985) that the basis for competitive advantage may lie with either product differentiation, low/competitive costs or market nicheing. The marketing audit should seek to identify the exact basis that an organization is using to establish its competitive advantage.

A marketing audit can be conducted in many ways, including the use of questionnaires and there is a strong case for using an outside agency to conduct the audit to ensure objectivity. The most important points about any audit are that it should be systematic and that it should canvass a wide variety of opinion within the organization. Ultimately, the marketing audit will enable an organization to identify its strengths and weaknesses with respect to marketing and this information will provide and important input to the process of strategy development.

Conclusions

Marketing information is essential for the development of an effective marketing strategy as well as providing an important input to other business functions. The provision of data and information is the responsibility of a marketing information system. This information system will consist of internally generated and maintained data, including the outputs of a marketing audit; externally collected marketing intelligence and externally collected marketing research. The final component of the marketing information system is the decision support system, which represents a set of procedures and personnel responsible for converting data from internal and external sources into meaningful information, which is then used in formulating and monitoring marketing and other business strategies.

Self-test questions

1. What are the differences between marketing intelligence and marketing research?
2. Explain the differences between primary and secondary data?
3. Explain the relative merits of different methods of collecting primary data?

4 Understanding the marketing environment

Introduction

The marketing environment is a phrase used to describe the range of external and internal factors that affect the way in which an organization interacts with its markets. Understanding the nature of the marketing environment is a key component in the development of any strategy, whether at a corporate or market level, since the ultimate aim of such strategies is to develop a match between the organization's capabilities and the environment in which it operates. By its very nature, the process of analysing the environment, and attempting to anticipate developments therein, is not a one-off but rather a continuous process. The nature of the operating environment and the ways in which it changes is one of the main sources of uncertainty confronting marketing planners. Environmental analysis cannot remove this uncertainty but can help to reduce it.

As the marketing environments become more complex and the pace of change increases, effective environmental analysis becomes more important and more difficult. In a simple, fairly static marketing environment, organizations can draw on past experience in predicting future developments, and the degree of uncertainty about those future developments will tend to be low. Increasingly organizations find themselves in complex, turbulent environments, where past experience can only offer limited guidance as to future developments and the degree of uncertainty associated with environmental analysis is high. Yet, in such environments, the benefits of anticipating environmental change and preparing an appropriate strategy can be considerable, as exhibit 4.1 shows. This chapter reviews the main factors influencing the organizations operating environment and discusses frameworks within which these influences may be analysed.

Exhibit 4.1   Anticipating environmental change

Morton International

In 1982, US chemical giant Morton International acquired Thiokol for its speciality chemical, space and defence businesses. One of the apparently less attractive products in the Thiokol portfolio was automobile air bags. These bags were designed to inflate in the event of an accident, to protect the driver or front seat passenger from injury. From a manufacturing perspective, air bags were difficult to manufacture and were dependent on the use of a highly volatile mix of chemicals to inflate the bag in the event of a crash. From a marketing perspective the product appeared to have little to offer, being positively disliked by the prime customer group – the car manufacturers. That air bags had a future was confirmed in 1983 when Morton signed a deal to supply the bags to Mercedes-Benz to be fitted to all cars being sold in the United States. Morton anticipated that given time, air bags would become a standard feature for all cars sold in the United States and probably elsewhere. Accordingly the company invested heavily in improving quality and reducing production costs. This approach is now beginning to pay dividends. Chrysler decided in 1987 to install driver-side air bags in all 1990 models with Morton as sole suppliers, and the new US law, which could become effective by 1995, would require air bags to be fitted to all vehicles sold in the United States. By waiting patiently and then investing heavily as change appeared to be imminent, Morton International now has a 55 per cent share in the world market for air bags with excellent prospects for future growth.

Source: Skelly von Brachel (1992).

The marketing environment

The overall marketing environment has a number of dimensions. At the simplest level, we can distinguish between the internal environment (conditions within the organization) and the external environment (conditions outside the organization). The external environment can be further subdivided into the macro-environment and the market environment. The macro-environment includes all those factors that may impact on all organizations, irrespective of the market in which the organization operates, while the market environment, as the name suggests, is concerned with market-specific factors. These external environmental factors may create opportunities for the organization to exploit or may pose threats to current or planned activities. An outline of the key elements of the marketing environment is presented in figure 4.1.

The aim of any marketing strategy is to find some match between the opportunities presented by the external environment and the strengths present in the internal environment. Increasingly strategy is not just about matching strategy to the environment; it is also about matching the environment to strategy. That is to say, the environment should not be viewed simply as a set of constraints within which the organization functions. The environment (or aspects of it) can be managed by the organization to fit the needs of strategy. The extent to which aspects of the environment can be managed varies. Typically, macro-environmental factors are seen as being least controllable, while market environmental factors are more controllable. Vertical or horizontal integration are both widely recognized as strategies for adjusting patterns of competition and managing supply and distribution arrangements. Similarly, corporate advertising and public relations are becoming increasingly important as mechanisms for altering consumer perceptions of an organization. Even at the macro-level, there is scope for environmental management, particularly in relation to legal/political environments, where the lobbying process has proved successful for many organizations, either individually or in groups, as exhibit 4.2 shows.

The external environment

As figure 4.1 shows, there are two components to the external environment. The macro-environment is concerned with broad general trends within the economy and society while the micro-environment focuses on the immediate features of the market in which the firm operates. The macro-environment is typically of much greater relevance when considering the development of broad strategies, while the micro-environment (or market environment) will be much more important when considering the development of specific business/product strategies.

Exhibit 4.2   Environmental management

The brewing industry in the United Kingdom

In 1989, the Monopolies and Merger Commission (MMC) published its review of the structure of brewing in the United Kingdom. The industry is dominated by six national brewers, of which five have extensive tied distribution networks. Brewery-owned public houses were heavily restricted in terms of the range of products offered. The MMC regarded these arrangements as uncompetitive and counter to the interests of consumers. The initial report recommended that brewers be required to divest all tied outlets above a specified 2,000 maximum. Following extensive lobbying by the Brewers' Association this requirement was changed to divestment of half of all tied outlets above the 2,000 maximum.

The macro-environment

There are seven key elements in the macro-environment:

Economic environment

The economic environment covers all aspects of economic behaviour at an aggregate level and includes government economic policy – both actual and intended – as a particularly important element. Clearly, factors such as the level and rate of growth in incomes will have important implications for the level of consumer spending. The impact of these factors may vary across sectors and will typically be more substantial for consumer durables than for basic food and household products. Interest rates and the availability of credit may also have a significant impact on expenditure in relation to durable goods. Often, it is not sufficient to consider individual economic variables by themselves, as the interaction between variables can be important. For example, the gradual fall in interest rates throughout 1991 and 1992 was widely expected to stimulate consumer spending. In practice, falling interest rates had only a limited impact because high levels of unemployment and the threat of redundancy made many consumers reluctant to make large, expensive purchases.

Fiscal policy can have far-reaching effects on consumer spending through changes in the levels of tax imposed both on incomes and on

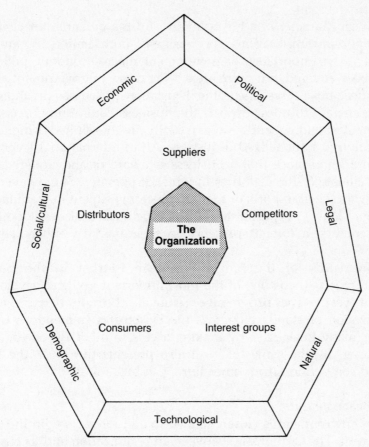

Figure 4.1 The marketing environment

products. In addition, for businesses operating in international markets, different rates and patterns of taxation can have a major impact on marketing strategies. Exchange rates may also be of particular relevance to organizations that rely on a high proportion of imported raw materials, or those with large export markets, or those whose domestic markets are subject to high levels of foreign competition.

In addition to taxation and exchange rates, firms operating in international markets will have to pay particular attention to relative income levels, income distribution and economic structure. The marketing opportunities offered by a rapidly growing, newly industrialized country (NIC) may be quite different to those offered in a slower growth, industrially mature country.

Political environment

The political character of a government, and the potential for change can have important implications for business, both nationally and internationally. The importance of government macro-economic policies has already been covered, but there are a wide range of government activities which affect businesses, including legislation (discussed in more detail below), general attitudes towards the business community, decisions on government spending and, more recently in the United Kingdom, the privatization of nationalized industries. At an international level, it is of paramount importance that a business is aware of and understands the political climate of the countries in which it operates. Some governments may actively solicit imports or foreign direct investment in manufacturing; others may look to concentrate on domestic industrial development and thus discourage a foreign presence in their markets either actively or passively.

The formation of the Single European Market in the European Community is perhaps one of the most important political developments in recent years. The progressive removal of trade barriers and the harmonization of standards across the EC creates tremendous opportunities for many businesses by making access to other European markets much easier. By the same token, it also presents threats in the form of increased competition from other European businesses.

The legal environment

The legal environment is closely related to and interacts with the political environment. The relationship between an organization and its customers, competitors, suppliers and distributors is constrained in various ways by existing and planned legislation, as are many activities within the organization. Furthermore, this legislation can vary considerably from country to country. In addition to the existing law of contract in the United Kingdom, there is a variety of statutory legislation which influences the way in which the organization conducts its business. Health and Safety legislation affects the internal activities of the organization, while the Food and Drugs Act 1955, the Trades Descriptions Act 1968, the Sale of Goods Act 1979 and the Consumer Protection Act 1987 all affect dealings between organizations and their consumers (whether final or intermediary consumers). The implications of this legislation are discussed in some detail in Palmer and Worthington (1992). A variety of legislation is also in place with respect to promotional activities (e.g. Advertising Standards) and the provision of consumer credit.

Exhibit 4.3   Burton Group plc

Responding to demographic change

The Burton Group has a portfolio of retail brands targeted at most sectors of the population. Top Shop and Top Man are targeted at 15–24 year olds, Principles and Principles for Men are targeted at 25–35 year olds and the 35+ age group is served by Debenhams and Harvey Nicholls. When the youth market was at its peak in the 1970s, Burtons invested heavily in Top Shop and Top Man. As this 'baby boom' generation grew older, Burtons placed increased emphasis on Principles and Principles for Men in the 1980s. More recently, Debenhams has been the target of new investment in recognition of the progressive ageing of the population.

Source: Palmer and Worthington (1992).

The relationship between organizations and their competitors is restricted through competition policy. Both the Monopolies and Merger Commission and the Office of Fair Trading are empowered to investigate and report on potential anti-competitive practices. In addition there is a further layer of competition policy operated at EC level. The significance of this legislation is well illustrated in the recent debate regarding the proposed Midlands Bank–Hong Kong Shanghai/Lloyds merger proposal. While the Hong Kong Shanghai bid was cleared at EC level, the Lloyds bid, because of its domestic impact, was to be referred to the MMC. Ultimately, the need to wait for an MMC recommendation (the outcome of which was by no means certain) combined with an increased bid by Hong Kong Shanghai, led to the withdrawal of the Lloyds bid.

The demographic environment
The demographic environment encompasses all factors relating to the size, structure and distribution of the population. The potential market for any product is affected not only by the number of individuals within the population but also by the age structure and regional distribution of that population. Although world population is growing at a rapid rate, the pace of change in developed countries is slow and in some cases virtually zero. By contrast, many of the developing countries are experiencing rapid population growth, largely as a consequence of high birth rates and falling

Table 4.1   Regional variations in income, cost of living and leisure

	Average weekly income (1989–90)[1]	*Cost of living (% above or below national average)*	*% of adults participating in DIY*	*% of households owning at least one car*
North	£265.62	–5.8	69.6	57.8
Yorks and Humberside	£263.52	–6.1	70.7	66.1
East and West Midlands	£302.74	–4.2	69.7	70.7
South East and East Anglia	£387.99	+2.5	66.2	78.5
Greater London	–	+21.5	60.5	63.2
South West	£317.36	–1.9	66.5	76.9
North West	£289.75	0.6	67.5	64.5
Wales	£263.08	NA	71.0	66.4
Scotland	£277.48	4.1	66.8	61.1

[1] South East and East Anglia includes Greater London
Source: Advertising Association (1992a).

death rates. One consequence of this is that developing countries tend to have very young populations, while the population of most developing countries is rapidly ageing. In the United Kingdom for example, the 50–54 age group is forecast to increase in size by 21 per cent by the year 2000, while for the 75–79 age group, the forecast increase is 18 per cent. This changing age structure has substantial implications for many companies. Those with products targeted at the baby, child or youth markets will find their markets under threat, while those organizations with products targeted to older age groups are presented with significant growth opportunities. Exhibit 4.3 presents as example of how one organization has responded to the changing demographic environment in the United Kingdom.

For many organizations, the regional distribution of the population may be of relevance along with the balance between urban and rural areas. In addition to regional variations in population, there are also regional

---

Exhibit 4.4   Environmental concerns

Müller falls foul of consumers

The German dairy product firm Müller has made rapid inroads in the UK market, with an 80 per cent share in the premium yoghurts sector and an 18 per cent share in the total yoghurt market. According to the company's UK spokesman, this success has been achieved by offering innovative and high-quality products. However, in its home market in Bavaria, Müller now faces a consumer boycott because of claims that it is despoiling the local environment. These claims include allegations of water pollution as a result of the discharge of 6,000 litres of cream into a local river and the allegedly illegal use of underground water supplies.

Source: Gow (1992).

---

variations in spending patterns and leisure activities, such as those shown in table 4.1, which can have important marketing implications.

Similarly, for many food manufacturers and domestic appliance manufacturers, the change in household structure and particularly the increase in the number of single person households has importance implications for the product range being offered. By the year 2001 it has been estimated that 14 per cent of households will be young single-person households. Thus, as well as family-sized microwaves, washing machines and dishwashers, many manufacturers now offer compact versions of the same products to meet the needs of the single person.

Social and cultural environment
Understanding consumer needs is central to any marketing activity and those needs will often be heavily influenced by social and cultural factors. These cover a range of values, beliefs, attitudes and customs which characterize societies or social groups. Some of the more significant cultural and social factors in the UK market include the growth of leisure time, the increased emphasis on healthy living and the quality of life, the changing role of women and the increased concern about the environment. Exhibit 4.4 indicates the potential dangers of ignoring consumer concern about the environment. Environmental concern has led to a tremendous growth in

the availability of 'eco-friendly' products, particularly in the markets for toiletries, cosmetics and household cleaning products, while concern about healthy lifestyles has led to a proliferation of fitness clubs, and low-calorie, low-fat and low-sugar foods.

At an international level, there can be tremendous variation in society and culture, and a failure to understand these country-specific factors can be a recipe for disaster for the international firm. This understanding is perhaps particularly important for culturally sensitive products such as food, toiletries, cosmetics and clothing, but can be equally important in affecting the ways in which non-culturally sensitive products are marketed.

The technological environment

Technology essentially refers to our level of knowledge about 'how things are done'. That is to say, understanding this aspect of the marketing environment is much more than simply being familiar with the latest hi-tech innovations. Technology affects not only the type of products available but also the ways in which people organize their lives and the ways in which goods and services can be marketed.

Clearly changing technology does have important implications for the types of products available, particularly as the increasing pace of technological change tends to result in the shortening of many product lifecycles. The long-playing vinyl record is now virtually obsolete as a result of the development of compact discs, the word processor is rapidly replacing the typewriter and the cine camera has been overtaken by the camcorder. Vacuum cleaners and irons were once expected to have useful lives of twenty and ten years respectively. Now, vacuum cleaners are replaced every seven years and irons every three years.

The impact of technology on manufacturing processes is arguably as important as its impact on products. Computer-aided design and computer-aided manufacturer (CAD/CAM) have shortened the time required for new products to reach the market and increased the variety of products that can be produced cost effectively. The benefits of CAD/CAM are clearly evident in the car industry. Mass production of standardized models, as championed by Henry Ford, to keep costs and prices low, is no longer the hallmark of the car industry. The use of CAD/CAM and robotics has meant that a large range of models can be manufactured cost effectively from one basic design.

The impact of technological development is equally in evidence in marketing activities. The development of sophisticated stock control, warehousing and distribution systems have reduced both order processing times and the need for high levels of stockholding, and have enabled

Exhibit 4.5   The changing natural environment

Marketing developments in the sun-care market

Consumers have become increasingly aware of the link between melanoma – the most severe form of skin cancer – and exposure to the sun. Furthermore, it is widely assumed that the depletion of the ozone layer (which protects the earth from ultraviolet light) will lead to an increased incidence of melanoma. The sun-care industry, which traditionally marketed products based on their tanning ability, has begun to change tack. Manufacturers are tending to use the phrase 'sun-care products' rather than 'sun-tan lotion' and the marketing message increasingly de-emphasize tanning ability and instead focuses on the sun-protection qualities of the product.

Source: Jones (1992).

organizations to offer a wider range of better-quality products more rapidly than was the case in the past. Bennetton, for example, uses computers to record sales at a range of strategic outlets. These sales figures are relayed back to headquarters and production plans can rapidly be adjusted to meet changing consumer needs. Computer systems have also contributed substantially to the growth of various forms of direct marketing such as direct mail and direct response marketing.

The natural environment
The physical or natural environment deals with factors such as the geography and climate of a particular market. Typically, we might expect that the natural environment is of greatest significance to firms operating in international markets, where climatic and geographic differences are likely to have a substantial impact on the types of product sold, distribution, storage and packaging (Hill and Still, 1984). Increasingly, however, the natural environment has become relevant to firms in domestic markets, not so much in the sense of what it is but rather in terms of how it is changing and consumer reactions to these changes, as exhibit 4.5 shows.

Other aspects of the natural environment which may increasingly affect marketing include the availability and cost of raw materials, energy and other resources, particularly if those resources and energy come from non-renewable sources (e.g. oil).

Clearly the importance of these various elements of the macro-environment will vary according to the particular situation of an organization. While each is important in its own right, environmental analysis must also recognize the importance of interactions between different elements in the environment since this can be a significant contributor to environmental complexity. Economic and political environments interact through government decisions regarding the management of the economy and the political pressures facing the party in power. For example, in an attempt to neutralize the political damage created by the Community Charge (Poll Tax), the 1991 budget incorporated a 2.5 per cent increase in Value Added Tax (VAT), the revenue from which was to be used to restrict the increase in Community Charge bills. For many organizations, this represented a significant increase in selling costs, which left them facing a dilemma. The increase had either to be passed on to the consumer in the form of higher prices in an already depressed market, or absorbed internally, reducing margins in organizations that were already suffering heavily from the effects of the recession. Similarly, there are important interactions between the cultural and physical environments, some of which have been mentioned already. For example, an increased degree of environmental consciousness has affected the marketing of a wide range of products. This can be attributed both to increased awareness of environmental problems and also to the increasing rate of degradation in the physical environment itself.

A key feature of the macro-environment is that, except in a few cases, it is largely outside the control of the firm. Most firms must accept the macro-environment as it is and develop strategies to match current and anticipated future developments.

The market environment

This includes all factors that impact directly on a firm and its operations in relation to a particular market or set of markets in which it operates. It requires a detailed analysis of conditions in the market place, including the following:

Suppliers
In effect, suppliers represent the first stage in the chain of activities that leads to products reaching markets. Consequently, although dealing with suppliers is not directly a marketing activity, an understanding of the

supply side of the market is an important component of effective marketing. The market power of suppliers, their number and size will all have an important impact on the price of the final product and on the degree of flexibility in pricing. Equally relevant will be the suppliers' ability to guarantee sufficient quantity and quality of the required inputs. Indeed, for many companies, effective supply management which reduces costs and/or allows an increase in product quality can be the key to gaining a competitive advantage.

Distributive network
In order to market a product effectively, management must understand the patterns of distribution that currently exist, how those channels can be used and the extent to which they can influence consumer buying behaviour. As with the supply side of the market, the strength and bargaining power of the distributors will have important implications for marketing strategies, particularly pricing, but if the market power of the distribution network is substantial, manufacturers may find themselves having to compete for distributors as well as customers.

Consumers
Understanding the factors that motivate consumers and influence their buying decisions is clearly crucial to effective marketing, so much so that it will be analysed in greater detail in the following chapter.

Competition
Strategic marketing requires a constant monitoring of competitors, including identifying who they are, their current market position, their strengths and weaknesses, and their strategic approach to their markets. As Kotler (1991) points out, competition arises at a number of different levels, as shown in figure 4.2. At the broadest level, consumers may have a number of different desires they may wish to satisfy, and given income constraints, the more money spent satisfying one particular desire, the less there will be available for satisfying other desires. At the next level, the firm faces generic competition, i.e. competition from the range of products which can satisfy the consumer's basic desire. Within a particular generic product category, the firm encounters product form competition from different variants of the generic product. In the car market, for example, this may take the form of competition between sports cars, estate cars, large family cars, small family cars and hatchbacks. Finally, the most immediate level of competition is brand competition between different brands of the same basic product. Although brand level competition is arguably the most

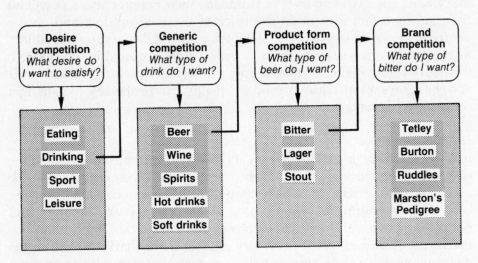

Figure 4.2   Levels of competition
Source: Adapted from Kotler (1991)

immediate and most relevant form of competition, the other forms of competition should not be disregarded because of their importance to the long-term health of a particular market.

By considering competition from other product forms and other generic product types the company can focus its attention on potential opportunities to expand its markets and ensure that it is aware of future threats from substitute products. The brewery that focuses attention only on competition between its brands of bitter/lager and those of its competitors runs the risk of missing the competitive threat posed by the growth of wine or soft drinks and the opportunity to develop low-alcohol or alcohol-free versions of its basic products to counter the threat of increased soft drink consumption.

Interest groups
For any organization, there is a variety of interest groups who can influence, either directly or indirectly, the success of a marketing strategy. Thus it is important to maintain an awareness of the attitudes of the

general public, the media, the government and so on, and consider how best to present itself to these groups. One group of particular importance is the organization's own employees, and internal marketing to these can be a key factor in business success.

An alternative approach to the analysis of the market environment that is widely used is Michael Porter's 'five forces' framework (Porter, 1980). Porter argues that industry profitability depends upon industry structure and specifically on five key features:

- bargaining power of suppliers;
- bargaining power of consumers;
- threat of entry;
- competition from substitutes;
- competition between firms.

Thus, the analysis of the market environment should focus specifically on these five aspects. The application of this approach is discussed in chapter 7, though it should be clear that there are many similarities between this method of analysing the market environment and the five features discussed above.

Understanding the market environment requires detailed consideration, not only because it will have a major impact on the operation of the firm, but also because it is an aspect of the environment that the firm can, in part, control and change. Thus, a business can encourage loyalty, preference from suppliers/distributors, influence what competitors do and what consumers think and, through the development of corporate image, influence perceptions held by various interest groups.

The internal environment

Clearly, the internal environment is the area in which the firm can exercise greatest control. Essentially it requires analysis of an organization's capabilities. At the broadest level, this means a consideration of the nature of corporate culture. Corporate culture refers to the prevailing value system within an organization. This value system may be one that has arisen through time or it may be one that is actively created and managed by senior staff. A corporate culture associated with rapid innovation and risk taking will have different marketing implications to a culture orientated towards high quality and an exclusive image, and this in turn will differ from an organization with a low-risk culture looking to follow the market with a standard product. At a more detailed level, there is a need to identify areas in which the company and its personnel have particular strengths and weaknesses, since these will help determine the type of product that the organization will be able to supply most effectively. The marketing audit outlined in chapter 3 indicates how organizations can gather information on their internal environment.

Evaluating developments in the marketing environment

Following an analysis of the internal and external environments the available information must be evaluated in order to identify the implications for marketing strategy. The process of SWOT (*strengths, weaknesses, opportunities, threats*) analysis is one of the simplest techniques for summarizing information about the marketing environment and guiding the direction of strategy. Information used in the development of strategy is either external (i.e. it relates to the outside environment) or internal (i.e. it relates to the organization itself). External information can be classified as either an opportunity or a threat and internal information can be classified as either a strength or a weakness. Thus any piece of information can be classified as follows:

Strengths
A strength refers to any particular skill or distinctive competence that will aid the organization in achieving its stated objectives. This may relate to experience in specific types of markets, specific skills possessed by employees either in relation to production, R&D or marketing. It may equally include aspects of corporate culture/image – e.g. Proctor & Gamble's reputation for quality and McDonald's emphasis on customer service can both be regarded as strengths.

Weaknesses
A weakness describes any aspect of the organization that may hinder the achievement of specific objectives. Weaknesses may include limited experience of certain markets/technologies, the nature of the organization's reputation, the financial resources available, staff skills and so on. Thus, for example, the building societies' limited experience of money transmission may have represented a weakness in relation to the decision to move into the provision of current accounts. Similarly, the image of

companies such as KwikSave and Superdrug as high-volume, low-price retailers might constitute a weakness should either organization consider moving into high-margin, low volume retailing.

Opportunities
An opportunity is any feature of the external environment that creates conditions which are advantageous to the organization, given the objectives it wishes to achieve. Thus, for example, the rise in the price of petrol is an opportunity for manufacturers of fuel-efficient cars or petrol/ oil substitutes. Equally, the growth of environmental concern among consumers is an opportunity for the manufacturers of environmentally friendly products.

Threats
A threat is any environmental development that will create problems for an organization in achieving its specific objectives. What constitutes an opportunity to some firms will almost invariably constitute a threat to others. Thus, for example, the growth in environmental concern among consumers, which has already been described as an opportunity for some organizations, is also a threat to others, such as the manufacturers of products that use CFCs. Similarly, growing consumer interest in healthy eating may be regarded as a threat to confectionery manufacturers.

This information is commonly presented as a matrix of strengths, weaknesses, opportunities and threats. In identifying SWOTs it is important to ensure that strengths and weaknesses are internal factors, specific to the organization, and that opportunities and threats are factors present in the external environment and independent of the organization. A common mistake in SWOT analysis is to confuse opportunities and threats with strategies and tactics. For example, the ability to cut prices is not an opportunity; it is a marketing tactic. The relevant opportunity would be the existence of a price sensitive segment in the market.

It is also desirable to attempt to attach some ranking to the various pieces of information to identify their importance, their likelihood of occurrence and the significance of their impact. Banning cigarette smoking in all public places would represent a major threat to manufacturers of tobacco products, but if the likelihood of this event occurring is small, it should not have a major impact on the formulation of strategy. Conversely, the increased taxation of cigarettes may seem less threatening, but may be more relevant to the formation of marketing strategies if the likelihood of

Strengths	Weaknesses
1. Large captive account base	1. Underdeveloped selling skills
2. Extensive branch network	2. High cost structures
3. Adequate capital for expansion	3. Inflexible technologies
4. Considered trustworthy	4. Historic banking culture

Opportunities	Opportunities
1. Increased demand for personal financial services	1. Competition from other suppliers of personal financial services
2. Rising personal wealth	2. Consumers becoming more critical
3. Growth in demand from older sections of population	3. Consumers have higher expectations of service
4. Easier access to European markets	4. Increased competition from Europe

Figure 4.3   SWOT analysis for a UK clearing bank in relation to the market for personal financial services
Source: Adapted from Thwaites (1991)

occurrence is high. In the example in figure 4.3 the information in each cell is ranked to account for these factors.

Having formulated this matrix, it then becomes feasible to make use of SWOT analysis in guiding strategy formulation. The two major strategic options are as follows:

Matching
This entails finding, where possible, a match between the strengths of the organization and the opportunities presented by the market. Strengths that do not match any available opportunity are of limited use, while opportunities that do not have any matching strengths are of little immediate value from a strategic perspective. Thus, for example, the bank

in figure 4.3 may consider using its captive account base to pursue a strategy of cross-selling other financial products through direct mail campaigns which emphasize the bank's trustworthy image.

Conversion

This requires the development of strategies that will convert weaknesses into strengths in order to take advantage of some particular opportunity or converting threats into opportunities which can then be matched by existing strengths. Thus, for example, many ice-cream manufacturers face a threat from the gradual ageing of the population, which is eroding their traditional markets. This threat can be converted into an opportunity by pursuing a strategy of developing new ice-cream products targeted more explicitly at the older, more sophisticated consumer, as Walls have done with products such as 'Vienetta'.

SWOT analysis is probably one of the most widely used tools in marketing and strategic planning and it is simply a method of structuring information of both a qualitative and a quantitative nature. Its advantages arise from the fact that it is easy to use, does not require formal training and therefore is accessible to all levels of management across a broad field. This simple technique provides a method of organizing information and identifying possible problems and future strategic directions.

Conclusions

The environment within which organizations operate is becoming increasingly complex and turbulent and, as a consequence, increasingly uncertain. Understanding the nature of this environment and its implications for the organizations is a key element in any marketing strategy. The environment must be analysed at a number of different levels, from broad, macro factors, through to market-specific and finally organization-specific factors. However, although these elements of the environment constrain the activities of the organization, it is increasingly important to recognize that the organization itself, through its marketing activities, can influence the environment to produce conditions that are more favourable to the success of its strategies.

CASE STUDY

Understanding the marketing environment

The DIY market

Introduction

After a period of general growth in the DIY industry a number of organizations are re-evaluating their marketing strategies in the face of a downturn in the economy. The DIY industry grew enormously during the 1980s. By 1989 DIY goods accounted for 1.15 per cent of total consumer spending, having grown by over 11 per cent during the year. The following section summarizes the results of a recent analysis of the key influences on the DIY market in the United Kingdom.

The macro-environment

(a)   The economy

The rate of economic growth had slowed substantially in the late 1980s and early 1990s. Interest rates had been high for some two years and despite gradual falls during 1991 and 1992, unemployment was rising and the level of consumer spending had fallen.

(b)   Demographic/social factors

Household formation is continuing to expand and estimates suggest that a further 2 million households will have been formed by the year 2001. However, the population itself is generally getting older and the number of households formed among the younger age groups is likely to decline. This could be counterbalanced if the trend towards more single-person households continues, though with the recent high interest rates this seems increasingly unlikely.

Between 1979 and 1989 the level of owner-occupation increased from 54 per cent of the population to over 65 per cent and there is evidence that this trend will continue in the medium term, but at a considerably slower rate. The number of private housing units (both new and sales from the public sector) grew by around 18 per cent between 1981 and 1987, but the housing stock itself is getting older and currently almost half of the housing stock was built prior to 1944.

(c) Political/legal factors

The dominance of the Conservative Party in UK politics and the active promotion of owner-occupation appears to be rather weaker in the 1990s than it was in the 1980s. In addition the future of active policies to stimulate new businesses (low rents, etc., on out-of-town sites) is debatable.

Market factors

(a) Consumers

Table 4.2 shows some of the main trends in consumer DIY activities. The main market for DIY goods is among men. During 1989, the majority of men indicated that they had undertaken some DIY activity, making this more popular as a form of leisure than either

Table 4.2   DIY activities in 1991

Percentage of adults	Adults	Men	Women	AB	C1	C2	D	E
Any DIY	67.1	77.6	57.4	66.5	67.5	70.8	68.5	57.2
Painting inside	57.6	66.2	49.6	55.3	57.0	61.4	59.8	50.1
Putting up wallpaper	37.9	45.0	31.2	31.4	36.8	42.5	40.4	34.9
Paint outer windows/ doors	26.7	38.0	16.2	30.5	27.4	29.0	23.6	19.1
Paint outside walls	11.0	15.5	6.8	10.7	10.4	12.7	10.9	9.0
Putting up shelves	21.8	33.9	10.5	23.9	23.2	24.4	19.3	13.7
Make/put up cupboards	12.1	19.1	5.5	12.1	12.3	14.7	11.1	7.0
Renovate old furniture	7.9	9.4	6.4	11.2	8.4	7.9	5.6	5.2
Strip paint/varnish	11.6	14.9	8.5	13.5	11.8	12.8	10.8	6.3
Laid garden patio	6.7	10.5	3.3	7.2	7.0	8.5	5.4	3.3
Built ornamental pond	2.3	3.3	1.3	2.8	2.4	2.6	2.0	1.1

Source: Advertising Association (1992b).

reading or gardening. Generally, DIY activities are more popular among social classes C1, C2 and D. Other research suggests that the proportion of 'DIYers' is greatest among the 30–44 age group. For women, DIY is rather less popular than it is for men and is most popular among women in the 25–35 age group. It is interesting to note that the role of women is most significant in relation to activities such as interior painting and wallcovering.

DIY activities cover a variety of tasks and the 1980s witnessed a change in the takeup of different activities. At the beginning of the 1980s the most popular activities were outside painting, tiling, plumbing and replacing windows. By contrast, towards the end of the decade activities such as shelving, assembling furniture and electrical work were more popular.

(b) Competition

The number of DIY stores declined markedly in the last thirty years from 23,000 in 1961 to 10,800 in 1988, with the smaller traditional hardware type outlets being replaced by larger units and by retail chains. The trend towards larger stores has enabled companies to cater for the extension of consumer requirements by offering a wider range of products than would have been feasible at high street sites. B&Q and Texas were among the first of the major chains to make the move to out-of-town sites. These were often available at very reasonable rents, offered extensive parking facilities and allowed the stores to carry an even wider range of products. The success of these superstores was attributable to both wider range of products and superior marketing.

The DIY superstores dominate in the area of paints and wall-coverings. Hand tools and woodcare show a more fragmented pattern of sales while powertools have a similarly wide variety of outlets including mail order and electrical goods suppliers.

With the rapid expansion in the number of DIY superstores in recent years, there is some concern that the market is reaching saturation level and there will be little scope for future expansion by increasing the number of outlets. However, the distribution of superstores is by no means even across regions. In particular there are relatively fewer stores in the north of England and Scotland.

The market is characterized by a high degree of non-price competition. Media advertising is dominated by B&Q with gross expenditure of £16m in 1989. In the same year, their nearest rival,

Texas, spent £13.9m. Expenditure by the other leading retailers, Do-It-All, Payless and Magnet chains, was significantly lower. Despite the downturn in economic activity towards the end of the decade, neither of the two market leaders cut back their advertising budgets. In part, this may be explained by the growth in new stores, which will account for significant media expenditure (largely local) when openings are announced. Equally, it may be attributable to the importance of both advertising and branding to maintain competitive advantage in recessionary periods.

Source: Adapted from Cook (1991).

Questions

1. What are the implications of this analysis of the marketing environment for the major DIY retailers?
2. What recommendations would you make regarding future strategy for a major chain of DIY retailers?

5 Understanding buyer behaviour

Introduction

Marketing is about supplying customers with goods or services that they want. To do this effectively requires that the organization understands its customers, is aware of their wants and needs, and is familiar with the way in which they make decisions. Understanding customers and their behaviour does more than simply ensure that the organization is providing products that best meet the needs of those consumers. By being aware of how customers behave and how they make decisions, the organization can determine how best to formulate the marketing mix to ensure that the right image is created for the product. An example of the potential benefits associated with understanding consumer needs is shown in exhibit 5.1.

Before we examine buying behaviour, it is perhaps worth pointing out the differences between customers and consumers. In most cases the words are used interchangeably, but they do have slightly different meanings and this difference can be significant in some circumstances. The customer is the person or organization who actually makes the purchase, whereas the consumer is the person who actually uses the product. When customer and consumers are quite distinct groups, the marketing task can be more complex since it may be necessary to market the product to both groups in a different manner. For example, the manufacturer of children's toys might wish to present the image of a toy as exciting and dangerous to the child (consumer), and at the same time convince the parents (customers) that the same toy is safe and reliable. For the purposes of this chapter, the two terms will be used interchangeably unless otherwise stated.

Depending on the type of market in which the organization operates it may face a variety of types of consumers: the individual final consumers, the industrial buyer, government consumers, buyers from retail or

---

Exhibit 5.1 Understanding customer needs

United States Surgical

United States Surgical reputedly has one of the most aggressive and successful sales forces in the surgical supply industry. The success of the sales force is based on thorough training and an emphasis on building and maintaining close relationships with both buyers and users of the company's products. The training programme involves courses relating to the company's products, surgical techniques and basic anatomy, to ensure that all sales staff are familiar with medical terminology and comfortable in the operating theatre. To understand the needs of surgeons, sales staff are expected to don gowns and accompany their customers into the theatre. There they can advise surgeons on the use of United States Surgical's products and observe what the surgeons do and do not like and what they do and do not need. Getting close to the customer in this manner gives United States Surgical a clear understanding of customer needs and has provided the basis for a much improved business performance. By the end of March 1992, sales had grown 55 per cent compared with the previous year and net profit was up 94 per cent, representing a 28 per cent return on equity.

Source: Reese (1992).

---

wholesale outlets or institutional consumers. In many senses, the basic ways in which these consumers will make their decisions will be similar; accordingly, this chapter will concentrate primarily on the buying behaviour of final consumers and will briefly review some of the particular issues and models that are relevant to organizational buyers.

How do consumers buy?

Marketing attempts to understand consumer behaviour by focusing attention on the buying process, which describes the ways in which the consumer decides or does not decide to purchase a particular product and how the consumer reacts to the product after purchase. Thus, under-standing consumer behaviour from a marketing perspective is concerned not only with analysing the purchase as such, but also with analysing the factors that precede and follow the purchase decision.

Most attempts to understand consumer behaviour treat the buying process as a problem-solving exercise. This problem solving involves rational evaluations of both products and their features but is also subject to emotional influences through the consumer's concern for subjective, hedonistic benefits. The simple decision-making process can be seen as having five stages (Engel, Blackwell and Miniard, 1990), as indicated in figure 5.1. This framework suggests that the buying process is initiated when the customer has a particular need or want to satisfy (problem recognition). He or she will then collect information concerning the different ways in which these needs can be met, and having evaluated this information, will then take the decision as to whether or not to make a purchase. Once this purchase is made, the customer will then register satisfaction or dissatisfaction with that particular product (post-purchase behaviour).

In order to market a product successfully to customers or consumers it is important to understand their needs and motivations to ensure that products are developed to meet these needs. It is equally important to understand the nature of each of the stages in the buying process in order to identify the best way to influence the consumer through the marketing mix. Each of the five stages will be examined in more detail below.

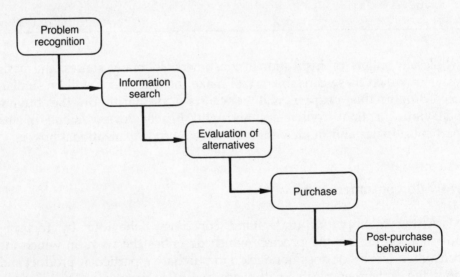

Figure 5.1 The consumer's decision process

Problem recognition

The phrase 'problem recognition' is used to refer to the situation in which the consumer identifies a difference between his or her actual and desired states. In other words, the consumer has a need that he or she would like to satisfy. Of course, consumers will have many needs that they would like to satisfy, but there will only be a certain number of situations in which the consumer will be motivated to act. The identification of a need will motivate the consumer only if that need is sufficiently great and if it is feasible for the consumer to satisfy it.

A discrepancy between the consumer's actual and desired states may arise as a result of changes in the consumer's actual state, changes in the desired state or changes in both. A change in the consumer's actual state will usually arise as a result of changes in current circumstances, but may also arise due to individual-specific factors. Thus, changing circumstances such as a new job, a new house, marriage, etc., may create new needs, as may the acquisition of a new product. For example, the purchase of a new computer may create a need for new software purchases. Equally, consumption of existing products may create a need for the purchase of replacements. Individual differences such as personality and lifestyle may also affect the consumer's actual state; the individual who is extrovert and aspirational is perhaps more likely to be dissatisfied with their actual state than is the case with an individual who is introvert and self-contained. Similarly, the consumer's desired state will change with time and will be subject to a variety of influences both personal and environmental. The factors that influence problem recognition are outlined in figure 5.2 and some of the more important influences are considered below. These factors are discussed in more detail in Engel, Blackwell and Miniard (1990).

- *Culture* Culture refers to the set of ideas, beliefs, values and norms of behaviour that are common to a particular group. Normally, cultures differ at national levels, but within any particular country there may also be important subcultures. Culture will influence the needs of consumers and the types of product they will seek in order to satisfy those needs. This is perhaps most obvious with food products but can be equally important across the range of consumer goods. The prevailing culture will also affect the way in which individuals react to certain aspects of the marketing mix.
- *Social influences* Problem recognition can be affected by a variety of social factors, including social class and occupation. Although, in practice, social class is difficult to measure, many products are seen by

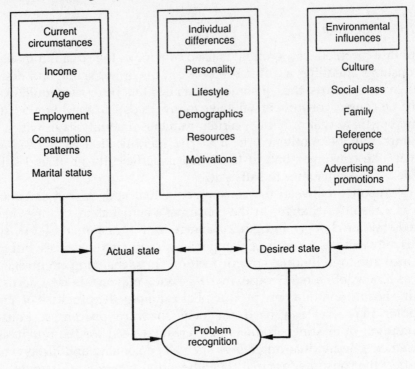

Figure 5.2 Influences on problem recognition

Exhibit 5.2   Reference groups

MD Foods

The Danish firm MD Foods is the world's fifth largest dairy company and had traditionally concentrated on core dairy products such as cheese, butter and milk. Following the acqusition of Associated Fresh Foods, MD Foods expanded its activities into dairy desserts. The Danish firm is also planning to use these products to move into the UK market. The summer of 1992 saw the launch of a range of yoghurts and fromage frais, all branded with Thunderbirds characters from the cult television series. The Thunderbirds characters were chosen to give the company an instantly recognizable brand association in the highly competitive children's segment of this market.

Source: Marketing (1992).

consumers as status symbols and are associated with particular social classes. The consumer's perception of their particular social class may therefore influence the needs they wish to satisfy and the types of products they wish to purchase.

- *Reference groups* Within particular cultures or socio-economic groups, consumers will still be influenced by other people around them. These groups may include opinion leaders, reference groups and family. Opinion leaders are those groups or individuals who indicate what is fashionable and who guide consumer choice. For example, chemists may be opinion leaders for consumers in the purchase of non-prescription medicines. Both reference groups and families are groups of individuals with whom the consumer may actively wish to be associated. The consumer's needs will then be influenced by the needs and purchases of this associative group. The extensive use of sports stars and celebrities in advertising a variety of products from sports equipment to Mars Bars is a clear attempt to appeal to consumers who associate strongly with these individuals. The use of reference groups can, of course, extend to fictional characters as exhibit 5.2 shows. Equally, reference groups and families can be dissociative in which case, the consumers will actively avoid the products which are linked with these groups.

- *Advertising and promotion* Another key external factor is advertising and promotion, since this can play an important role in creating the feeling of an unsatisfied need among consumers. Advertising, for example, may present a product as something everyone of a particular status should have, or something that you owe to your family. Similar effects can be achieved with other forms of promotion, particularly personal selling.

There are also a number of internal factors that will influence the consumer's perceived needs. The most obvious individual specific factor is probably the availability of consumer resources. At one level this simply refers to the consumer's spending power, but it has a broader dimension in that it is also concerned with the time available to the consumer and the consumer's capacity to collect and analyse information. However, the availability of consumer resources will simply determine whether it is possible for the consumer to satisfy a need. Other important internal influences on the problem recognition process include:

- *Individual personalities* All consumers are different; they have different personalities, different attitudes and different aspirations. The purchase of designer clothes may be essential to one individual and totally unimportant to another. Personality can therefore have an important influence on a consumer's perceived needs. Although this is a difficult characteristic to measure, there have been a number of attempts to develop personality profiles. These will be discussed in more detail in the chapter on segmentation.

- *Demographics* Age and gender are obvious factors that can influence consumer's needs, although the notion of a family lifecycle is often cited in this context as a contributory factor. This idea suggests that consumers' needs will vary according to whether they are single, married without a family, married with a family, etc. Indeed, as we shall see in the following chapter, this approach is widely used for market segmentation.

- *Motivation* Motivation has already been mentioned in the context of the problem recognition stage of the consumers' decision-making process. Motivation is derived from the consumers' needs, but as we have indicated, consumers have many needs and not all those needs can be satisfied. Individual motivation will affect which needs consumers regard as important and therefore the priority in which they should be satisfied. For example, Abraham Maslow (see Kotler, 1991) suggested that individuals had a hierarchy of needs ranging from basic physiological needs through to self-esteem and self-actualization needs. The consumer would seek to satisfy needs that were lower on the hierarchy (e.g. physiological or security needs) before progressing to the higher esteem and satisfaction needs. From a marketing point of view, this approach might give some indication of how particular needs are likely to be translated into purchasing actions.

These factors combined will stimulate problem recognition in consumers. From a marketing perspective, understanding the interaction between these factors in relation to the purchase decision for a particular product or a particular consumer group will provide a key input to marketing strategy. For example, if the influence of opinion leaders is strong, then the marketing campaign will need to be directed towards these groups. Equally, if the individuals who buy, say, Porsche cars are concerned with self esteem and reward then these are attributes that the marketing effort should emphasize.

Information search

This is concerned with the process whereby the consumer collects information in order to identify the best ways to meet particular needs.

The amount of information that is collected depends on the nature of the decision process. For products that are purchased regularly, the consumer may collect little in the way of new information, relying instead on past knowledge of the product or the brand name. In the case of a large-scale, complex purchase, a much larger volume of information will be collected. There are two sources of information:

- *Internal information* Internal information is information that the consumer already possesses about the product. This may be based on past experience of the product, information collected from word-of-mouth recommendations or information that has been absorbed from past marketing campaigns. Internal information is often manifested in the form of brand loyalty. It is often assumed that internal information is favourable to the product, but this is not always the case. Consumers may have formed and retained negative views about a particular product that are unfounded, in which case trying to change such attitudes can be an important aspect of marketing.
- *External information* External information is collected by consumers from a variety of sources, including promotional materials, sales staff, trials, families, friends, opinion leaders, etc. From a marketing point of view, however, it is not sufficient simply to make information available. The information itself is only of use when it has been processed by the consumer and it is important to recognize that information may be lost or distorted in the processing phase. The stages in information processing are outlined in figure 5.3.

The first stage in information processing is ensuring that the consumer is exposed to the information, that it is available at the right time and in the right place. For example, if media advertising is being used to communicate with consumers, then it is important that the appropriate media are used. If the target consumer group is in social class AB, advertising in, say, the *Daily Star* is likely to be ineffective since less than 1 per cent of ABs read this paper. By contrast, advertising in the *Daily Telegraph* is likely to be rather more appropriate since 24 per cent of ABs read this paper (Advertising Association, 1992c).

It is then necessary to ensure that the consumer's attention is attracted through the use of a combination of visual, verbal and audio stimuli. Having attracted the consumer's attention, the information provided must be understandable; if the organization presents information in a form that is complex or difficult to understand, the consumer will lose interest and look elsewhere. For the information to be used, the consumer must accept

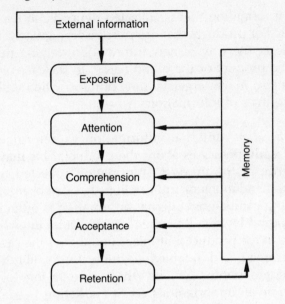

Figure 5.3   Consumer information processing

that what is said is genuine and then retain this information in memory. The nature of information already in the memory can affect the consumer's willingness to acknowledge, understand and accept the information. For example, someone who is aware of product names or understands technical details may be rather more responsive to particular types of information than other consumers who do not have this knowledge.

An important point to note is that all information must pass through these stages before it can be used by the consumer. At each stage there is the possibility of bias or distortion in the information flow. It is therefore important to ensure that information being provided to customers is clear, precise and consistent so as to minimize the possible distortion. However well the flow of information from an organization is managed, only a small proportion will ever reach the consumer's memory. For example, in the case of information conveyed through television advertisements, it is suggested that only 24 per cent of viewers actually retained message information by the following day.

Evaluation of alternatives

The evaluation of alternatives by the consumer is probably the most complex part of the decision process and the one that is least understood.

In very simple terms, the customer will compare different products against a set of evaluative criteria and, on the basis of comparison, will select a particular product for purchase. These criteria are partly determined by the nature of the need that the consumer initially perceived. For example, if the initial need was for something to quench a thirst, then a range of different drinks might be evaluated on the basis of their thirst-quenching properties. Exhibit 5.3 gives an example of the evaluative criteria used by consumers when buying cars and the impact these criteria can have on marketing strategies.

Although evaluative criteria will vary across different consumers it is useful to establish what the most important criteria are. Although this can often be achieved through marketing research, as was explained in chapter 3, it may not always be possible to identify the consumers' real reasons for choosing a particular product. At the same time, it is important to remember that marketing can play a role in influencing the evaluative criteria used by consumers. By using promotion to emphasize certain distinctive product attributes, an organization can encourage consumers to include such attributes in their set of evaluative criteria. For example, the television advertising campaign for Radion washing powder/liquid focused particular attention on the products' ability to eliminate odours

---

Exhibit 5.3 Evaluative criteria

Safety can sell cars

With the increased volume of traffic on the roads and with the continual increase in the number of accidents, the safety features of cars have become an increasingly important criteria for consumer choice. According to market research in the United States, safety is now the second most important feature that consumers look for when purchasing a car. The increased importance of safety in guiding consumer choice is reflected in the increased emphasis that car manufacturers are placing on safety features in product design and marketing. Traditionally, in the UK market, only Volvo placed particular emphasis on the safety features of its models in promotional activities. Now the competition are following suit with Audi, VW, Ford and Vauxhall all increasing the emphasis on safety in their marketing.

Source: Engel, Blackwell and Minniard (1990).

---

from clothes in order to emphasize the importance of this particular attribute to consumers.

Purchase decision
Based on the evaluation of alternatives, the consumer will choose whether to buy and if so, will select that product which has the most satisfactory performance in relation to the evaluative criteria. In the absence of sudden or unexpected changes in the consumer's circumstances or in the marketplace, the decision to purchase will lead to an actual purchase. Marketing can facilitate this process by ensuring that the actual purchase is as easy as possible, perhaps by offering attractive financing arrangements, free delivery or simply by ensuring that sufficient sales staff are available to take customer orders.

Post-purchase behaviour
Post-purchase behaviour describes the consumer's actions and feelings following a purchase. The significance of this stage of the buying process is that it will affect future purchases by that same consumer and also the information they may convey to other consumers. Indeed, for many products and services, word-of-mouth can be an important source of information for potential purchasers. Kotler (1991) notes that a satisfied consumer may communicate his or her experience to around three people, while a dissatisfied consumer may convey dissatisfaction to around eleven people. Hence marketing does not end with the purchase – rather there is a need to reinforce the consumer's belief that the right purchase has been made and minimize the extent of any 'cognitive dissonance', i.e. minimize any feelings of doubt that the consumer may experience about the nature of the purchase that has just been made.

When consumers make a purchase, particularly if it is a large or expensive item, then it is quite common for them to experience doubts about whether they have made the correct decision, whether they have got the best value for money, whether the product will be able to fulfil their needs, etc. If those doubts are ignored, then the consumer may well come to believe that the wrong decision was made and thus develop negative attitudes to the product. Marketing therefore has an important role in reminding consumers that they have made the correct decision. Initially, it is important to ensure that the organization does not raise expectations too high by trying to claim that the product can do something which it cannot. At the same time, back-up calls from sales or technical staff or reinforcement promotions can be beneficial, because they serve to remind and reassure consumers that choice they have made is correct.

The idea of understanding consumer buying behaviour as a sequential decision process is one that is common in marketing. This approach has, however, been subject to some criticism. In particular, it has been suggested (Foxall, 1987) that this type of decision process assumes a highly rational approach by the consumer that may not be justifiable in practice. Furthermore, the same author argues that the nature of these models is such that they are virtually impossible to validate through empirical studies of buying behaviour. An additional problem with this decision process approach is that the emphasis tends to be placed on one-off purchases rather than recurrent ones. While recognizing that these criticisms have some validity, the idea of a decision process is a useful tool from a marketing perspective as it provides a framework for trying to understand how consumers buy and for identifying how best to formulate a marketing mix to influence those buying decisions.

Different decision processes

The decision process described in the previous section is quite substantial and lengthy and an obvious criticism of this model of consumer buying would be that not every purchase will involve such an extensive decision-making exercise. It is usual, therefore, to see this five-stage model as the broadest framework, and then to recognize that the consumer does not necessarily go through all these stages when making every purchase. In particular, three broad types of decision process can be identified:

High involvement
The high-involvement decision process usually refers to the purchase of a large item where there is considerable choice, the product itself is expensive and is often important to the buyer's self-image. Products such as cars or houses are typical examples of high-involvement decision processes. The nature of the decision process is such that the problem recognition stage will occur only rarely, the consumer will engage in extensive information search and evaluation prior to purchase and the purchase itself will be a relatively long process. Risks associated with the purchase decision are high, leading the consumer to input a considerable amount of effort to ensure that the correct decision is taken.

Medium involvement

The medium-involvement decision process typically deals with moderately expensive products such as consumer durables. There is usually a considerable variety from which to choose and the risks associated with the purchase are also moderate. Typical examples include electrical goods, furniture and holidays. These types of purchase, though not frequent, will occur with some regularity, so the consumer does have some past experience to draw on. Nevertheless, the decision process will be characterized by reasonably extensive information collection and evaluation prior to purchase.

Low involvement

The low involvement decision process refers to the more regular, day-to-day purchases of small items where there is little risk associated with the purchase. In this situation, the actual 'problem recognition' or identification of need may not occur explicitly; there may be little or no information search and the consumer may rely heavily on brand loyalty or on simple criteria such as price. Although this suggests that such buying is habitual, it does not mean that marketing does not have an important role. Low-involvement decision processes are typical of fast-moving consumer goods such as food and household products, which are sectors where companies market their products very actively in order to build and maintain brand loyalty.

Are organizational buyers different?

So far we have discussed buying behaviour from the perspective of the final consumer, but many organizations do not deal with final consumers; they simply sell to other organizations. This raises the question of whether the type of decision process outlined above is appropriate in the case of organizational buyers. In general terms, the answer is probably 'yes'. Organizations will only buy if they recognize a need; they will require information and evaluation prior to purchase and they too may experience some post-purchase doubts. Furthermore, we should remember that organizational buying decisions are made by people and they themselves are subject to the same types of influences as they are in making their own personal buying decisions. Despite these general features of buying processes, there are some areas in which important differences exist between final consumers and organizational buyers. Specifically:

- Organizations will only purchase products if those products are required as an input to some aspect of the organization's activities. That is to say, organizations buy to fulfil organizational requirements, whereas personal customers buy in order to fulfil their own needs.
- While final consumers buy products for their own use, organizations demand products to be used in the process of producing their own goods or services. In that sense, organizational demand is usually thought of as being a derived demand and as such tends to be less price sensitive.
- Final consumers typically make decisions individually or in family groups, whereas in organizations the decision to purchase is normally the responsibility of a larger number of individuals. This group is often described as the buying centre or the decision-making unit.
- Organizations often buy a complex product which can involve a high level of technical support, staff training, delivery scheduling, finance arrangements and so on.
- Organizations are more likely to employ experts in the buying process and these buyers are often trained specifically for this type of work; they are likely to be much more rational, better informed and more rigorous in the ways in which they evaluate products and services. Indeed, the purchasing function is increasingly acquiring the status of a profession in much the same way as marketing and planning functions are being recognized as *professional*.

The significance of these differences is the subject of some debate. Although most marketing textbooks present final consumer and organizational buying as separate (but related) subjects, others argue that the extent of the differences between the two types of buyer is relatively small (Fern and Brown, 1984). For example, many high-involvement decision processes for final consumers will have more in common with the process by which an organization makes a major purchase than with low-involvement purchases by final consumers. Similarly, the organizational purchase of items such as pens, pencils, drawing pins, etc., will have more in common with a low-involvement consumer purchase than with a high-involvement organizational purchase. Thus, it is perhaps useful to consider the underlying decision processes for final consumers and organizational buyers as being in some way similar, while recognizing that some differences will arise according to the specific buying situation.

As we saw in the case of final consumers, there are different types of organizational buying behaviour, which range from simple reordering (e.g.

of a firm's stationery supplies) to complex purchasing decisions (e.g. the purchase of a mainframe computer system). The different types of buying behaviour in organizational markets can be categorized in a manner similar to that drawn up for final consumers:

Extensive problem solving

This situation focuses on the purchase of unfamiliar products from unfamiliar suppliers and is often referred to as a *new buy* or *new task* situation. This process will require extensive information search, it will normally require a considerable amount of time and effort and may also require that the buyers develop new criteria with which to judge the purchase.

Limited problem solving

This category deals with the purchase of a relatively unfamiliar product or service but where the suppliers are known and the buyer has some experience of the basic product type. This type of purchase is often described as the *modified rebuy*. Since there is something new about the purchase, the business will typically not depend quite so heavily on existing suppliers. Accordingly there is likely to be a reasonable degree of information collection, probably in the form of quotes or tenders from a variety of possible suppliers prior to evaluation and purchase.

Routinized buyer behaviour

This category deals with habitual buying where the buyer knows the product and the item is frequently purchased. This is often described as a *straight rebuy* since the business will simply continue to purchase the product without actively seeking new information or re-evaluating existing information. Indeed, it is likely that the buyer has well developed supplier preferences and any deviation from habitual behaviour is likely to be influenced only by price and availability considerations.

Clearly, when marketing to organizational buyers, it is important to be able to identify the buying situation facing the organization. When an organization is engaged in a straight rebuy, the opportunities for a new supplier may be limited; by contrast, if the purchase is a modified rebuy, the chances of a new supplier attracting business are much greater. However, in addition to knowledge of the buying situation, there are a number of other aspects of organizational buying that can have important implications for marketing. In particular, to market effectively to organizations it is important to have a clear idea of how the buying process works (both formally and informally) and be aware of who is involved in this process. Specifically, it is important to be aware of the following:

Identifying responsibility for the purchase decision
In some organizations and in some situations, individuals may be responsible for purchase decisions; in others, responsibility may lie with a committee. Organizations will also vary as to whether purchase decisions are made centrally or locally.

Understanding the composition of the buying centre
Identifying who makes the purchase decision may not be sufficient for marketing staff who are trying to understand the organizational buying process. The final purchase decision may simply be a process of approving recommendations made by other individuals involved in the buying process. Accordingly, effective marketing to organizational customers will depend on identifying the range of individuals involved in the buying process. This range of individuals is often described as the buying centre. The typical buying centre includes:

- *The user*   The user may have influence on the technical characteristics of the equipment (and hence the cost) and on reliability and performance criteria. For example, within a specified range, the buyer of company cars will be guided by the choices of the users of those cars.
- *The influencer*   The influencer is particularly useful where the purchase relies on technical knowledge. The influencer may be inside or outside the buying organization but will have a major input to the purchase decision because of specific technical knowledge. Unlike personal purchasing behaviour, where opinions may be sought from colleagues, friends, family, etc., competitive pressures and trade secret constraints may limit the sharing of information between companies. In this environment the salesman can be a respected technical link with the buyer and able to influence the purchasing process.
- *The decider*   The decider is the individual or the group of individuals who formally specify the requirements for a product or service and make the decision to purchase. Deciders, like any individual, will be affected by social personal, organizational and environmental factors.
- *The buyer*   The buyer has specific responsibility for making the purchase and arranging the terms and conditions for the purchase. The buyer may or may not be the same as the decider. For example, the

decision to purchase a particular type of computer system may be made by information technology specialists, but the actual purchase may be made by an individual within the organization's purchasing department.

- *The approver*   Approvers are the individuals who formally authorize a purchase. Often such individuals are in senior positions and may have limited involvement in the process leading up to the purchase decision, but this does not preclude the possibility of an approver having influence on the final outcome of the purchase process.
- *The gatekeeper*   The gatekeeper controls the flow of information about the purchase. This role can be senior or junior but is important because it influences the communication flow within the organization.

Although the precise composition of the buying centre can vary from company to company and can vary according to the nature of the purchase, identifying the members of the buying centre and their relative importance will provide the basis for more accurate marketing to industrial buyers.

Understanding buying procedures
The formal buying procedure will vary from organization to organization. Nevertheless, effective marketing to organizational customers depends on a clear understanding of this process. This process extends beyond identifying the range of individuals involved and entails developing an awareness of organization-specific procedures and practices, including being able to identify the different stages of the purchase process (specification, obtaining quotes, supplier selection, order and delivery, etc.), the timescale over which these procedures operate and the degree of formality that is expected.

Effective marketing to organizational consumers therefore depends on being able to identify who is responsible for buying, the range of individuals involved in buying and the formal buying procedures. Much of this information is organization specific and usually only acquired over a prolonged period of contact with the relevant organization. In this context, the supplier's sales staff have an important role to play, not just in generating business, but also in gathering information.

In understanding the buying behaviour of organizational customers, it is important to recognize that these customers are undertaking a decision process in much the same way as final consumers do. The influences on industrial buyers may be different and, in particular, may be more 'rational'. We should also remember that industrial buying is complex in organizational terms and that understanding these organizational arrangements is a prime requirement for any company marketing to organizational buyers. It is particularly important to identify how the buying centre or decision-making unit works as this will help to determine where marketing should be targeted.

An alternative perspective on industrial buying

One of the criticisms often voiced about the view of industrial buying as a problem-solving exercise is that it tends to place the buyer in a relatively passive role, reacting to various stimuli provided by the supplier in the form of a marketing mix and making decisions. Implicitly it also tends to treat each purchase decision as somehow separate. In practice, it is often argued that organizational buying is heavily dependent on interactions between buyer and seller, that both are active participants in this process and that many buyer–seller relationships are on-going rather than one-off events.

An alternative perspective on organizational buying has been suggested by the Industrial Marketing and Purchasing Group (Ford, 1990). This model views industrial marketing and purchasing as an interactive process which takes place within the context of long-term relationships between buyers and sellers. The model argues that buyers are not passive: having identified specific purchasing needs, organizational buyers will often actively seek out suppliers and in many instances will not be purchasing a standardized product and will instead be actively seeking a product tailored to meet their particular specifications. The framework for this model is shown in figure 5.4. There are essentially four elements: the interaction process itself, the participants (buyers and sellers), the atmosphere surrounding the interaction and the environment within which interaction occurs.

The interaction process
The interaction process is concerned with the relationship between buyers and sellers and both are seen as active participants in the market. This relationship is seen as being composed of a number of episodes, and these episodes relate to particular forms of exchange, including product/service exchange, financial exchange, information exchange and social exchange. Thus, the IMP framework stresses that the interaction process extends

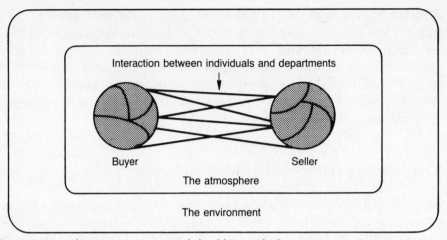

Figure 5.4   The interaction model of buyer behaviour

beyond the simple purchase transaction to include a variety of forms of personal contact. Long-term relationships are created as a result of an accumulation of episodes and these relationships are characterized by particular contact patterns and by varying degrees of willingness to adapt to the needs of either party.

The interacting parties
The relationship between buyer and seller is also affected by the characteristics of the interacting parties, and in particular by the characteristics of the organizations concerned. These characteristics include technology, organizational size, structure and strategy, and organizational experience. Given that one aspect of interaction is concerned with linking the production technology of the seller to the production technology of the buyer, the relationship between the two and the degree of adaptation will be influenced by the relative technology levels of the two parties. Similarly, the relationship will be affected by the size and relative market power of the two interacting parties and also by the degree of formalization, centralization and specialization in the organizational structure. Furthermore, an organization's experience of previous buying and selling relationships will affect they way in which existing relationships are managed and what is expected from these relationships. Finally, the nature of both parties' strategies will affect how the relationship is managed; the management of a relationship between an organization pursuing a low-cost, high-volume strategy and one pursuing a high-price, low-volume strategy may be quite distinct from the

management of a relationship between two organizations with largely similar strategic directions.

The atmosphere
The atmosphere within which relationships are formed and develop can have important implications for the processes of interaction. The atmosphere is typically described in terms of the degree and direction of dependence surrounding the relationship, the extent to which one party can exercise power over another, the mutual expectations of the two parties and the degree of cooperation, adaptation and conflict. This atmosphere is created over time as a product of the various interaction episodes, and the atmosphere created may then affect subsequent interactions.

The environment
The conditions under which relationships are formed and buyers and sellers interact will be influenced at the broadest level by aspects of the operating environment. Of particular importance will be factors such as the extent and pace of change in the environment, market and distribution structures, the degree of internationalization in the relevant markets along with other broader social influences that impact on business practices.

Thus, the IMP framework views the organizational buying process as being influenced by patterns of interaction that occur within the context of a long-term relationship, which in itself is influenced by changes in the atmosphere surrounding the relationship and changes in the broader business environment. The role of marketing in this framework is essentially one of developing and maintaining long-term relationships between the supplier and the buyer.

Conclusions

In order to be able to identify and anticipate customer needs and develop appropriate marketing strategies it is essential that an organization understands why and how those customers buy. Understanding why customers buy and the needs they seek to satisfy provides a basis for future product development, while understanding how those customers buy provides a basis for formulating the sort of marketing mix that will be effective in influencing the buying process. The orthodox approach to understanding consumer buying tends to centre on the notion of buying as a decision process. Briefly, this type of model suggests that consumers become aware of a need or want, collect information on how to satisfy that need or want and finally make a purchase, once the various alternatives have been evaluated. Although there is a good case for applying this approach to both final consumers and organizational buyers, there is an alternative view which argues that it is more useful to treat organizational buying within the context of long-term relationships between buyer and seller.

Self-test questions

1. How can advertising and promotion influence the problem recognition stage among final consumers?
2. What strategies could a car dealer pursue to ensure that a prospective customer wishing to purchase a particular make of car will actually do so?
3. What is *cognitive dissonance* and what is its significance in marketing?
4. Explain the differences between high-, medium- and low-involvement decision processes. How significant are these differences from a marketing perspective?
5. To what extent do final consumers and organizational buyers differ?

6 Market segmentation

Introduction

The purpose of any marketing strategy is to identify, build and maintain a competitive edge for an organization in its chosen markets. These markets are typically heterogeneous. They consist of a range of consumers with different needs and expectations who respond differently to the elements of the marketing mix. Market segmentation is an attempt to take these differences into account by identifying groups (segments) of customers. Within these segments, the customers have similar needs, but each segment differs in some definable way from the others. By using marketing approaches tailored to the characteristics of each segment it should be possible to increase the profit contribution compared with using a blanket marketing approach to the whole market. This chapter presents an analytic framework for segmenting markets and reviews some of the different segmentation approaches that are used in both final consumer and organizational markets.

Criteria for effective market segmentation

Segmentation is used in both final consumer and industrial markets and there are many approaches which can be used to identify segments. Whatever approach is used there are a number of requirements for effective market segmentation:

Measurability
This refers to the degree to which information already exists, or can be obtained cost effectively, on the particular buyer characteristics of interest. Thus, for example, it is fairly easy to identify the age distribution of the

population but much more difficult to identify the different personality types.

Accessibility

This is concerned with the degree to which the organization can focus its marketing activities on the chosen segments. For example, the organization that wants to focus its marketing activities on sports enthusiasts might look to advertise in sports magazines or on television during live sports coverage. This segment could be regarded as moderately accessible. By contrast, the company looking to direct its marketing campaign towards independent, career-women might find it considerably more difficult to identify these consumers and direct a campaign towards them.

Viability

This refers to the degree to which the segments are large enough to be worth considering for separate marketing cultivation. Since it is expensive to devise different marketing approaches, it is desirable to identify a minimum size for a segment, measured perhaps by volume of sales or potential profitability. After all, at one extreme, every consumer could be treated as a distinct segment, but this approach would be both highly costly and managerially infeasible except in the case of tailor-made/customized products.

Homogeneity

Individuals within the group should be homogeneous, but groups should be heterogeneous. In practice perfect segmentation is impossible and there will always be some overlap between different segments. The aim of good segmentation is to minimize the extent of this overlap.

Relevance

This refers to the degree to which the segmentation approach that is used actually explains why people behave differently. Thus for example, in the case of Porsche, income would probably be reasonably effective in defining the market segments that are likely to aspire to owning a Porsche, but it may not be the most relevant factor. By contrast, the view of Porsche owners as *achievers*, as successful individuals who wish to reward their own success, is perhaps a much more relevant description of the characteristics of that market segment.

A number of variables can be used to identify different market segments. These are used either singly or in combination and the type of variable used depends very much on the type of product and the nature of the market.

Approaches to market segmentation

In practice, organizations usually adopt one of two general approaches to segmenting their markets – either *a priori* segmentation or *post hoc* segmentation. *A priori* segmentation draws heavily on the analyst's experience of a particular market. On the basis of this experience, market segments are identified prior to any market research being undertaken. The role of market research is to explore in more detail the characteristics of the identified segments. In contrast, *post hoc* segmentation entails grouping consumers into segments on the basis of research findings. This approach can prove to be more costly than *a priori* segmentation because of the complexity of the research techniques used in establishing segments, but may be essential in new or rapidly changing markets where the researcher is unable to draw on past experience to guide segment identification.

Whichever approach is being used, market segmentation needs to produce answers to two basic questions.

- How do consumers differ?
- Why do consumers differ?

Both sets of information are essential for an effective marketing strategy. In relation to any product or service, customers will differ in terms of level of use, occasion of use, benefits sought, etc., and these differences will arise as a consequence of a variety of factors including age, social class, income, personality and so on. Thus, any market segmentation exercise requires two categories of variable:

- *Segment basis* The variable that explains how consumers differ, usually measured in terms of the buyer's response to particular marketing stimuli.
- *Segment descriptor* The variable or variables that explain why consumers differ in their response to marketing stimuli. The segment descriptor provides important information both on why consumers differ and also on the characteristics of particular segments. In statistical terms, the segment basis can be thought of as a dependent variable and the segment descriptors as the independent or explanatory variables.

Within these two categories, the variables used can be of two types – objective and subjective. Objective variables are usually directly measurable characteristics such as quantity purchased or frequency of purchase for the basis variable, compared with age, income or social class for the descriptor variable. Subjective variables, by contrast, are not directly measurable and will usually be inferred from customer behaviour and attitudes. Examples of subjective variables include benefits sought or degree of brand loyalty for the basis variable and personality or lifestyle for the descriptor variables.

Unfortunately, there are few clear guidelines as to which variables are most appropriate to use. Objective variables usually have the advantage of being easily available and easily measured. Segmentation based on objective variables is likely to perform well in relation to the criterion of accessibility. Subjective variables by contrast, although difficult to measure, are often more relevant, in that they can perform well in terms of explaining why consumers differ. In practice, the choice of variables may be heavily constrained by the availability of data and the costs of data collection, and many segmentation exercises will involve a combination of objective and subjective variable, with the objective variables being incorporated to aid in the process of profiling the chosen segment.

The segment basis

Either objective or subjective variables can be used as the segment basis. Objective variables typically measure some aspect of consumption for the product in question, while subjective variables usually measure some aspect of consumer behaviour in relation to the product. Consumption-based (objective) variables are relatively easy to measure and will include usage level, usage occasion and user stature. Thus, a brewer may segment consumers as light, medium and heavy drinkers, while an airline may segment consumers into business and non-business users. One of the particular attractions of segmenting according to usage rates is the so-called Pareto effect – that 20 per cent of customers can account for 80 per cent of sales. The ability to identify this 20 per cent and target a marketing campaign to their specific needs can yield substantial benefits. Behaviouristic (subjective) variables tend to be rather more difficult to measure but can potentially offer useful marketing insights. For example, Haley (1968) suggested that four segments could be identified in the toothpaste market on the basis of benefits sought, namely decay prevention, bright teeth, good taste and low price. Similarly, research by

---

Exhibit 6.1   Benefit segmentation

Nike

Phil Knight, CEO of Nike, attributes much of the company's recent success to market segmentation. He describes the process as 'breaking things into digestible chunks and creating separate brands or sub brands to represent them'. In the mid-1980s Nike launched the Air Jordan Basketball shoe to appeal specifically to the basketball segment within the sports shoe market. However, segmentation did not stop at the level of a specific sport. Within the basketball market, Nike recognized that there are different styles of play. Not every basketball player played in the style of Michael Jordan. Two further market segments were identified. One was based on an aggressive, muscular style of play, typified by David Robinson and Charles Barkley, the other on a quick, high-flying style of play typified by Scottie Pippin. The result was two further brands of basketball shoe, Force and Flight, targeted at these two additional segments. The result of this is that Nike now have the number one, number two and number four brands of basketball shoe.

Source: Willigan (1992).

Timex identified three segments in the watch market: the low price segment, the durability and quality segment and the status symbol segment. As exhibit 6.1 shows, Nike use a form of benefit segmentation in the market for sports shoes. In addition to using benefits, other behaviouristic variables for market segmentation include price sensitivity, brand loyalty and buyer readiness. The use of these variables is discussed in more detail by Wind (1978).

Segment descriptors

Descriptor variables typically serve two purposes in market segmentation. First, they explain why consumers differ, and second, they help in providing a profile of the segment for subsequent marketing activities. This profiling procedure is an important component of any segmentation because it enables the organization to identify the individuals to whom it wishes to direct its marketing activities. Often, the segment descriptors will provide a segment profile directly. If age is used as a segment descriptor, it will also act as a profiling variable. However, when markets are segmented using subjective variables, it may be necessary to collect further information to profile the segment. In the case of Porsche, the target segment might be identified in psychographic terms as achievers and then profiled in terms of age, income, reading habits, etc. Some of the more commonly used segment descriptors are outlined below.

Location
Segmentation based on different geographic locations is one of the most common forms of segmentation. Despite improved communications, significant geographic differences between markets appear to persist – particularly so at an international level where cultural and climatic variations can lead to important differences in purchasing patterns. Even at a national level there are some significant differences. For example, a family living in the south of England is much more likely to purchase a dishwasher than one living in the north. However, the relevance of geographic segmentation can be questionable in some instances. Geographic differences between markets may simply reflect variations in the relevant variables between different regions. In the dishwasher example, greater likelihood of purchase in the south of England may simply reflect the fact that incomes are higher in the south-east than in the north. The geographic difference does not then 'explain' differences in behaviour, but it does provide an indicator of the existence of those differences. As such, it can be useful from a managerial perspective in providing a method for organizing markets administratively. For example, many companies will organize their sales forces on a geographic basis and will structure promotion around the use of certain regionally based media.

Socio-economic variables
Socio-economic variables encompass various measures of income, wealth or social status. Income is often used in market segmentation because it relates directly to individuals' abilities to make a purchase. However, in some circumstances, the relevance of income as a variable for segmentation may be questioned because of the focus on the consumers' ability to purchase rather than the consumers' need or desire to own a particular product.

The notion of different buying behaviour across different socio-economic groups is widely used. The UK market research industry uses standardized

Table 6.1 Social group classification

Social grade	Social class	Occupation	Approx. % of UK population
A	upper or upper/ middle class	higher managerial, professional or administrative	2.7
B	middle class	intermediate managerial, professional or administrative	15.1
C1	lower middle class	supervisory, junior managerial or administrative, clerical	23.9
C2	skilled working class	skilled manual workers	27.8
D	working class	semi-skilled and unskilled manual workers	17.8
E	subsistence level	state pensioners, unemployed, casual workers	12.7

Source: Advertising Association (1992d).

social groupings that are based entirely on occupation. Each occupation has been categorized into one of the following groups shown in table 6.1.

Demographic variables
Here the market is divided on the basis of age, gender, housing, family characteristics or family lifecycle stage, or by some combination of these factors. Many products show a marked difference in take up between these demographic groups, and although there are difficulties in assigning people to particular classes, the approach has generally been effective.

One important demographic variable that is increasingly used in marketing is the notion of the *family lifecycle* (FLC). The FLC is a summary demographic variable, i.e. it combines the effects of age, marital status, career status (income) and the presence or absence of children; and this is the basis of its appeal, for it is able to identify the various stages through which households progress. An example of the different stages in a basic FLC are outlined in table 6.2.

Table 6.2 The family lifecycle

Lifecycle stage	Description
1	Young and single, living at home *few financial burdens, recreation orientated, strongly influenced by opinion leaders, tend to make a large volume of leisure purchases*
2	Young and single, away from home *possible homeowners, probably moderately well off but with patterns of expenditure slightly more orientated towards the house*
3	Newly married, no children *at present better off financially than they will be in the near future, high level of purchases of both household goods and consumer durables*
4	Full nest 1 – young children *likely to be financially stretched at this point in time, child-dominated household, expenditure probably restricted to the necessities*
5	Full nest 2 – older married couples with dependent children *rather improved financial position, some expenditure required to support children, but children no longer dominate the household*
6	Empty nest 1 – older married couples, still working, children left home *financial position much improved, mortgage probably repaid, increased volume of expenditure on leisure, travel and consumer durables*
7	Empty nest 2 – older married couples, no longer working, children left home *expenditure reduced, may consider moving, probably increased expenditure on health and medical products*
8	Solitary survivor – still working *income probably adequate, but expenditure patterns likely to be modest, may be selling the house to move to smaller accommodation*
9	Solitary survivor – no longer working *significant reduction in income, may move to sheltered accommodation, concern with health*

Table 6.3 The sagacity lifecycle grouping

Lifecycle stage	Description	% of adults
Dependent	Mainly under 24s, living at home or full-time student	14.9
Pre-family	Under 35s who have established their own household, but no dependent children	9.5
Family	Housewives and head of household, under 65, with one or more children in the household	32.3
Late	Adults whose children have left home or who are over 35 and childless	43.4

Source: Advertising Association (1992d).

In practice, this type of classification may often be too fine for market segmentation and a simple example of a lifecycle classification for the United Kingdom is shown in table 6.3. This particular lifecycle uses only four stages, but does give market analysts the option to further subdivide these stages according to income and occupation.

In general, demographic segmentation methods are powerful tools to specify target market segments. This conclusion is particularly true when each of the bases is used in combination with other methods. It will have become clear that the descriptors for demographic segmentation are not independent but are interdependent. Age and family lifecycle stage are, for example, closely linked. By using descriptors in combination it is possible to be highly specific in selecting targets for marketing campaigns.

Geo-demographic variables
Geo-demographics is a relatively new approach to segmentation and attempts to combine locational and demographic information. The underlying principle of geo-demographics is the belief that households within a particular neighbourhood exhibit similar purchasing behaviour, have similar attitudes and expectations, and similar needs. Neighbourhoods can therefore be classified according to the characteristics of the individuals who live there and can then be grouped together, even though they are widely separated. Geo-demographics is thus able to target customers in particular areas who exhibit similar behaviour patterns.

Table 6.4 Acorn classification

Group	Title	% of 1991 UK population
A	agricultural areas	3.3
B	modern family housing, higher incomes	17.6
C	older housing of intermediate status	17.9
D	older terraced housing	4.2
E	recent, better-off council estates (category I)	13.2
F	council estates, older age groups (category II)	8.8
G	council estates, overcrowded, greatest hardship (category III)	7.0
H	mixed inner metropolitan areas	3.8
I	high status non-family areas	4.1
J	affluent suburban housing	15.8
K	better-off retirement areas	3.8
U	unclassified	0.5

Source: Advertising Association (1992d).

A number of commercial systems for this type of segmentation are available, including MOSAIC (CCN Systems Ltd), ACORN (CACI) and PINPOINT (PiNPOINT Analysis Ltd). These systems are typically constructed on the basis of information from the national Census of Great Britain, which is then updated by each organization on a regular basis and may also be supplemented with additional information such as postcodes. The ACORN Profile (A Classification of Residential Neighbourhoods) for Great Britain is shown in table 6.4 based on 1981 Census of Population data and updated by the suppliers of ACORN data, CACI.

Although this classification differs from the traditional social class groupings, there will of course be a considerable amount of overlap between the two. ACORN has the advantage of providing a much finer classification. The table above gives twelve geo-demographic groupings, compared to six social class groupings, and the twelve ACORN groups can be further split into thirty-nine ACORN types. Similarly, MOSAIC is based on fifty eight different housing types and PINPOINT on twelve Pin groups, which further subdivide to twenty-five Pin types.

Psychographic segmentation

Psychographics or lifestyle segmentation is a method that seeks to classify people according to their values, opinions, personality characteristics, interests and attitudes. It focuses on the person and aims to identify common types of attitudes or patterns of behaviour that can influence the purchase decision. By its very nature, it is arguably one of the more relevant types of segmentation, but the fact that it is very much a subjective approach means that there are measurement difficulties. Collecting and interpreting the relevant data can be a complex and costly exercise and empirical work to date has been less than successful in identifying links between personality and buying behaviour. In part, this lack of success may be due to a heavy reliance on clinical scales for measuring personality when in practice it may be more appropriate to identify brand personality types (Foxall, 1987) or develop scales that relate specifically to a particular product.

Lifestyle refers to distinctive ways of living adopted by particular communities or subsections of society. Lifestyle is a manifestation of a number of behavioural factors, such as motivation, personality and culture, and its effectiveness in segmenting markets depends on how accurately a lifestyle can be described and whether the number of people conforming to that lifestyle can be quantified. If distinctive lifestyle groups can be identified and profiled, then marketers can target products and promotion towards particular lifestyle groups. Lifestyle is a controversial issue, and a full analysis of the argument is beyond the scope of this text. The implications of lifestyle for marketing, and the problems of definition involved, can perhaps best be illustrated by some examples.

One simple example generalizes lifestyle in terms of four categories, thus:

- *Upwardly mobile, ambitious* Consumers who are seeking a better and more affluent lifestyle, principally through better paid and more interesting work, and a higher material standard of living. Consumers in this group will typically be innovative and more willing to try new products.
- *Traditional and sociable* Individuals who seek social approval and reassurance. These needs will usually be met through compliance and conformity to group norms. Purchasing patterns will therefore be 'conformist'.
- *Security and status seeking* Typically individuals for whom *safety* needs and *ego-defensive* needs are predominant. This lifestyle links status,

income and security. It encourages the purchase of strong and well-known products and brands, and emphasizes those products and services that confer status and make life as secure and predictable as possible. Products that are well established and familiar inspire more confidence than new products, which will be resisted.

- *Hedonistic preference* Individuals who typically place emphasis on *enjoying life now* and are oriented towards the immediate satisfaction of wants and needs.

From a marketing perspective, there may be much to be gained from identifying customer groups in this way, since the attitudes and behaviour that characterize each group seem to have obvious links to purchasing patterns. At the same time, there are obvious difficulties in measuring, for example, *conformism* and *compliance*. Furthermore, even when methods have been identified for measuring such concepts, there may still be difficulties in actually reaching consumers who fall into these groups.

As with geo-demographics, there are commercial systems available for profiling lifestyles. An example of such a system is given in table 6.5. This system is described as behaviourgraphics and is based on consumers' shopping and leisure behaviour.

Segmenting organizational markets

Much of the discussion so far has focused on segmentation in final consumer markets, but the principles are equally valid in organizational markets. In organizational markets, segmentation tends to be more heavily based on objective variables such as organizational size, main business activity and turnover. Thus, for example, the UK market for paint can be segmented according to the way in which the product is used (Chisnall, 1985). The two main segments are decorative paints used mainly on buildings, and industrial paints used mainly for manufactured products.

Similarly, a computer manufacturer may segment its market to distinguish between office use (word processing), scientific research use and production control use. Turnover can give some indication of the likely needs and expectations of customers. In the banking sector, for example, corporate customers are commonly segmented by size in recognition of the vast difference between the needs of a local small shopkeeper and a multinational oil company.

Table 6.5 Persona behaviourgraphics classification

Name	Description	% of UK households
Golf clubs and Volvos	husband/career orientated, materialistic	3.7
The got set	higher income, well-educated, interested in arts	1.8
Bon viveurs	winers and diners, articulate conversationalists	4.3
Fast trackers	young, middle income, interest in active sports, leisure	3.6
The high techs	motivated by technology, not necessarily high earners	6.2
Faith, hope and charity	churchgoers and charity donators, generally with older/grown up children, community minded	3.9
Safe, steady and sensible	mostly self-employed with health and accident insurance, savings and pensions plans	3.9
Craftsmen and homemakers	little education but useful craft skills	6.1
Trinkets and treasures	older, middle-income group, intellectual rather than physical	4.7
Cultural travellers	often elderly, love foreign holidays/theatre/concerts	5.0
Carry on camping	outdoor types, like camping, walking, often in industrial and white collar work, particularly public sector	3.8
Health and humanities	has spiritual values, political/social change	4.2
Wildlife trustees	older, better off with country pursuits, enjoy travelling	5.5
Factories, fishing and football	active, outdoor, mostly blue-collar	4.6
Lager, crisps and videos	sociable materialists, pleasure seekers, poorly paid with little education	5.3
Instant chic	lower-income young people, interested in modern styles, eager for new experiences	4.9
Gardeners' question time	older, suburban/rural owner occupiers	5.9
Pools, horses and pubs	poorer, less educated, few material comforts	5.5
Survivors	very poor, little education or confidence	9.1
Reading, religion and routine	low-income elderly, 'respectable' folk, give to charity and like to read, usually in small towns	8.1

Source: CCN Systems Ltd (quoted in Advertising Association, 1992b).

Some organizations have adopted approaches to segmentation based on more subjective variables. As shown in exhibit 6.2, Girobank employed attitudinal data for segmenting the small business market while Ciba-Geigy have used a benefit segmentation for herbicide (Naert, 1990). This distinguishes between:

- *Brand loyal*   Prefer an established product, distrust new products, tend to be influenced by colleagues. Typically older farmers with less income and less education.
- *Performance*   Prefer high-performance herbicide with the ability to control all types of weed. Typically younger farmers with higher incomes and more formal training.
- *Versatility*   Prefer herbicides that are suitable for a variety of crops on a variety of soil types with a variety of methods of application. Typically farmers with a mixture of crops on heavy soils.

The third segment was identified as providing Ciba-Geigy's best customers.

Conclusions

Segmentation is the process of identifying groups of consumers with broadly similar needs and wants, who are also broadly similar in the way in which they respond to the marketing mix. By understanding the characteristics of each segment within a market, an organization has the opportunity to develop distinct products and marketing campaigns that are closely tailored to the needs of these segments. Provided each segment is large enough to be profitable, this approach is preferable to simply offering the same product to the market as a whole. There are a variety of approaches to segmenting markets, but all have common elements, namely the need to establish how consumers differ and why they differ. Two broad categories of data can be used in market segmentation: objective data and subjective data. The advantage of objective data, such as quantity purchased, age, income, etc., is that the required information is easily available and it is relatively straightforward to identify which consumers fall into which segments. Subjective data, by contrast, is less readily available and more difficult to collect. However, subjective, data such as benefits sought, lifestyle, personality, etc., may often have the advantage of

Exhibit 6.2   Attitudinal segmentation in organizational markets

Girobank

Launched in 1968 as a basic money transmission service, Girobank developed into a full clearing bank and by the mid-1980s was the sixth largest in the UK market. In 1984 Girobank decided to expand its business by offering banking services to the small business sector. Given the bank's organizational structure, it was recognized that a target marketing strategy would be appropriate and therefore some consideration had to be given to how the market segmented. After much discussion it was decided that the segmentation exercise should be based on products used and attitudes towards banks. The segments would be identified using cluster analysis.

Eight clusters were identified, including:

- Would be big companies.
  Relatively large, typically manufacturing firms, tend to be major users of international payments and interest earning facilities. Generally heavy users of bank services and tend to be self confident in their financial dealings.
- The simple life.
  Largely retailers and suppliers of consumer services. Tend to be low users of bank services and are primarily concerned with convenient access in choosing a bank.

These clusters were profiled according to location, turnover and sector as well as product usage to allow Girobank the potential to target its marketing to specific segments.

Source: Roach (1989).

being able to explain why groups of consumers differ far more effectively than objective data. Thus, the choice between the different approaches is not always clear cut and often there is much to be gained in combining both types of data in order to segment markets.

Self-test questions

1. What are the criteria for effective segmentation?
2. What is the difference between a segment basis and a segment descriptor?
3. What are the advantages of geo-demographic segmentation over simple demographic or socio-economic segmentation?
4. What problems do organizations encounter when trying to segment a market psychographically?
5. Why are objective variables more common when segmenting organizational markets?

7 Market targeting

Introduction

Having identified how a market is segmented and established the characteristics of each segment, the next stage in formulating a marketing strategy is to identify which markets to target. As explained in chapter 2, this requires some consideration of the needs of consumers in each segment, the nature of the competition, and the skills and capabilities of the organization. Many organizations will either not wish to or may not be able to target every segment in the market. Consequently, the process of market targeting can be divided into two stages. This chapter examines both stages of the market, targeting process in turn. The first stage is to examine the characteristics of market segments and assess their degree of attractiveness from the perspective of the organization. This leads to the second stage which involves the organization making a decision with regard to market coverage, i.e. whether to target the market as a whole or whether to concentrate on specific segments.

At this stage it might be useful to clarify what is meant by the term market since this word may be used to describe individual segments as well as much larger groups of consumers. To avoid the marketing myopia trap, it is preferable, at least initially, to think of markets in a broad sense as consisting of groups of consumers with similar needs, which may be satisfied by a range of similar products. Thus, for example, the computer market can be thought of as encompassing business, engineering, scientific, educational and personal customers and covering products from mainframes, minicomputers, microcomputers and portable computers. Diagrammatically, we could represent this market as a matrix of product–market combinations as shown in figure 7.1. The final outcome of the market targeting process is that the organization should be in a position to identify which products to offer in which segments of the market; in other

		Markets				
		Business	Scientific	Engineering	Educational	Personal
Products	Mainframe computers					
	Minicomputers					
	Personal computers					
	Portable computers					

Figure 7.1   Product – market combinations in the computer market

words, market targeting enables the organization to specify its product/ market scope.

Evaluating segment attractiveness

Once segments have been identified within a particular market, the organization must assess the relative attractiveness of those segments in relation to its own particular skills and objectives. In many senses, this entails a smaller scale version of the market environment analysis explained in chapter 4. Thus, for example, Kotler (1991) suggests that each segment is assessed in terms of its size and growth and then in terms of its structural attractiveness using Porter's five-force analysis. Given the potential variability across segments within a particular market, a five-force analysis of the individual segments may produce results that are quite different to those produced at the level of the market as a whole. Size and growth rate are clearly important features of any market segment, but these must be evaluated in conjunction with the following:

Degree of segment rivalry
The level and intensity of competition within a segment requires specific consideration, particularly so given that those segments which are apparently the more attractive (large, high growth rates, etc.) are also the segments that are likely to be characterized by higher levels of competition.

Suppliers' bargaining power
As was the case at the overall market level, the degree of supplier bargaining power can have a significant impact on the attractiveness of a particular segment, particularly when the products relevant to a particular segment require distinctive inputs. For example, the market power of suppliers of pointing devices (the computer mouse) may be of little relevance in the mainframe segment of the computer market, but may be of much greater significance in the microcomputer or portable computer segments.

Bargaining power of buyers
Again, because of segment differences, there may be considerable variations in the bargaining power of buyers. The bargaining power of computer distributors is of little significance to the mainframe computer market but could have a substantial impact in the microcomputer or portable computer markets.

Threat of substitute products
The potential impact of substitute products may vary across market segments. Electronic personal organizers, for example, may be regarded as a substitute product in the notebook segment of the portable computer market, but would not be considered as a substitute in other segments of the computer market. Furthermore, the threat of substitutes may arise within the market itself, broadly defined. The pace of technical change in computer technology has resulted in high-powered personal computers becoming a threat to the market for minicomputers.

Threat of new entrants
Many organizations concentrate their efforts on serving only particular segments within a broad market, so the threat of new entrants will vary across segments. Toshiba, for example, although operating in the computer market, chose to concentrate their efforts on portable personal computers. Thus, at the time at which they entered the market, they represented a threat in this particular segment, but would have had little or no impact elsewhere in the market.

Analysing each segment in terms of these features can give some indication of the structural attractiveness of a particular segment. However, it is not sufficient simply to consider how attractive a segment is in terms of is own features; the organization must also consider how well the features match the organization's own skills and objectives. Boyd and Walker (1990) suggest that the balance between the intrinsic structural attractiveness of a segment and its suitability as a target market for a particular organization can be assessed using a variant of the General Electric (GE) business portfolio matrix. In principle, the GE matrix is similar to the BCG matrix outlined in chapter 2 and is commonly associated with decision making regarding the composition of the product portfolio. The fact that it is rather broader in the way in which it assess markets also makes it suited to other applications. The matrix measures market attractiveness against business strength and competitive position. The five-force analysis discussed above can give some indication of market attractiveness, and the use of some form of scoring system would allow segments to be classified as being of low, medium or high attractiveness. Business strengths and competitive position can then be assessed by considering factors such as:

- the organization's relative market share and rate of growth in market share;
- the sources of the organization's competitive advantage (actual or perceived);
- the degree of consistency between the opportunities offered by the segment and the organization's objectives;
- managerial skills and competencies within the organization relative to market expectations;
- production capability and capacity;
- marketing strengths;
- technological strengths.

Again by using some form of scoring system, possibly based on information collected during a marketing audit, business strengths and competitive position can be assessed as being either low, medium or high.

Each segment can then be positioned on the matrix according to market attractiveness and business strengths, and the position of each segment gives some indication of the appropriate strategic response. The specific recommendations for each position are outlined in figure 7.2. Segments in the top left-hand corner of the matrix clearly offer considerable potential for the organization either to enter or maintain and build a position. Those in the bottom right-hand corner should ideally be avoided, and the organization that is already present in such segments may need to consider a gradual withdrawal. As figure 7.3 shows, each segment can be represented in the matrix as a circle which is proportional to the size of

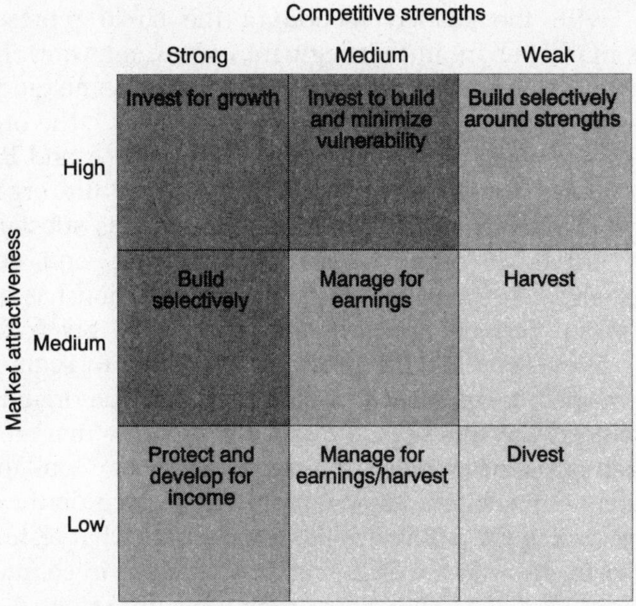

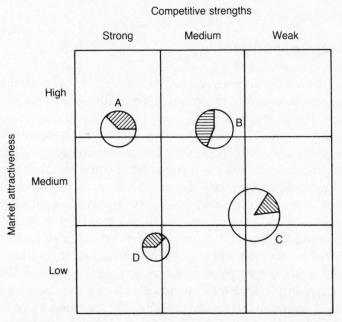

Figure 7.2 The General Electric business screen
Source: Adapted from Boyd and Walker (1990)

Figure 7.3 Positioning market segments using the General Electric business
screen

that segment, with the shaded section of the circle representing the organization's market share in that segment (where relevant). Positioning segments in this way can then offer the organization some guidance with respect to market targeting. In the example in figure 7.3, the organization has placed four segments on the GE matrix. Segments A and B both look attractive for future development, particularly given the organization's relatively large market share. By contrast, segment C is substantially less promising in terms of both market attractiveness and competitive strengths. It is also a segment in which the organization has a relatively low market share. Serious consideration should be given to possible harvesting or divestment for the products marketed to segment C. The position with respect to segment D is less clear cut. The organization has competitive strengths in this segment and a reasonable market share, but the market itself is less attaractive. The organization may look to strategies that concentrate on developing income from this segment in the short term as well as considering the possibility for a more active harvesting strategy in the longer term. As with the BCG matrix (discussed in chapter 2), these recommendations should not be seen as definitive, but rather as guidelines to help planners think about whether particular segments should be targeted, and if so, what sort of strategy might be appropriate.

Market coverage strategy

Once the relative attractiveness of each segment has been established, the organization must use this information to establish its market coverage strategy. Few, if any, markets are entirely homogeneous. Even within some of the simplest markets, there are typically identifiable segments. The existence of these segments, however, does not automatically indicate that the most appropriate strategy is to develop specific products and specific marketing campaigns to meet the needs of each segment. For some organizations, it may make business sense to try to offer a narrow product range to the market as a whole, while for others it may be more appropriate to develop products for specific consumer groups.

In broad terms we can identify two approaches to market coverage, namely full market coverage and selective market coverage. Full market coverage would imply that the organization looks to provide products to most, if not all, segments in the market. Within the category of full market coverage strategies, we can identify two basic options, namely undifferentiated and differentiated marketing.

Undifferentiated (mass) marketing

This entails targeting the entire market, perhaps because the market does not easily segment, or because the organization has chosen to ignore the differences between groups and offer a standardized, relatively low-cost range of products to all consumers. This approach to marketing is broadly similar to what Porter (1980, 1985) would describe as a cost leadership strategy. Henry Ford's Model T is probably the classic example of an undifferentiated mass marketing approach. The key to an undifferentiated strategy is to ignore differences between consumers and concentrate instead on similarities. The products offered will typically be highly standardized and the product range narrow. Products would normally be widely distributed and competitively priced, supported by a highly standardized marketing campaign and a major objective of the marketing strategy for these products would be one of maximizing sales. Profits would be based on a high sales volume and low unit costs. In particular, the firm would hope to benefit from any economies of scale that may be present, both in production and marketing. A narrow product range will tend to reduce production, transport and inventory costs, and will also tend to reduce promotional expenditure.

The popularity of mass marketing has declined in recent years as a result of the reduced importance associated with economies of scale. Increasingly, the application of information technology in the production process and the development of flexible manufacturing systems has meant that many organizations benefit more from economies of scope (cost savings associated with the production of many different varieties) than from economies of scale. Thus the potential to produce cost effectively a wide range of differentiated products has increased and many organizations have taken advantage of this opportunity to move away from undifferentiated marketing strategies. Exhibit 7.1 presents an example of a move away from a largely undifferentiated marketing strategy. Traditionally the major clearing banks in the United Kingdom had pursued an undifferentiated strategy in relation to the market for current accounts on the implicit assumption that the product itself was not easily differentiated and that customer needs were largely homogeneous. Midland Bank launched a range of accounts – Vector, Orchard and Meridian – targeted at three different customer groups. These segments were identified according to demographic and lifestyle characteristics. Although the move was widely recognized as successful, the bank has recently started to reverse this process and dropped the Vector account from its product range.

Exhibit 7.1   Midland Bank

Targeting the yuppie market

Segmenting personal customer markets provides a basis for product differentiation and more accurate targeting of customer needs. The Midland Vector account, launched in May 1987, was an attempt by Midland Bank to extend the range of accounts available to its customers, offering a current account with a number of new features targeted at a specific group of consumers. The Vector account was based on lifestyle segmentation, concentrating on the young, affluent, independent consumer – the 'yuppie' market. It was targeted specifically at the 25–44 age group with salaries in the region of £12,000–25,000 and the typical customer was considered to be someone who was well educated, confident, with a sophisticated and easy lifestyle.

This particular segment was seen to have considerable growth potential; the number of Bs and C1s in society was forecast to grow and they were expected to become increasingly affluent as inheritance windfalls from property continued to rise. Furthermore, the bank recognized the importance of trying to break down the traditional view of the banks and the 'superior attitudes adopted by many branch managers'. The importance of relationship banking was growing on the personal side as well as on the corporate side.

The account offered a moderate rate of interest, free overdrafts up to £250 and no unexpected charges. In return, the account holder paid a fixed fee of £10 per month. The account was essentially designed to run itself, provided that a monthly salary cheque appeared, to cater for the needs of consumers who were willing to incur the monthly charges in order to save themselves the time and effort associated with running their finances. The monthly charge provided Midland with a guaranteed income, which contributed to the estimated 9 per cent costs of running current accounts. The initial take up was in the region of 70,000, which provided Midland with a fee income in the region of £8.4m.

Source: Marketing (1987).

Differentiated marketing

The aim of differentiated marketing is to select a number of segments and tailor specific products to the needs of those segments. In many respects, this approach can be seen as an efficient method of increasing sales since the products concerned are targeted more precisely at the needs of particular customer groups. Thus, the focus is on differences between consumer groups rather than similarities across groups, but the success of this approach is dependent on the organization having the necessary skills and competencies to meet the needs of differing segments. Organizations pursuing a differentiated marketing strategy will have a wide product range, possibly with a variety of brands and a distinctive marketing campaign for each segment. The products will typically attract a premium price and distribution and promotion will be tailored to the needs of the relevant segments.

By differentiating, the organization aims to increase the value of sales, if not the volume. At the same time, differentiation means that the firm incurs an increase in costs. Since separate production runs are normally required, marketing costs increase because of the need to develop a number of distinctive campaigns and, finally, inventory and distribution costs may be higher. Increasingly however, improvements in manufacturing technology and the adoption of just-in-time (JIT) ordering and delivery mean that production and inventory costs can be kept low, and for many organizations, the cost of differentiating is primarily a marketing cost. A possible problem with differentiated marketing is that of over-segmentation, which occurs when the organization identifies too many market segments, some of which are not large enough or sufficiently distinct to justify separate marketing campaigns. Consequently the increase in costs is greater than the increase in revenue, which results in falling profits. Companies such as Ford and Vauxhall provide good examples of firms pursuing a differentiated strategy with a range of cars from the small hatchbacks (Nova, Fiesta) through to the large executive models (Carlton, Granada). As table 7.1 shows, each type of car within the overall product range is targeted at a different segment of the market, and within each range there is further differentiation to meet the needs of sub-groups within the relevant market segment. Thus, for example, both the Nova and Fiesta range from the basic, low-powered model through to the luxury, high-powered model.

Table 7.1   Product ranges for Vauxhall and Ford

	Hatchbacks		Small family car		Executive cars	
	Vauxhall	Ford	Vauxhall	Ford	Vauxhall	Ford
Basic	Nova 1.2i 3-door (£5,652)	Fiesta 1.1 3-door (£6,231)	Astra 1.4i Merit 4-door (£9,060)	Escort 1.3 3-door (£7,923)	Carlton 1.8i L (£14,333)	Granada 2.0 LX (£17,548)
Mid-range	Nova 1.4i Luxe 5-door (£8,995)	Fiesta 1.3LX 5-door (£9,163)	Astra Si 1.6i 5-door (£11,011)	Escort 1.6 LX 5-door (£10,606)	Carlton 2.0i CDX (£20,008)	Granada Scorpio 2.0i (£20,558)
Top of range	Nova GSi 1.6i (£11,188)	Fiesta RS 1800 (£12,712)	Astra 2.0i Convertible (£14,371)	Escort XR3i Cabriolet (£17,135)	Carlton 2.6i Diplomat (£21,351)	Granada Scorpio 24v (£26,798)

Source: What Car Magazine

Selective market coverage entails offering products or services to a limited set of segments within a market. The chosen segments should correspond to areas in which the company has distinctive skills/capabilities and is well placed closely to match the needs of consumers in those segments. The actual size of the segments is not always that important; it may often be preferable to aim for a large share in a comparatively small market segment where the competition is easier, rather than aim for a position in a larger and more competitive segment. Following Kotler (1991), we can identify four particular types of selective targeting.

Single segment concentration

The organization concentrates only on a single segment in the market and supplies products tailored specifically to the needs of those customer groups. Such an approach is often described as niche marketing, and Porsche and Gucci provide classic examples of organizations pursuing this type of approach. Such a strategy can potentially be highly profitable provided the segment itself is large enough in value terms, though it need not be large in volume terms. It is also important that the segment is reasonably stable, since in pursuing such a strategy, the firm is effectively *putting all its eggs in one basket*. Sudden changes in customer needs or sudden changes in technology could result in either the disappearance of the niche or a substantial increase in competition, either of which could result in a substantial loss of sales.

Selective specialization

This can also be described as a type of niche marketing strategy, but rather than concentrating on a single segment, the organization chooses to operate in several, possibly unrelated market segments. Compared with single segment specialization, this approach has the advantage of being rather less risky, as the organization is not dependent on a single segment for all its business.

Product specialization

Most markets can be seen as comprising a number of different customer groups and a number of different but related products. The organization that concentrates on supplying a particular product type across a range of customer groups is pursuing a product specialization strategy. This approach may be particularly appropriate to organizations with specific strengths or knowledge in relation to a given technology or product. Thus, in the footwear market, Nike have built on their knowledge of the design and construction of sports shoes to specialize in providing this type of product to a variety of different customers, ranging from the professional sports person through to the weekend tennis player.

Market specialization

This is the opposite approach to product specialization. Rather than concentrating on a particular product, the organization chooses to specialize in meeting the needs of a particular customer group. This strategy may be particularly appropriate where knowledge of the customer groups specific needs is a particularly important basis for establishing a competitive advantage. Certain publishers, for example, concentrate only on supplying textbooks for schools, universities and colleges, while organizations who offer staff training course may choose to specialize in providing a range of training courses to businesses in specific sectors.

Exhibit 7.2   Targeting new markets

Durex

Traditionally, men have been the main target market for manufacturers of condoms. However, with a growing awareness of AIDS and changing social attitudes to the product, a new target market has appeared among women. The size of the condom market as a whole had doubled over the last five years, and within this, the proportion of women buying their own condoms is in excess of 20 per cent. Durex has introduced what is thought to be the first condom targeted at the female market and specifically at young, single women. The product is a coral-coloured condom attractively packaged and sold under the name Assure. It will be displayed and sold with sanitary products to ease the embarrassment felt by many women when buying condoms from general counters.

Source: Marketing Week (1992a).

Clearly, the process of establishing which markets to target is crucial in the development of the overall marketing strategy since it defines the scope of the organization's business. It is also important to recognize that targeting is a continuous process and regular reviews of the organization's product–market scope are essential to the success of a marketing strategy. Although the pace of change may vary, there are few markets that are not in a state of flux due to both changing consumer needs, changing patterns of competition and changing technologies. This process can lead to the appearance of new product–market combinations, the disappearance of others and will certainly result in changes in the structural attractiveness of remaining product–market combinations. Exhibit 7.2 shows the importance of adjusting targeting decisions in response to such changes. The spread of AIDS has led to a growing awareness of the importance of taking precautions against infection. The impact of this change in consumer attitudes was twofold. First, the market for condoms became more competitive with a number of new entrants looking to exploit the growth potential created by AIDS. Second, new segments began to appear in what had traditionally been viewed as a largely homogenous market. In order to strengthen its competitive position *vis-à-vis* new entrants, Durex developed a strategy to target these new segments.

Conclusions

The process of identifying target markets can best be described as a search for the most appropriate product–market combinations for a particular organization. Thus, the targeting decision is essentially concerned with deciding what products to market to which consumer groups. The first stage in this process is an assessment of the attractiveness of each segment from the perspective of the organization. This requires a consideration of both the organization's skills and competencies, along with an evaluation of the structural attractiveness of each segment. Once the various segments have been evaluated in this way, a decision can be taken with respect to market coverage. Two options present themselves: targeting the vast majority of segments through a full market coverage strategy, or targeting a smaller group of segments through a strategy of selective specialization.

Self-test questions

1. How can the structural attractiveness of a segment be assessed?
2. What are the attractions and the problems associated with differentiated marketing?
3. What are the differences between product and market specialization and what might lead an organization to pursue one or the other of these approaches?

8 Product positioning

Introduction

Market targeting is concerned with identifying the organization's product–market scope to determine which products will be marketed to which segments. For each product–market combination an appropriate product position must be established. The process of positioning is concerned with the establishment and maintenance of a strong competitive position within particular market segments. Product positioning describes the way in which the organization wishes consumers to perceive its products and the way in which consumers actually perceive those products. The basis for any positioning exercise is the identification of the product's differential advantage, given the needs of the target market and the existing and potential competitive offerings. Where there are a number of target markets to be served, a variety of positions may be required for products that are superficially quite similar.

While consumers will obviously position products on the basis of their experience and information, that positioning can be reinforced, or altered by the marketing campaign. The marketing strategy will aim to identify product positions, whereas the marketing mix will be concerned with creating and maintaining those positions. While any product position should reflect the organization's differential advantage in a particular market, it is important to recognize that this differential advantage may exist not only in relation to the physical attributes of the product itself, but may also relate to the perceived image of the product. Furthermore, in many service industries, the differential advantage may be based not on the product itself but on the reputation of the organization supplying the product. This chapter examines, first, how organizations can identify the attributes on which products may be positioned. It then moves on to consider the information that is needed for product positioning and finally reviews a number of positioning strategies.

Identifying a differential advantage

Effective product positioning depends upon marketers being able to identify a differential advantage for a product. This differential advantage, whether actual or perceived, should be some feature that is considered to be important by consumers and which competitors do not, or cannot, offer. Identifying a differential advantage requires a thorough understanding of organizational skills and capabilities and the needs of the target market. Kotler (1991) suggests that Porter's value chain can be used as an analytical framework for identifying sources of differential advantage.

The value chain, shown in figure 8.1, decomposes the activities of an organization into primary activities and support activities. Primary activities include inbound logistics, operations, outbound logistics, marketing and customer service, and these represent a series of sequential stages in the provision of products to consumers. Support activities include the organization's infrastructure, human resource management, technology and procurement, and these affect all primary activities. An analysis of the value chain can help an organization to identify its strengths and weaknesses and its potential sources of competitive advantage. For example, if outbound logistics (order processing and delivery) is identified as an area of strength, it may be feasible to use this as a basis for establishing a differential competitive advantage in markets where speed of delivery is important. However, it is not enough to examine the value chain in isolation because a particular strength can only be turned into a differential advantage if the organization outperforms its competitors in this respect. Thus, by analysing costs and performance throughout the value chain relative to the competition, the organization can identify areas in which improvement is required and, more importantly, areas in which it appears to have a differential advantage.

Porter (1980, 1985) also argues that there are two basic options for developing a differential advantage: costs and differentiation. A cost-based differential advantage requires that the organization attempts to control the market through being the low-cost producer. Typically, the product is undifferentiated, though differentiation cannot be ignored, since the cost savings for the consumer must compensate for the loss of product features, while the discount offered by the organization should not be so high as to offset cost advantages associated with a highly standardized product

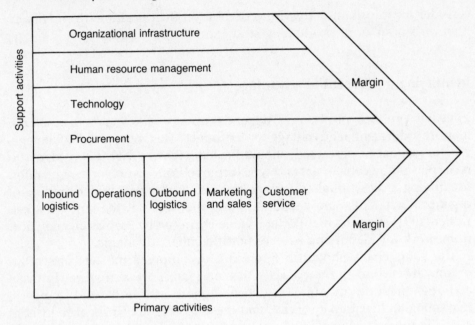

Figure 8.1   The value chain
Source: Adapted from Porter (1980)

range. This approach to building a differential advantage is described as cost leadership if pursued in the context of full market coverage and cost focus if pursued in the context of selective specialization.

The alternative approach is to concentrate on offering products that can be regarded as unique in areas highly valued by the consumer. It is the products' uniqueness and the associated customer loyalty that protects the organization from competition. For this strategy to be successful, however, the price premium received by the organization must outweigh the costs of supplying the differentiated product. At the same time, the customer must feel that the distinctive image of the product and the additional features offered more than compensate for the additional cost of acquiring the product. When this approach is pursued in the context of full market coverage it is usually described as differentiation leadership; when pursued in the context of selective specialization it is termed as differentiation focus. Porter argues that organizations must look for either cost or differentiation as a basis for building competitive advantage, but not both. The organization that tries to compete on both dimensions will be *stuck in the middle* and is likely to be out-performed by competitors who concentrate their efforts on either cost or differentiation. In practice, however, there are examples of businesses such as Sainsburys which are successfully emphasizing both cost and differentiation in their positioning (Dobson and Starkey, 1993).

For any factor to qualify as the basis for a differential advantage, it must fulfil three criteria.

Uniqueness
A differential advantage must be able to create an actual or perceived uniqueness in the mind of the consumer. Unless a product can be seen as unique in some sense, the organization faces the risk of having to compete purely on price and price competition can be highly destabilizing. In the personal computer market, the Apple Macintosh range of computers held a unique differential advantage based on a user-friendly operating system; in the hi-fi market, the Danish company Bang & Olufsen have a unique differential advantage based on the design and style of their products. A differential advantage need not be simply based on product features; other elements of the total offering may provide a basis for uniqueness. Waterstones, for example, created a differential advantage in book retailing through extended opening hours, while Lloyds Bank have built a differential advantage through advertising and branding, particularly in the form of the Black Horse logo.

Importance
Identifying a unique differential advantage is not, by itself, sufficient to create a competitive advantage for the organization's products. This differential advantage must exist in areas that consumers regard as important. National Westminster Bank, like many other financial institutions, anticipated that a differential advantage could be gained by adopting the status of independent intermediary under the terms of the Financial Services Act 1986. In practice, this strategy proved less than successful because independent financial advice was not an attribute that most consumers regarded as particularly important when purchasing financial products. Where a differential advantage exists in an area that consumers regard as unimportant, organizations have two options. First, the organization may take a reactive stance and simply seek alternative differential advantages in areas that consumers regard as important. Second, the organization may take a proactive stance and actively try to convince consumers of the importance of an aspect of the product in which they have a differential advantage.

Sustainability
For a differential advantage to be effective, it must be sustainable; it must be something that the organization can continue to offer and it must be possible to protect the relevant features from copying by competitors. For example, a differential advantage based on price is often difficult to maintain because competitors can easily match low prices, unless the ability to keep prices low derives from a fundamental superiority in terms of production or distribution costs that competitors cannot copy. Many organizations build competitive advantages around accumulated experience and these competitive advantages are potentially more difficult to copy and thus easier to sustain. Porsche, for example, has a strong competitive advantage based on engineering and design. In industries such as chemicals and pharmaceuticals, patents provide a basis for sustaining a competitive advantage based on product features, but patent protection is not available in many markets. For example, in the service sector, products are easily copied by competitors, so a differential advantage based on product features may be difficult to sustain. Thus, Midland Bank relied on heavy branding in an attempt to maintain their differential advantage in relation to the Vector account because the basic product features could easily be copied by competitors.

By identifying a differential advantage that gives the organization something to offer consumers that is unique, important and sustainable, the organization has the basis for developing an effective position in its chosen market.

Information for product positioning

In order to formulate a positioning strategy, an organization must first identify the features of products (including its own) that are currently being offered in the target market. It must also, through market research, establish which features are considered to be important by consumers. This provides the basic information for a positioning strategy. Ideally, however, further analysis should be conducted to establish more precisely how consumers perceive the current range of products. This information can be obtained through market research. Having identified the attributes of products that consumers consider to be important, further survey work can be undertaken to identify the extent to which these attributes are present in the available products. Figure 8.2 presents an example of this type of information for a number of products in the UK confectionery market. Simply plotting the average scores for each product in relation to each attribute produces a profile of how consumers perceive each brand of confectionery. The same technique can be employed to identify consumers' ideal brand profile, and by comparing actual with ideal, the marketer can gain some indication of how new products should be positioned or how existing products should be repositioned. Figure 8.3 shows a comparison between an existing brand and the desired brand profile. In this example, Bounty comes close to matching consumers' perceptions of an ideal brand

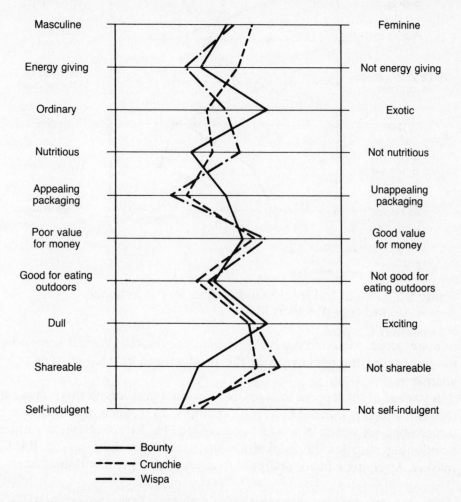

Figure 8.2 Brand profiles for confectionery
Source: Adapted from Watkins (1986)

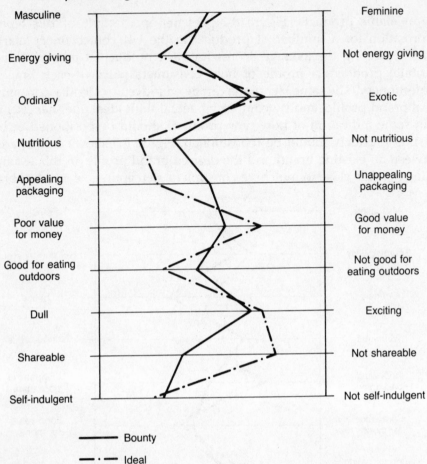

Figure 8.3   Actual and ideal brand profiles for confectionery
Source: Adapted from Watkins (1986)

in many areas, though there is evidence to suggest that there is some scope for improving the packaging of the product and making it appear less shareable.

A variant of this approach is to use a product positioning map. This uses the same basic information but attempts to reduce the number of dimensions on which a product is assessed. Figure 8.4 shows a product positioning map for the market for small/medium-sized cars in the UK market. Applying a factor analysis[1] to data on a range of variables, such as

---

[1] This technique uses correlations within a large number of variables to identify a smaller number of factors that are themselves combinations of the individual variables. The resulting factors can then be interpreted as measuring a particular dimension of the product offering.

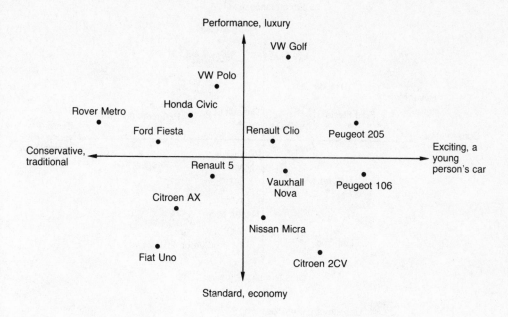

Figure 8.4 Product positioning in the UK car market (smaller cars)

engine size, top speed, number of doors, features, consumers' image of the car, etc., enables each model to be described in terms of its underlying features (or factors). In this instance, two factors are used, one relating to performance/luxury and the other relating to the car's image (either young and exciting or conservative and traditional). These data could be combined with information about consumer preferences (collected on a similar range of variables) to given a comparison between actual product positions and desired combinations of attributes. Again, a visual examination of the resulting product position map, as shown in figure 8.5, may offer some guidance on the appropriate positioning strategy. An analysis of this nature may indicate the existence of gaps in the market which the organization may wish to exploit. These gaps can be thought of as areas where there is a cluster of consumer preferences (as indicated by the clusters of dots) but no product that matches those preferences. However, in undertaking an analysis of this nature, it is important to be aware of the fact that it may not always be technically possible to offer a product that perfectly matches the target market's desired profile. Rather,

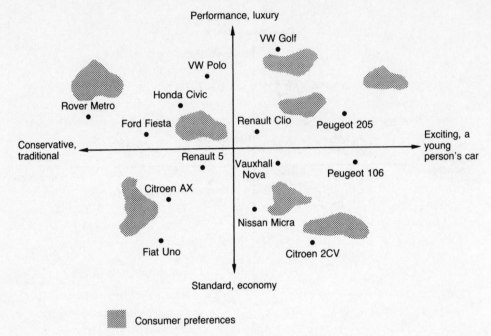

Figure 8.5 Product positioning and consumer preferences in the UK car market (smaller cars)

the intention would be to develop a match that is as close as possible, given the positions of competing products.

Strategies for product positioning

There are a number of positioning strategies that an organization can adopt and these may be used independently or together.

Positioning in relation to attributes

This essentially involves positioning the product on the basis of very specific attributes such as performance, durability, quality, reliability, style and design. Volvo cars are positioned on the basis of their safety features, while Volkswagen emphasize the extent to which their cars can be recycled. An example of positioning in relation to attributes is given in exhibit 8.1, which outlines a repositioning exercise for a Dutch brand of lager in the UK market.

Exhibit 8.1 Repositioning

Allied Breweries relaunch Oranjeboom

The Oranjeboom brand of lager was initially launched by Allied Breweries in the 1980s. The product was formulated and positioned to compete in the market for standard draught lager. The product itself was not the original Dutch lager but rather a weaker, UK-brewed imitation. The product was less than successful and was ultimately withdrawn. With the increase in competition in the market for standard draught lagers and the increasing cost of maintaining market share, Allied have decided to reposition and relaunch the Oranjeboom brand as a premium bottled lager. The decision to move Oranjeboom was supported and guided by demographic and psychographic trends. The market for premium lagers is primarily among social groups B and C1, and is typically young, single males with a high level of education and high incomes. The prospects for market growth within this target market were considered to be strong, making the premium lager segment an attractive one for Allied. Psychographically, this segment attached considerable importance to the authenticity and heritage of the product, to European influences and to design and quality. Thus, the relaunch of Oranjeboom emphasizes its Dutch origin, premium strength and the fact that it is imported, not manufactured domestically. The ultimate aim is to position Oranjeboom as the crown prince of lagers.

Source: Marketing Week (1992a), Meller (1992).

Positioning in relation to the user/usage

This can involve positioning the product according to the occasions on which it is used. Ovaltine and Horlicks, for example, have traditionally been positioned as bedtime drinks, though the launch of Ovaltine Light some years ago was an attempt to alter this image. Similarly, Lucozade was initially positioned as something to drink when ill; increasingly it is being repositioned as a healthy drink to restore and provide energy for sport and for anyone leading an energetic lifestyle. Equally, it may be possible to position the product in relation to specific types of users or specific user lifestyles. Thus, for example, the perfume 'Charlie', marketed by Revlon, was initially positioned to appeal to the independent career woman on its launch in early 1970s; it has recently been repositioned to appeal to the more feminine and romantic consumer.

Positioning in relation to competitors

This involves emphasizing features that are to some extent directly comparable with those of competitors. There are several variants of this strategy:

Positioning directly against competitors

This involves presenting the product as having all or most of the important features of the competing product at a comparable or lower price. This is potentially an aggressive and risky positioning strategy, since it involves challenging the competition *head-on*, but if successful it can offer considerable benefits in terms of improved sales and profits. The effective implementation of such a positioning strategy is heavily dependent on production efficiencies and innovative marketing. For example, the success of Compaq in the personal computer market has been achieved by positioning its products directly against IBM, the market leader, but aiming to present those products as being of even higher quality.

Positioning away from competitors

This involves positioning the product as having quite distinct or different features but fulfilling the same consumer requirements. This may be appropriate if the competitor's product is patent-protected or if it not feasible to produce a comparable product. An obvious example comes from the soft drinks market. The manufacturers of 7-Up could not compete directly with Coca-Cola and Pepsi, the market leaders, so they positioned 7-Up as the 'un-cola' drink. The product satisfied consumer requirements, but also offered something different. The campaign was a success and 7-Up became the number three best-selling soft drink.

Positioning in relation to a different product class

This entails positioning products in relation to competing offerings from a different but related product class. The rationale behind this approach to positioning is that it should enable the organization to attract consumers who might not otherwise have considered purchasing a product of this nature. For example, the recently launched margarine 'I Can't Believe Its Not Butter', is positioned in relation to butter rather than margarine to

---

Exhibit 8.2   Organizational positioning

Mencap

Mencap is a charity that represents mentally handicapped children and adults. Steve Billington, the organization's Marketing and Appeals Director, was concerned about the low level of awareness and the general perception of Mencap as a child-oriented, out-of-date, negative organization. The charity is looking to a new advertising campaign to help it shed its image of pathos and reposition itself in a more positive light. This advertising is based round a poster campaign designed to emphasize the similarities between people with and without learning difficulties. This campaign is being supported with a new logo and a new direct mail campaign.

Source: Marketing Week (1992b).

---

emphasize the idea that the product has the attributes of both butter and margarine. A similar approach was used in the positioning of Krona Margarine. Both products were successful in gaining market share from both margarine consumers and from butter consumers.

Corporate positioning

The idea of developing a position for the organization as a whole rather than for individual products is becoming increasingly important in many markets. Organizational positioning is perhaps most important for markets in which the purchase decision is driven as much by the organization as it is by the product. In retailing, for example, organizational positioning can be particularly important in attracting consumers into a particular store. Thus, for example in the UK grocery market, Sainsburys has attempted to position itself as the high-quality, value-for-money grocery chain, while Aldi, a new entrant, has actively positioned itself as the low price supplier. Organizational positioning is also important in many service industries since consumer choice is often guided by organizational reputation because of the difficulties associated with evaluating a service prior to purchase (Parasuraman, Zeithaml and Berry, 1985). Exhibit 8.2 shows an example of organizational positioning for the charity Mencap. Although a non-profit organization, positioning is still important for Mencap as it must compete with other charities in attracting support and donations from its target markets.

Conclusions

Product positioning refers to the way in which an organization's products are perceived by the target market. In developing a positioning strategy, the organization is attempting to create a unique place for its product in the minds of consumers. For a positioning strategy to be successful requires a thorough understanding of the organization's capabilities and the needs of the target market, such that a clear differential advantage can be identified for the product. This differential advantage may be actual (i.e. based on the physical attributes of the product) or perceived (based on the image of the product or the supplier). To be effective, the differential advantage must relate to some aspect of the product that consumers consider to be important; it must be distinctive and it must be sustainable. Once identified, the differential advantage provides the basis for product positioning. This position must be created and maintained by the appropriate use of marketing mix variables. Furthermore, consumer perceptions of the product and of competing offerings must be monitored to ensure that the marketing effort is creating and maintaining the desired product position.

CASE STUDY

Market targeting and positioning

Derwent Valley Foods

In the early 1980s, the snack food market was characterized by a fairly uninspiring range of crisps and nuts. Product innovation appeared to be largely confined to the children's market in which products such as Monster Munchies and Horror Bags were making significant market share gains.

Traditionally, the view had always been that the basic range of crisps and peanuts would be adequate to satisfy the adult market, particularly as adults were not seen as large-scale consumers of such snack foods. However, the nature of the adult market was changing. More extensive travel abroad had increased the number of consumers who were willing to try new and unusual foods and quality in food products was regarded as increasingly important. Other significant developments were the increased consumption of wine on a regular basis and the increase in social drinking in the home.

For two graduates from Newcastle University, Roger McKechnie (then working for Tudor Crisps) and Ray McGhee (European vice-president of the US advertising agency NCK), this suggested that there was a gap in the market. They strongly suspected that there was an unsatisfied demand for interesting, exciting and high-quality snack foods in the adult market. However, they did not expect such a product to appeal to all adults. The likely buyer was in social class AB, a regular wine drinker, with a concern for quality and the desire to project a sophisticated image. Their problem was how to enter this market. Preliminary calculations suggested that to launch a new business producing sophisticated snack foods for the adult market would require an investment of around £0.5m. To have any chance of raising this sort of money the two partners needed a clear and well thought out marketing strategy.

The basis of this strategy was to collect information, to determine what sort of product the consumers would want, what image should be created, what price would they pay and how the product should be promoted. The results of the market research were encouraging and McKechnie and McGhee were able to get their new company, Derwent Valley Foods (DVF), off the ground. Further market research was required to ensure that the company was producing a product that would meet the needs of the market. This involved surveys and discussions with both final consumers and the retailers who would stock the product. The result was an adult snack to be produced in four different varieties: Mexican Tortilla Chips, Californian Corn Chips, Mignons Morceaux and Shanghai Nuts. The products were marketed under the family brand name of Phileas Fogg. The use of the name of a famous explorer was chosen to reinforce the cosmopolitan nature of the product and associate the product with the image of adventure and excitement. With budgets fairly tight, extensive media advertising to accompany the product launch was out of the question. The packaging was the only real form of promotion that DVF could use, and consequently a lot of time was spent getting the packaging right. To keep with the image being created for the brand, the packaging was a distinctive, metallized foil bag with top quality gravure printing. The result was a product that would stand out when placed on supermarket shelves.

Phileas Fogg was regarded as probably one of the most innovative new brands of the 1980s, and by 1989 it had sales of over £10m and advertising support of around £1.5m. However, its market is being eroded by a series of copycat products from competitors. In 1987, KP launched its World Snacks brand, supermarkets have produced their own brand copies of the Phileas Fogg range and the quality and variety of crisps and nuts has improved. DVF have been able to counter with some new snacks, but increasingly they are finding that the adventurous image of Phileas Fogg is no longer as strong as it was in the early 1980s.

Questions

1. What do you think were the key factors in the success of DVF?
2. What features of DVFs chosen market make it particularly attractive?
3. Why was it important to conduct market research with both retailers and final consumers?
4. What are the strategic options facing DVF for the future?

9 Understanding the marketing mix

Introduction

The four elements of the marketing mix – product, price, promotion and place – are the essential toolkit of any marketing strategy. These elements represent the marketing variables that are directly controlled by the organization. It is by developing an appropriate balance between these elements that the organization can tailor its product offerings in order to meet the needs of its target market and achieve its own specified objectives. In a sense, the concept of the marketing mix provides a bridge between marketing strategy and marketing tactics. The aim of marketing strategy in any organization, as the previous chapters have outlined, is to establish the organization's differential advantage and identify a product position that reflects this differential advantage. Marketing tactics, by contrast, are concerned with actually creating and maintaining the chosen product position (Greenley, 1986). This chapter reviews the concept of the marketing mix and examines ways in which this mix can be managed over the course of a product's lifecycle.

The concept of the marketing mix

The marketing mix, as a concept, has both strategic and tactical dimensions. The strategic dimension of the marketing mix is primarily concerned with decisions about the relative importance of the mix elements for a particular product–market combination. Promotion, and particularly television advertising, for example, may play a key role in the marketing mix for fast-moving consumer goods, but may be almost irrelevant for specialized industrial goods. The tactical dimension of the marketing mix works within the framework created by decisions regarding the balance of the mix and is concerned primarily with the specification of precise details for each element in the mix. To develop an effective marketing mix requires a clear understanding of the chosen product position and of the way in which consumers are likely to respond to the individual mix elements.

The notion of the 'four Ps' is one that is widely used in all marketing textbooks and it is a useful framework for the analysis of marketing decisions. However, it is important to think of each of the 'Ps' in their broadest terms. *Price* is more than simply the amount of money that the consumer pays when making the purchase; it also encompasses credit or finance deals, any discounts, special offers, additional delivery charges, etc. Similarly, *place* (distribution) is not just about the physical movement of products from manufacturer to consumer; it is also about the ease of access to products, the way they are displayed and the environment in which they are presented. *Product* is not just the physical item presented for sale; it also deals with the image that is created for the product through branding and the level of customer service that accompanies it. Finally, *promotion* is more than advertising; it covers all aspects of the way in which the organization communicates with its customers and other interested groups, including its own employees. Furthermore, as well as considering product, price, promotion and place in their broadest terms, it is also important to remember that the elements of the marketing mix must be consistent with one another. Each element in that mix is ultimately contributing to the way in which the customer perceives the product and in order to convey the desired image effectively, each element must convey the same message.

The term *marketing mix* was first coined by the Harvard academic Neil Borden, who drew on a colleague's description of marketing managers as *mixers of ingredients* (Borden, 1965). If marketing managers were *mixers of ingredients*, then what they produced could be described as a *marketing mix*. According to Borden, the success of marketing management depends on developing a suitable blend of the marketing mix elements given the environmental constraints that confront the organization. These constraints include consumer behaviour, competition, the nature of distribution systems and government restrictions on marketing activities.

Borden's initial review of the marketing mix identified twelve distinct elements, though, as shown in figure 9.1, these are more conventionally grouped under four headings – the four Ps. Thus, the typical marketing mix consists of a product that is offered at a certain price, in particular locations (place) accompanied by promotion to inform the target market. There are a number of variants of the basic four Ps framework. Some authors suggest that packaging should be added as a fifth P, rather than being incorporated as an element of the product; others argue for the inclusion of public relations as the fifth P. Service marketing texts often suggest that in the services sector, seven Ps are necessary, with people, processes and physical evidence being added to the list (Cowell, 1984). More recently, Kotler has suggested that the four Ps formulation is essentially seller-driven and that what marketing needs is a consumer-oriented marketing mix, which he described as the 'four Cs' – consumer value (product), cost to consumers (price), communication (promotion) and convenience (place) (Mazur, 1992).

The concept of the marketing mix has been criticized in more general terms in the context of industrial marketing, where the idea of marketing managers mixing together ingredients to persuade organizational customers to purchase their products appears to be a long way removed from the practicalities of building personal relationships and managing the process of interaction between buyer and supplier. Clearly, the view of the industrial marketing manager preparing and offering a particular marketing mix to a passive organizational consumer is both simplistic and misleading. As mentioned in chapter 5, organizational buying is an

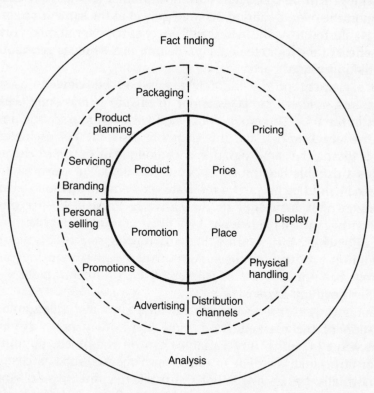

Figure 9.1 Borden's concept of the marketing mix and the 'four Ps'

interdependent and interactive process and the final marketing mix, such as it is, will be the product of negotiation, adaptation and conflict resolution between the two parties. However, this should not preclude marketing managers from thinking about the overall offering that they make to customers in terms of a mix consisting of four elements, provided it is recognized that those four elements must be defined broadly and managed flexibly. Prices may need to be negotiated, as may product specifications and distribution procedures. Furthermore, sales staff (whether described as part of promotion or place) will provide the key to managing the relationship and negotiating the final combination of product, price promotion and place which produces the purchase.

Irrespective of how the marketing mix is defined, the task of the marketing manager is to create and maintain a marketing mix that matches the needs of the target market as closely as possible, bearing in mind the impact that any of the often unpredictable and largely uncontrollable environmental variables might have on any or all of the marketing mix variables. Each element of the mix is given a substrategy, and these four substrategies must be consistent with one another so that they coordinate and support the overall marketing strategy, yet at the same time contribute to what is referred to as the synergistic effect of the overall mix. This means that the effect of the four elements on the mix as a whole is greater than the sum of the individual parts.

No one element of the marketing mix can be viewed in isolation; constant cross-referencing is essential to ensure consistency with other elements in the mix. The mix is concerned with communicating an overall offer to the target market and it is therefore essential that each element of the mix is giving the same signal to consumers. For example, the image of Swatch as a durable fashion accessory which could be worn by everyone and anyone would be harmed if the watches were only available through a limited range of exclusive outlets. Similarly, the Porsche 924 was ultimately withdrawn because its relatively low price was not consistent with the image of Porsche. More recently, Stella Artois lager, a product positioned as a premium product, has been supported by an advertising campaign with copy that reminds the consumer of the product's quality – 'Stella Artois: Reassuringly Expensive'.

Of course, in practice, there are no hard and fast rules guiding the specification of the marketing mix and there are usually a number of different ways in which mix variables can be combined, in spite of the nature of target markets. For example, in a market such as cosmetics, it would normally be assumed that the marketing mix would emphasize television and media advertising, with distribution through chemists, department stores and supermarkets. However, the American company, Avon, has had considerable success with a marketing mix that places heavy emphasis on personal selling with little or no conventional promotion.

The marketing mix and the product lifecycle

Although there are no hard and fast rules that can be used to guide the formulation of a marketing mix, either in strategic or tactical terms, there are some analytical frameworks that can help marketers when thinking about this problem. One such approach that is widely used is the product lifecycle (PLC). The basic idea of the PLC is that a product will follow a lifecycle from development and introduction, through to growth, maturity and finally decline. A typical product lifecycle is shown in figure 9.2. The concept of a PLC can be applied to broad product categories (e.g. beer), to product forms (e.g. lager) and to specific brands (e.g. Carling Black Label). Lifecycles tend to be longer for product categories and product forms than they are for individual brands, though of course the brand name itself may

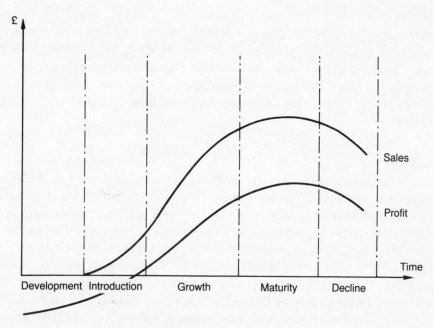

Figure 9.2 The product lifecycle

have a longer life than the specific products to which the brand name is attached.

From a marketing perspective, the PLC can be used in a variety of situations. At the broadest level, it can be employed as a tool for planning the product portfolio and in this context it has some similarities with the BCG matrix described in chapter 2. Products that the BCG matrix identifies as question marks can be viewed as products in the early stages of their lifecycle; stars are products in their growth stage, while mature products are similar to cash cows and declining products can be viewed as dogs. There are different cashflow implications associated with each stage of the lifecycle and an understanding of the relative positions of different products can be employed to guide an organization in the determination of the appropriate balance of products in its portfolio. The PLC is also widely advocated as a framework for guiding the development of a suitable marketing mix strategy.

The nature of the target market can vary during the product's lifecycle, as will patterns of competition and distribution systems. Thus, as the market environment changes through time, so the marketing mix may also need to change and the PLC offers some insight into the sort of changes which may be required at each stage.

Development

At this stage, the product has not reached the market, though it will be absorbing resources for development and testing. While there are no specific marketing mix tasks as such at this stage, the process of test marketing the product requires that some consideration be given to the types of marketing mix that might be employed when the product is finally launched.

Introduction

This is a period of slow growth, with sales being primarily to the more innovative customers. With considerable marketing effort being devoted to obtaining widespread acceptance for the new product, cashflows and profits will often be negative. From a marketing perspective, the priority is to raise awareness and appreciation of the product with the result that the marketing mix will place a high degree of emphasis on informative promotion. The product range will typically be relatively narrow and distribution will probably be limited to a selected number of outlets. Kotler (1991) identifies four basic price–promotion combinations for products in the introductory phase, and these are outlined in table 9.1.

Table 9.1 Marketing mix strategies in the introductory phase of the PLC

Marketing mix	Price	Promotion	Comments
Rapid skimming	High	High	Suitable if a large part of the market is unaware of the product, potential demand is strong and potential competition imminent
Slow skimming	High	Low	Suitable if the market is already aware of the product, demand is strong, the market is limited in size and the competitive threat is weak
Rapid penetration	Low	High	Suitable if the market is large but unaware of the product, buyers are price sensitive and there is the threat of significant competition
Slow penetration	Low	Low	Suitable if the market is large and aware of the product, buyers are price sensitive and the threat of competition is less substantial

Source: Kotler (1991)

These four combinations can be divided into two types of strategy – skimming and penetration. In essence, skimming strategies look to produce a rapid return on investment in product development in situations where buyers are less price sensitive and market share is less important. By contrast, penetration strategies concentrate on gaining market share in price-sensitive markets. The supporting level of promotion is guided by the existing level of consumer awareness and the strength of potential competition.

Growth
At this stage, sales volumes increase steadily, the product is accepted across a much broader range of consumers and it begins to make a significant contribution to profitability. Increases in sales can be maintained by improvements in the features, extending the distribution network, targeting at more segments or increasing price competitiveness. It

is at this stage, however, that the new product will begin to attract significant competition, though profitability will usually be high because the competition may not yet be fully established in the market.

Maturity
When a product reaches maturity, the rate of change in sales begins to stabilize and the product is known to the majority of consumers in the market. At this stage of the lifecycle for many consumer and industrial goods, replacement purchases tend to be more common than new purchases. The market itself is mature and the marketing campaign and product are well established. Pricing policies are likely to be closely linked to competitors' pricing, distribution will be at its most extensive and promotion will tend to be oriented towards attracting consumers from competing brands. Competition is probably at its most intense at this stage and it may be necessary to consider modification and rejuvenation of the product to arrest future decline.

Decline
Sales begin to drop away noticeably, leaving management with a number of strategic options. First, the product could be retained and cash flow maximized by price cutting and/or reduced marketing support. Second, if the product is seen as one with a potential long-term future, then the appropriate strategy may be one of rejuvenation by redesigning the product, altering features or changing quality. Third, if neither of these strategies are deemed appropriate, then the product could be withdrawn entirely. This may be in the form of divestment to a smaller company or alternatively, it may be by simply ceasing production. If the latter is chosen, there will still be important decisions to be taken with respect to the degree of service and parts provided for past customers.

There is some debate about the validity of the lifecycle concept (see, for example, Dhalla and Yuspeh, 1976). To many it is seen as a rather crude attempt to apply a biological law to an inanimate object. There may be no underlying reason why any product should automatically grow, mature and decline, and it is not too difficult to think of examples where this pattern has not been realized. Furthermore, there are no clear guidelines to enable managers to distinguish between the different stages in the lifecycle. Hence, it may be unwise to take the analogy too literally and assume that every product follows the sort of stylized lifecycle shown in figure 9.2. Lifecycles may take many different forms, some very short, others very long, and the time period associated with each possible phase can vary considerably. The underlying idea that the product lifecycle attempts to convey is that the position of a product in a particular market will change with time and that the understanding and analysis of those changes can be of use in guiding marketing decisions and maintaining some balance within the product portfolio.

Furthermore, the role of marketing is generally considered to be one of prolonging the growth and maturity phases, often using strategies of product modification or product improvement which are frequently regarded as less risky than new product development. If this is the case, then the fact that many products have not followed the patterns suggested by the traditional lifecycle may simply be indicative of the success of the marketing effort rather than the fact that the lifecycle concept is invalid.

Conclusions

The marketing mix represents the set of tools that can be used to communicate the organizations' chosen product position to the target market. Although various forms have been suggested for the marketing mix, the most commonly used presents the marketing mix as four Ps: product, price, promotion and place. Although each P is usually examined separately, it should be clear from our discussion that there is a tremendous amount of overlap between each of these elements. The purpose of the marketing mix is to create a particular image for the product and convey information to the consumer about that product. To do this successfully, the features of the product, the way in which it is priced and promoted, and the way in which it is distributed must be appropriate to what the consumer wants, different from the competition and consistent with each other to ensure that a distinctive image is created for the product.

CASE STUDY

Managing the marketing mix

Porsche

In a recent survey, Porsche was voted fifth most powerful brand in Europe and is one of the leading brands in the UK car market. The company produces some 3,500 exclusive sports cars each year. Ferrari, in contrast, produces only 300, while BMW produces over 50,000. In effect, Porsche as a company falls somewhere in between the mass-market producers and the small specialist manufacturer. Like many other German companies, the success of Porsche is built on strengths in engineering and quality. The company's research and development centre in West Germany is world renowned and over half the work undertaken there is for outside organizations. However, skills in research and development and expertise in production were not enough to ensure a strong competitive position for Porsche. Effective marketing was equally important to ensure that the full potential of these strengths was realized.

The typical Porsche customer is male, in his late thirties, owns his own business, has an income that is in excess of £50,000 per annum and probably has more than two cars. Seventy per cent of their customers have owned a Porsche before. This type of customer would regard himself as a success and the ownership of a Porsche is a visible manifestation of that success. These customers are not thought to be particularly price sensitive though they are still likely to be concerned about value for money and service. The attraction of a Porsche is its exclusive, elitist image.

The marketing philosophy within Porsche is that they are producing an exclusive product and the elements of the marketing mix seek to reflect this. Porsche UK has specialist centres (the word 'dealership' is considered inappropriate) throughout the United Kingdom who seek to build close relationships with their custo-mers. Within these centres, corporate identity is important and is created and supported by the use of extensive point-of-sale displays and striking signage. A key element in Porsche's marketing is personal service, which is an area in which it feels it can excel because of its size. However, the exclusive image and the personal touch cannot be sustained without the appropriate product range. In the early 1980s Porsche fell into the trap that has affected many manufacturers of luxury goods. It launched a new model – the four cylinder 924 – which was marketed at a relatively low price (by Porsche standards) and would extend market coverage beyond the target customer group. The 924 pushed Porsche towards the mass market. This expansion foundered in the late 1980s, the model was withdrawn and Porsche returned to cultivating its upmarket image. The cheapest car in the range now costs around £35,000.

Questions

1. How has the formulation and management of the marketing mix contributed to the success of Porsche?
2. In what ways can the size of the company be seen to provide Porsche with a competitive advantage?

10 Product decisions

Introduction

Although the relative importance of the marketing mix elements will vary over the life of the product and according to the needs of the target market, the nature of the product itself is arguably the most important component of any marketing mix. After all, if the product does not offer the features expected and required by consumers, a competitive price combined with imaginative promotion and efficient distribution will not compensate for the product's intrinsic weaknesses. Without a well-designed and well-developed product, the organization will lack an effective basis for long-term success in a competitive market place.

Since consumer needs and therefore product offerings are not constant, it must be recognized that some products will no longer be appropriate to the market; they will not be profitable and therefore must be dropped. At the same time, existing products will need modifications and new products must be developed. In this process, the overriding objective is to ensure that the range of products offered is consistent with the overall marketing strategy. In particular, where there are different markets and different market segments, the product range must be managed to ensure that the range of products available matches the needs of different consumer groups. Gaps in the product range leave areas of the market unsatisfied and provide the perfect entry route for new competitors. This chapter reviews the activities associated with managing product ranges, modifying existing products and developing new ones.

The concept of a product

Consumers do not buy a product for its own sake, only for the benefits that the product offers them. The consumer who buys a drill does not generally do so for the pleasures of owning a drill but in order to have a facility to make holes in things. Focusing too much attention on the product itself can lead an organization into the *marketing myopia* trap described in chapter 1. When thinking about products it is necessary to think in terms of the needs that the product fulfils.

The concept of a product is, however, a little more complex, as figure 10.1 illustrates. Any product can be thought of in terms of a number of different layers above and beyond the basic consumer need that is being satisfied. For any particular type of product, there are certain basic or essential features, and these are likely to be identical across all products. Thus, for example, all cars must provide a means of transport. These basic features can be thought of as the core or generic product. However, at this level, all products are effectively the same. Differentiation begins to appear at the next layer – often described as the tangible or expected product. At this stage various features, which might be regarded as desirable from the point of view of the consumer, are added to the product. These features will include brand names, certain types of packaging, different quality levels and other additional, non-essential features. It is typically at the level of the tangible or expected product that the greatest competition between different suppliers will emerge.

There is also a third layer in the product concept, that of the augmented product. The augmented product covers the additional aspects of the product offering, which go beyond what consumers might generally expect and hence provides a basis for the organization to gain a competitive edge. Features of the augmented product are often in the form of customer service facilities. Kotler (1991) suggests that organizations might also think in terms of a further layer, the potential product, which encompasses aspects of products that may become part of the standard offer in the future.

Understanding and managing the product mix

Many of the decisions regarding the composition of the product mix are essentially strategic decisions. The allocation of resources across different product groups is typically a decision taken in the early stages of the

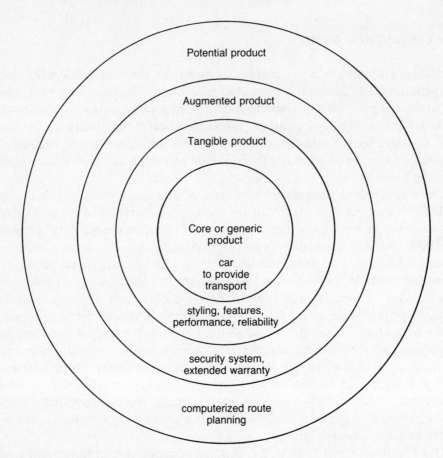

Figure 10.1 The elements of a product

development of a marketing strategy, often guided by the use of techniques such as the BCG matrix and the product lifecycle. The same can be said of decisions regarding the addition of new products and the deletion of existing products. The effectiveness of these decisions requires an input from product managers who are usually much closer to the market than strategic planners. Even when these decisions have been made, however, there is a variety of issues relating to the management of the product mix which will necessarily devolve to those involved in the specification of the marketing mix.

Most organizations will offer a range of different products (the product mix) to a variety of markets and consumers. The product element of the marketing mix concerns itself with the management and development of the product range and the items in this range to ensure that the organization maintains and improves its competitive position in the various markets in which it operates. An example of the product mix for an academic publisher is shown in figure 10.2. The product mix refers to the set of all product lines and items that an organization offers for sale. Any product mix can be described according to its width, length, depth and consistency. Width simply refers to the number of different product lines on offer, while length refers to the total number of items on offer. Depth is concerned with the number of variants of each brand and consistency is concerned with the closeness of the relationship between the different product lines. In our example, the publisher has a number of basic product lines (e.g. business books, engineering books), each with a series of sub-lines (e.g. marketing books, management books) and within each sub-line there will be a range of product items. These together describe the product mix. The product lines are closely related so we could describe the product mix as consistent. For major retailers, the product mix can be extremely large – a large supermarket may handle something like 5,000–10,000 product items, while in a specialist manufacturing businesses, the mix may consist of less than 100.

In addition to establishing the appropriate product mix, attention must also be paid to consideration of the length of a particular product line or product range. The product line or range refers to a group of products that

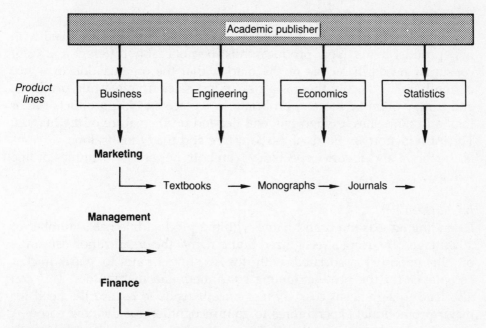

Figure 10.2 The product mix for an academic publisher

are broadly similar in terms of the customer groups they serve and the types of need that they satisfy. Identifying the optimal length (number of items) in a product range is an important marketing decision. In part this decision is conditioned by strategic considerations. Where an organization is pursuing a differentiation strategy it will need a long product line, while a cost-based strategy will normally imply a much shorter line. Although product lines tend to lengthen over time without any particularly conscious effort by the product manager, there are systematic policies for changing the product line.

Line stretching

This entails lengthening the product line, either upwards into higher quality items or downwards into lower quality items or in both directions at once. The introduction of the Lexus by Toyota targeted at the luxury end of the car market is an example of an upward stretch in an existing product line, while the move by IBM into personal computers may be seen as an example of a downward stretch in a product line. An upward stretch may be difficult if the product is perceived as low quality, since consumers may not recognize high quality in new product items. Conversely, if a downward stretch is used there is the danger of devaluing the line's quality image and taking sales away from existing products.

Line filling

The basic length of the product line is not changed, but gaps are filled with new product items. New products must be noticeably different and fulfil consumer needs in sectors of the market that the organization does not currently serve. Again, there is a risk of lost sales from existing products, and it may often be more appropriate to replace existing products rather than add new ones, though this will depend on the nature of the market. The introduction, by Ford, of the Sapphire and the Orion (saloon versions of the Sierra and Escort respectively) can both be seen as examples of line filling.

Brand extension

Extending an existing brand name within a product line has a number of advantages. By using a recognized brand name, the organization can trade on the goodwill associated with the existing brand to gain quicker acceptance for the product among consumers and distributors. This can also lead to significant cost savings since it tends to reduce the need for major promotional expenditures to gain recognition for the new name. A potential disadvantage is that if the product to which the brand name is extended proves to be unpopular or unsatisfactory in some respects, there may be some loss of goodwill in relation to the existing brand. Brand extension can take two basic forms. The first entails using the existing brand name to introduce new varieties of the existing product. For example, both Unilever and Procter & Gamble have extended their Persil and Ariel washing powder brands to include washing liquids and concentrated washing powder. The second form of brand extension entails extending the brand name to apply to new but related products. This strategy was pursued by Unilever, with the launch of Persil Washing-Up Liquid. Similarly, Mars and a number of other confectionery manufacturers have successfully extended confectionery brands into ice-cream bars. Exhibit 10.1 gives a further example of brand extension in the petfood market.

Strategies of brand extension must be pursued with care. If the brand is extended too widely, it may result in a dilution of the brand image. Nike, the manufacturers of training shoes, encountered this problem when attempting to extend their brand name to casual shoes. Not only did the brand extension prove ineffective, in that sales of casual shoes were weak, it also damaged the Nike brand in its core market for running shoes. Because casual shoes were included under the Nike brand, a brand that had traditionally been associated with running shoes, the message being

---

Exhibit 10.1   Brand extension

Pedigree Petfoods

The market for petfood is worth more than £1bn per annum and future growth is expected to be strong. This market is dominated by two companies, Pedigree Petfoods and Spillers. Some 90 per cent of sales in this market are in the form of canned petfoods and Pedigree's Whiskas brand is one of the largest selling products, with sales of over £175m. Despite the dominance of canned petfoods in this market, many manufacturers believe that much of the future market growth will come in the form of dry foods. To exploit this growing sector of the market, Pedigree Petfoods plans to launch two new products, one for dogs and one for cats. In both cases, the company is building on the success of its existing brand names by launching these dry foods under the Chum and Whiskas brands respectively.

Source: McMurdo (1992).

conveyed to customers became confused and many started to consider the purchase of competing products.

This process of managing and changing the product lines offered essentially deals with the product offering as a whole. It is also necessary, however, to give specific consideration to the individual features or attributes of the products offered

Product attributes

As the product moves away from its core or generic form, a number of attributes will be added in order to differentiate that product from its competitors. These attributes will include a variety of additional features, quality levels, design, branding, packaging and customer service. In each case attributes should be developed to meet the needs of the target market and provide a competitive advantage for the product.

Product quality refers to the ability of the particular product item to perform its intended functions, and as such it summarizes factors such as durability, reliability, precision, performance and ease of operation. The selection of a quality level depends on the nature of the market or market segment being targeted and also on the position selected for the product. Initially, the firm must select a particular quality level – low, standard, high, superior, etc. – which is consistent with the needs of its target markets. Profitability generally increases with quality, though the major gains occur when moving from low to standard or standard to high. In addition to selecting an initial quality level the firm needs to select the appropriate strategy for the management of quality. In particular, there must be a clear indication of whether to opt for quality maintenance, quality improvement or quality adulteration. Although the latter is often seen only as a short-term strategy to deal with financial problems, it may also be a way of managing products in the decline stage of their lifecycle. Exhibit 10.2 provides an example an organization pursuing a quality adulteration strategy.

Product features also qualify as an important source of product differentiation. In addition to the core product, the firm must offer a range of necessary features, i.e. the features that a consumer would expect to see in the product. In 35 mm cameras, for example, this might include autofocus and built-in flash. Features considered necessary will, of course, vary according to the market targeted. Additionally, however, the firm

---

Exhibit 10.2   Changing quality

Harp Lager

The market for standard lager has becoming increasingly competitive in recent years. There appears to be little to distinguish between the various brands in terms of taste and as a consequence, brand image and advertising have become increasingly important in maintaining market share. Guinness spent around £6.5m in 1991 in an attempt to maintain market share for Harp, its standard lager brand. The company has now abandoned its hopes of revitalizing the brand and is intending to move downmarket and reposition Harp as a value-for-money product by offering the product in 500 ml cans rather than the standard 440 ml can, to provide the consumer with more lager for their money.

Source: Marketing Week (1992d).

---

may choose to offer additional features. These will typically be features that consumers do not expect to be present but which differentiate a product from that offered by competitors. Because consumers may not expect such features, they may need to be persuaded of their value. For example, some customers may not expect motorwind on 35 mm compact cameras and the company that offers this feature may gain an advantage over the competition, but only if they can convince the consumers that this feature is genuinely useful.

Products can also be distinguished because of a unique style or design which helps to create a distinct 'personality' for the product. Examples might include Bang & Olufsen stereo equipment or Habitat furniture. A distinctive design is difficult to create, relatively rare and usually expensive. In consequence, most mass market goods are not characterized by distinctive designs and if anything, there is a tendency for businesses to use fairly standard styles for their products. Even at this stage, however, attention to design and product appearance is important, since if two products are similar in most respects, appearance may prove to be the deciding factor in the consumer's purchase decision.

Branding

Branding is an important method of differentiating a product. It simply entails attaching an image to a product which is associated with a particular name. Although typically associated most closely with fast-moving consumer goods, branding can be equally important in the market for industrial goods. Almost all products that are currently sold are branded in some way, though the use that is made of the brand from a marketing point of view varies.

The process of branding offers a number of distinct benefits:

- It provides the buyer with information on the quality, performance and features attached to the product, and in so doing it reduces the consumer's need to collect information about that product.
- The brand name or trademark can provide legal protection for specific product features.
- Branding can assist in market segmentation and targeting because it enables a business to offer a variety of product forms to different market segments.
- Branding provides the business with an opportunity to develop a strong relationship with its customers through by providing a basis for building brand loyalty.
- Branding can help in promoting corporate image.

There are of course some disadvantages associated with branding, with the most obvious being the increase in packaging, labelling and promotional costs. The process of branding is also often criticized on the grounds that it creates unnecessary product differentiation. Despite these problems, most organizations seem to feel that the benefits of branding outweigh the costs.

If active branding is chosen as part of a marketing campaign, then there are a number of key decisions that have to be made. These are:

Brand sponsor
The term 'brand sponsor' simply refers to the organization that is to be responsible for the brand. There are four basic choices available:

- *Manufacturer's brand* This is the standard approach to branding in which the manufacturer is identified as being directly responsible for the brand, e.g. Amstrad, Sony, Heinz. The individual brands are then able to build on the manufacturer's reputation and image.

- *Licensed brand*   Products are sold under a recognized brand that is not the manufacturer's. The manufacturer has a licence to use the particular name but the ultimate responsibility for the brand is effectively with the licensor who is often the designer. Typical examples of this type of branding would be Christian Dior, Pierre Cardin and Calvin Klein.
- *Distributor's brand (own brand)*   The product is sold under the name of the distributor, whether wholesaler or retailer. Provided the difficulties associated with finding a reliable supplier can be overcome, this has the advantage of giving the distributor an exclusive range which cannot obviously be copied. This approach is probably most common and noticeable in the grocery and household goods markets, where the major retailers rely heavily on sales of own brand products.

Although most manufacturers prefer to sell under their own brand, the growing market power of the retailers and the growing popularity of distributor's brands has threatened market share. As a consequence, many organizations now sell part of their output under a manufacturer's brand and part under the distributor's brand.

Brand family

Having identified the appropriate brand sponsor, it is then necessary to determine the brand family and the way in which it should be named. Again, there are a number of basic options:

- *Individual names*   Each product item is given its own distinctive name, as in the case of Procter & Gamble's range of detergents, which includes Ariel, Bold and Tide. The advantage of individual brand names is that the products are not directly linked or explicitly associated with the manufacturer. This approach may be particularly useful if the company is introducing a product that is considered to be quite different from it terms of image and quality. For example, the new up-market addition to Toyota's range of cars, the Lexus, was deliberately not called a Toyota because the car was seen as a major departure from Toyota's middle-market image.
- *Blanket name*   A common name (often the manufacturer's) is used for all product items, usually accompanied by a product specific description. Heinz adopt a blanket name for all their products, as do many other FMCG companies. The advantage of the blanket brand name is the potential for *halo* effects. The strength of the brand in any one area (Heinz Baked Beans, for example) will be carried over to other products with the same brand name (Heinz Potato Salad, for example).

Additionally, there are potential cost savings in relation to advertising and promoting the brand.

- *Family brand (umbrella brand)* Family branding describes a situation in which a number of different brands names are used for different product lines or sub-lines. This can be particularly useful in cases in which the products are distinct and the company actively wishes the consumer to see the products as different. Thus, for example, Pedigree Petfoods uses different family brands for its dog food and cat food, namely Whiskas (cat food, kitten food, milk) and Pedigree Chum (dog food, puppy food and dry mixer).

Brand name

Formulating the name for a new brand can be a particularly problematic aspect of branding (Murphy, 1987). Ideally, the chosen name should be easily recognizable, memorable and concise. In addition, it is common to look for brand names that say something about the products benefits/features (e.g. Sunkist Oranges, Portakabin). Of course, there are many successful brands which have none of these characteristics. The name Kodak has no meaning as a word and says nothing about the benefits of the product and yet has proved to be a highly successful brand. Similarly 'I Can't Believe It's Not Butter' is hardly the most concise brand name, but yet again has been highly successful. Considerable care is required in selecting a brand name to ensure that it does not infringe upon any currently registered brand names or trademarks. In addition it is also important to ensure that the chosen name is not open to any misinterpretation, particularly where products are being sold to international markets. Thus, for example, Nestlé's Bonka Coffee may be less than successful in the UK market and the same might be said of the Plopsies brand of cereal. Equally, the Chevrolet Nova was initially less than successful in Latin America because the name, when spoken, sounded like *no va* (doesn't go).

The value of a brand name is such that it is rare to see name changes. More commonly, a brand name may be maintained long after the product to which it was initially attached has disappeared. Nevertheless, some brand name changes do occur. One recent example is the rebranding of Marathon chocolate bars as Snickers, a change that was pursued in order to present a common brand name for the product across a variety of international markets. By contrast, Kattomeat cat food was recently rebranded as Arthur's, following the name of the cat used in television commercials. In this instance the rationale for the rebranding was that the advertising personality was well known but the link with the existing brand was weak. Spillers chose rebranding in order to capitalize on the success of their advertising.

Packaging, labelling and customer service

The role of packaging and labelling varies considerably across products, but can be an important contributor to the branding effort and contribute to elements of the tangible or expected product. Packaging has increased in importance as a marketing variable for a number of reasons. It adds convenience to the product and improves its appearance, an attribute that consumers are more willing to pay for as incomes increase. In addition with the growth in self-service, packaging is important as a means of making a product distinctive and conveying information to consumers.

Carefully designed packaging can also aid in the process of brand and image creation. For example, the distinctive appearance of Coca-Cola cans and Kodak films illustrate the potential contribution the packaging can make in consumer recognition of the product, as do the distinctive shapes of Orangina and Grolsch bottles. In addition, the design of packaging – particularly where it is innovative – can provide an important means of differentiating a product. The winebox, when originally introduced, was probably one of the most important packaging innovations and gave its manufacturers a distinct edge in the wine market.

Any inclination to underestimate the importance of packaging can easily be quashed by recent developments in the marketing of non-durable consumer goods. The growing importance of environmental factors in consumers' buying decisions has presented a threat to the manufacturers of many environmentally unfriendly products such as detergents. If the product itself cannot be presented as environmentally friendly, then an alternative is to use packaging that is. A number of recent advertisements for fabric conditioner and washing powder testify to the importance of this marketing appeal. Indeed, the importance of environmentally friendly packaging is increasing and presents important marketing challenges to a range of businesses as exhibit 10.3 shows.

The final product attribute that needs to be considered is customer service, and in particular, the level of service that should be offered in conjunction with the product. The service decision is relevant primarily in the case of durable rather than non-durable products. A company needs to identify, perhaps through market research or competitor analysis, the appropriate level and type of customer service to provide, the main aim being to provide services in those areas regarded as important. The

---

Exhibit 10.3   Packaging and the environment

New legislation in Germany

In April 1992, a new law came into force in Germany which allowed customers to return packaging materials to retailers, and retailers to return packaging to suppliers. The suppliers are then required to take responsibility for the disposal of that packaging. The law was intended to force companies to recognize that they had a genuine responsibility for the environment. In anticipation of the new legislation, many companies drastically cut back on their packaging. Kaufhof, for example has forced suppliers to cut back on outer packaging by nearly 80 per cent since 1990 and Union Deutsche Lebensmittel has dropped all outer packaging where possible. Similarly, Henkel, Procter & Gamble and Lever GmbH have devoted resources to the development of recyclable packaging materials for detergents and cleansers.

Source: Schypek (1992).

---

provision of customer service is, again, a potentially important mechanism for differentiating products, but it is also costly and an increasingly used strategy is to offer a basic, essential level of service, backed up by an optional, more comprehensive service for an added charge.

Standardization or customization

Most products are developed with the needs of specific, and usually domestic target markets in mind. An increasing proportion of goods and services are, however, marketed internationally as well as nationally, and this presents marketing managers with a further product decision. Products marketed internationally can be standardized for all markets or customized to meet the needs of specific markets. The case for standardization is based on the idea that the similarities between consumers in international markets are more important than the differences and that most products will therefore have a universal appeal. By standardizing, the organization can maintain a high degree of strategic consistency across markets as well as benefiting from economies of scale. Coca-Cola, Pepsi-Cola and McDonald's are all examples of organizations following standardization strategies in global markets; their products are almost identical, wherever they are purchased.

The standardization approach to global markets is similar to the mass marketing approach described in chapter 8 and inevitably has the same weaknesses. It ignores what may be very significant differences between markets and relies on gains from economies of scale, though it is not always clear that such gains actually exist. Customization, by contrast, entails tailoring the product to the needs of the specific market, and though it results in increased costs, this approach also aims to increase revenues by meeting consumer needs more closely than the competition. In practice, in international marketing, the gulf between standardized and customized products may not be as wide as it may seem. Pure standardization is virtually impossible to achieve because of language and cultural differences. Furthermore, country-specific legislation may require some product modification before a product can be legally marketed. The middle-ground position would appear to one of standardizing where possible and customizing where necessary, and in general, the more culturally sensitive a product (e.g. food, toiletries, cosmetics), the more it will need to be adapted to the needs of the specific market.

Product modification

Irrespective of the attributes that may be assigned to a product initially, some adjustments may be required at later stages in the product's life. Product modification is often pursued in the maturity stage of a product's lifecycle to attract new customers and differentiate the product from the competition. Product modification does not add to the product line as such but instead involves effectively replacing an existing product with a new and improved version. Related to the process of product modification is that of product development. This is a form of product modification, which results in the appearance of new but related products. Effectively, this involves some form of product line stretching or product proliferation. Exhibit 10.4 describes how Ford has modified one of its products to meet more accurately the needs of the market.

The importance of product modification is considerable in an increasingly competitive market place. Improvements in existing products can be an important strategy for maintaining and expanding the existing customer base, and while there are clearly risks associated with devoting additional resources to existing products, particularly at the maturity/

Exhibit 10.4   Product development

Ford launches Rapid Fit

The recent recession has resulted in a substantial fall in car sales and put increasing pressure on car manufacturers to look for alternative forms of revenue generation. Ford has always recognized the importance of after-sales service but has a poor record in this area, with only 30 per cent of Ford owners making use of Ford dealers for servicing cars. Typically, the company loses customers on the resale of cars. Most purchasers of second-hand Fords do not use Ford dealers because they are seen as expensive and uncompetitive. Consequently many dealers have underutilized repair and maintenance facilities. Ford is looking to target these Ford owners by launching a national chain of fast fit operators to rival Kwik-Fit. Some 400 dealerships are to be rebranded as Ford Rapid Fit, with new facilities and staff trained to cater for exhaust, tyre and battery replacement. In developing this new service, Ford is aiming to show its customers that the company cares about their needs and by doing so, hopes to engender brand loyalty among the owners of older Ford cars.

Source: Boulding (1992).

---

decline stage of the lifecycle, these risks may well be small in comparison with those associated with new product development and diversification. Product development and modification aim to further differentiate existing products in order to appeal to more specific segments of the market. These two strategies involve the organization operating in markets with which it is familiar, and consequently the risks associated with such developments tend to be relatively low. At the same time, it is important to ensure that markets are not oversegmented as this will result in a reduced profit contribution from the different items in the product range.

New product development

The process of new product development (NPD) is in itself an important component of the management of the product portfolio. The whole pattern of product development, product modification and product deletion is a key element in the development and maintenance of a product range that meets the constantly changing needs of consumers. NPD is one of the most costly and risky aspects of marketing. The genuinely new product is a rare phenomenon and innovativeness is no guarantee of success; there may be many innovators who can 'build a better mousetrap' but if the market does not require it then the product will fail. Furthermore, for every new product that actually reaches the stage of being launched, there will be perhaps hundreds that have failed to get through the development phase. Given the costs and risks involved, and the importance of NPD in marketing strategies, it is important to develop an organized and systematic approach to the process. Such an approach cannot in itself guarantee that new products will be successful, but it can at least attempt to reduce the possibility of failure.

The process of NPD covers a wide range of activities and the development of original new products is only one component of that process. As was discussed in the previous section, any organization must constantly monitor and review its product range to ensure that it provides the desired extent of market coverage. Where the aim is to provide a varied range of products to a number of market segments, then it is necessary to ensure that the range of products on offer meets the needs of those segments. By contrast, if the aim is to focus attention on specific market niches and supply a narrower range of products to meet the needs of specific customer groups, then again regular monitoring is important to ensure that aim is achieved. Furthermore, since customer needs will change over time, product ranges should be monitored and modifications made as and when necessary. Indeed, such modifications are often implemented when products have reached the maturity stage of their lifecycle in order to stimulate a renewed interest from consumers and encourage an expansion in sales.

Accordingly, in considering NPD we must first identify the different forms that it may take. We will concentrate on products that are new to the organization and classify those products according to whether they are new to the market or whether they already exist in some form.

- *Genuine innovations* The genuine innovation is a product that is new to both the organization and the market. Innovations of this sort are few and far between. Although genuine innovations offer potentially high profits, they are also inherently risky. The development, launch and successful marketing of a genuine innovation will often require high levels of investment, the use of different and new technologies and may involve the organization moving into areas in which it is comparatively inexperienced.

- *New product lines* These refer to products that although new to the organization are not new to the market – at least not in their basic form. The development of a new product line will typically involve developing an organization's own variant of a particular product which is already available, but possibly adding additional features to differentiate it from existing variants of the product.

The development of new product lines is arguably the most common form of NPD in any business area. When NPD takes the form of adding new product lines, however, the organization must be aware that, since there are competing products already established in the market, the potential returns may be lower. At the same time, the organization is moving into an area with which it is considerably more familiar, either in terms of the technology or the markets, and so the risks associated with this form of NPD are rather less.

Since NPD is a costly and risky activity and is also one that is important to the long-term competitive success of a business, a systematic and structured approach to NPD is important. Adopting such an approach will ensure that new product ideas which are consistent with an organization's strategies can be fully tested and evaluated such that only those with a real chance of success will actually reach the market place. There are a number of different approaches which can be used to NPD but all will involve broadly similar sets of activities and stages. The key stages in NPD are outlined below.

Rationale
Any NPD exercise should begin by identifying why the organization is involved in NPD and what it expects to achieve. In essence, this can almost be thought of as a statement of the organization's NPD strategy. By clearly identifying the motivations for NPD it is possible to provide some guidance to those involved in the process of formulating ideas. Thus, for example, if the process of NPD is to be orientated towards taking advantage of new market segments, then those involved need some clear indication of the needs and expectations of customers in the particular segments. By contrast, if NPD is to be concerned with reducing excess capacity or evening out fluctuating levels of demand, then the focus of attention, particularly in generating ideas, will be different.

Idea generation
Ideas are the basic raw material for any NPD process; since only a very small proportion of ideas ever become products, the importance of generating many and varied ideas should not be overstated. The possible sources of new product ideas can be classified according to whether they are internal or external. Internal sources include any ideas generated by employees within the organization; the most obvious being:

- *New product development groups* Groups within the organization who meet on a regular basis to 'brainstorm' ideas for new products.
- *Marketing research department* Through regular monitoring and analysis of the market place, management within the marketing research function are potentially well placed to come forward with new ideas. These ideas may stem from the analysis of changes in consumer requirements but may equally well arise from an appreciation of changes in technology or changes in legislation.
- *Informal management suggestions* Management, both within the marketing department and elsewhere in the organization, can also be a useful source of ideas.
- *Employee suggestions* Staff involved in day-to-day dealings with customers are often encouraged to submit their own suggestions for new products. This is a potentially useful source of ideas, because such staff, by virtue of their regular contact with customers, may have a clearer understanding of customer attitudes and problems with the existing product

A significant number of new product ideas are developed either formally or informally from external sources. There are numerous possible external sources, but the major ones include:

- *Customers* Ideas may be generated by an organization's customers either through informal suggestion or as a result of formal market research.
- *Outside agencies* These include suggestions from market research agencies, advertising agencies and specialist new product development agencies. The advantage of ideas generated from these sources often stems from the fact that an outside agency is able to distance itself from the organization, and is not constrained by internal traditions and cultures. This will tend to encourage the generation of new ideas from a different perspective.

- *Competitors* Copying and modifying products developed by competitors is a common source of ideas for new product development in many organizations.

Since very few ideas will ever reach the stage of product launch, it is important to ensure that ideas are generated regularly and in significant numbers to increase the probability of finding a successful idea. At this stage ideas should be encouraged, however unusual or eccentric they may seem; their suitability will be evaluated at a later stage.

Screening

The next stage of the NPD process is to screen the available ideas in order to establish which should proceed to the development stage. Essentially, screening will seek to establish whether the ideas will be of benefit to the organization in attempting to achieve its objectives. In order to do this, each idea must be judged according to a variety of criteria. Typically the screening process will fall into two stages. The primary screening will seek to eliminate those product ideas that are clearly outside the company's capabilities, that do not fit the current strategies, which duplicate existing products or are technologically, politically or legally impractical. The precise criteria used for a primary screening will vary according to the nature of the organization's NPD strategy, but it is important that a clear set of criteria are determined and clearly laid down in advance.

The primary screen may well eliminate as many as 80–90 per cent of new product ideas. While this may seem to be a particularly high failure rate it is nevertheless necessary because once beyond the primary screen and into secondary screening and product development, the costs of ideas begin to increase substantially. Thus it is important to eliminate ideas that are clearly impractical. At the same time, it is important not to be too ruthless and eliminate potentially successful ideas. At the primary screening phase, it is possible to err on the optimistic side, since the secondary screen should identify any obviously weak ideas that have escaped the primary screen.

The secondary screen is a much more detailed evaluation of the potential of an idea and is often referred to as the business analysis stage of NPD. Again, it involves comparing and ideally ranking products according to their performance over a set of evaluative criteria. Obviously there is a variety of criteria which can be used and their precise nature will again differ according to the requirements of the organization. At the end of the secondary screening process as few as 5 per cent of the original ideas may proceed to the stage of development and testing.

Development and testing

The ideas that have passed through the screening phase must now be transformed into product concepts and images. The product concept involves translating the basic idea into a specific set of features and attributes that the product will offer to potential consumers. The product image, meanwhile, is concerned with determining the way the product should be perceived by the customer, and included in this is some notion of how the product will be marketed to those consumers. For these purposes, products under development would typically be assigned a modest development budget.

Once a clear product concept has been developed, it would be normal to progress by testing either the concept or a sample product or both in the market. This is the clearest source of real evidence on the suitability of the product and will provide the development team with information on consumer and market reactions. The feedback from the testing process will identify any modifications that may be necessary and perhaps more importantly will provide some indication of whether the product is likely to be successful. The product concept is often tested by the use of consumer discussion groups, consumer panels or consumer experiments; the test marketing exercise involves the actually marketing of the product to a small group of consumers who should ideally be representative of the targeted market as a whole.

Product launch

The product launch provides the true test of the viability of a newly developed product. At this point the organization makes a full-scale business commitment to the product and the product moves from the development phase of its lifecycle, into the introductory phases. As far as the actual launch is concerned, the key decisions are essentially of an operational nature – decisions regarding the timing of the launch, the geographical location of the launch and the specific marketing tactics to be used in support of that launch.

The use of a structured and integrated framework for new product development will not, by itself, guarantee success. It is also important to generate an organizational structure and a corporate culture which encourages NPD. Actively soliciting suggestions from within the organization and allowing all ideas to go forward, without criticism, to a screening phase will be important. This has been described as 'creating a climate of trying'. Furthermore, it is important to maintain regular contacts with the external environment to identify changes in market characteristics and customer requirements. There is also a need to develop a flexible management structure which stimulates and encourages the NPD process. Finally, it is important to identify key individuals with specific responsibility for the NPD process.

Conclusions

The product forms the central element of any marketing mix and it can best be thought of in terms of the basic need that it satisfies along with a range of features which serve to differentiate that product from the competition. Most organizations offer a variety of products to a variety of markets. In addition to managing this portfolio of products, the individual lines and product items must also be managed to ensure that the needs of a constantly changing market are being met. This process will involve changes to the number of items in the lines, decisions regarding the features and attributes of products, branding, packaging, labelling and customer service, as well as the initiation and management of new product development.

CASE STUDY

Product management

Rank Hovis McDougall and Mother's Pride

Rank Hovis McDougall (RHM) is one of the largest food-processing companies in the United Kingdom. Its existing portfolio includes the Bisto, Mother's Pride and Mr Kipling brands. In the late 1980s, RHM faced a dilemma over the future of one of their best-known brands, Mother's Pride. In the late 1970s and throughout the 1980s the consumption of brown and wholemeal breads increased significantly. The declining popularity of white sliced bread was evident throughout the industry and Mother's Prides main rival, Wonder-loaf, had already disappeared from the shelves. The development of on-site bakeries within supermarket chains, along with extensive price cutting, meant that margins were squeezed and the position of national brands generally weakened. The marketing group at RHM had to decide whether there was a future for the Mother's Pride brand or whether it should simply be killed off.

Research conducted by RHM suggested that consumers saw Mother's Pride as unhealthy, old-fashioned, unattractive in appearance and with a poor taste – results that seemed to confirm the rather negative attitudes which existed within the company. At the same time, it became clear that there was another side to the brand. The name itself was incredibly strong and it was associated with warmth, friendliness and reliability. If the brand was to survive, RHM needed to exploit these positive aspects of the brand's image and counteract the negative elements.

The proposed solution was to revitalize Mother's Pride through umbrella branding, that is to say, RHM planned to apply the Mother's Pride brand name to a series of related products. These included soft-grain bread (Mother's Pride Champion), high-quality white bread (Mother's Pride Premium) and 'morning goods' (teacakes, chelsea buns, croissants, etc.). The launches of Champion and Premium were supported by advertising campaigns to the value of £2m and £1.5m respectively. This approach was in stark contrast to that adopted by RHM's main rivals, Allied Bakeries, who dropped the traditional Sunblest brand and opted for two new brands: Kingsmill Top Grade for the premium market and Mighty White for the soft grain market. The Sunblest brand had experienced similar problems to Mother's Pride, but in this instance, Allied opted to kill the brand name and start afresh with new brands. Although this was a much simpler strategy, it was also more expensive, requiring far more extensive advertising than would be the case for an existing brand.

Questions

1. What were the advantages and disadvantages of RHMs branding strategy?
2. What other marketing issues should RHM consider in relation to Mother's Pride?

11 Pricing decisions

Introduction

The price paid for a product is a measure of the value of that product to the buyer. Ultimately, the consumer's decision to make a purchase will depend upon the belief that what is given up (the price) is less than the value of what is gained (the product). Usually, this price is simply measured in monetary terms, but it may also be measured in terms of other products if the exchange is based on barter. It is a common suggestion that the aim of marketing is to make price unimportant in the consumer's decision-making process. There is certainly some truth in this view, in that the other elements of the marketing mix are ultimately concerned with adding value to the product and tailoring it to the consumer's needs to ensure that the choice between two products is not simply based on their different prices. However, this should not be seen to devalue the role of pricing as an element of the marketing mix.

Unlike the other marketing mix elements, pricing decisions affect profits through their impact on revenues rather than costs. Pricing is the only element of the mix that generates revenue rather than creating costs. In addition, it also has an important role to play as a competitive tool which can be used to differentiate a product and an organization and thus exploit market opportunities. It is also important that pricing is consistent with other elements of the marketing mix since it contributes to the overall image created for the product. No organization can hope successfully to offer an exclusive, high-quality product to the market with a low price – the price must be consistent with the overall product offering. This chapter provides an overview of the objectives of pricing, the factors that influence pricing decisions and examines some of the main approaches to pricing that organizations can adopt.

The objectives of pricing

Ultimately, the objective of pricing, as with other elements of the marketing mix, is to ensure that the required level of sales is generated to enable the organization to achieve its specified objectives. Two broad categories of objectives may be specified for pricing decisions: they may not be mutually exclusive but they are different.

- *Maximizing profits* This approach to pricing will be one that concerns itself with maximizing the returns on assets or investments. This may be realized with a comparatively small market share depending on the patterns of cost and demand.
- *Maintaining or increasing market share* The alternative approach, which is concerned with increasing or maintaining the customer base, may require a different and possibly more competitive approach to pricing, since the firm with the largest market share may not necessarily be the firm which earns the best profits.

Either of these approaches may be used, though ultimately the objectives of pricing will effectively be determined by the nature of overall corporate objectives and corporate strategies. It is possible to identify a third pricing strategy, that of pricing for survival. Survival is a basic objective for any organization and consequently, because of the impact of price on revenue, there are circumstances in which pricing decisions may be formulated simply to ensure survival during periods of difficulty. Thus, during a recession, some organizations may cut prices and possibly incur short-term losses simply to ensure that sufficient revenue is generated to keep the organization in business.

Influences on pricing

The pricing decision is potentially a very complex one because it often has to adjust to the requirements of different groups within the firm. For example, finance and accounting may be concerned with price only in relation to costs and the organization's ability to meet certain specified financial targets. Marketing may focus attention on general market reactions and the ability of price to generate a required level of sales, while a sales department may be rather more concerned about the reaction of individual customers. Furthermore, the complexity of the pricing decision can be compounded by the degree of uncertainty that exists in relation to the marketing environment in general, and consumers, competitors and distributors in particular. Indeed, in general terms a variety of factors will affect the outcome of the pricing process:

The nature of consumer demand

Basic economic theory suggests that there is a relationship between price and the level of demand, and that demand will be lower at high prices and higher at low prices. This general principle probably holds for most markets; however, there are always instances of higher prices leading to higher demand. These typically occur when the price is taken as an indicator of quality, so that demand is higher for a higher-quality product. Some consideration must be given to the basic principle of a negative relationship between price and quantity because revenue depends not just on price but on quantity sold. Furthermore, costs may also be affected by quantity in that some products may be significantly cheaper when produced on a large scale. When a high level of sales is a target, then it must be recognized that this will often only be achieved by adopting a relatively lower price.

In addition to considering the negative relationship between price and quantity, however, it is also important to consider the responsiveness of price to quantity (price elasticity of demand in economic terms). If demand for a product is described as elastic, it means that quantity is responsive to demand and only a small change in price may be required to produce a large change in quantity demanded. From a marketing perspective, this suggests that it will be relatively easy to increase sales with only a small reduction in price. By contrast, when demand is described is inelastic, then it suggests that quantity demanded is not very responsive to price. In such circumstances, reducing price will have very little impact on the level of sales, unless that price reduction is very substantial.

The economic approach to consumer demand considers reactions to price in a narrow sense. From a marketing perspective, we would also want to think about consumer perceptions of value and the benefits they receive from the product. If additional features, which are highly valued by the consumer, can be added to a product, then the price of that product can be increased significantly, irrespective of the cost. If on-site warranties for personal computers are highly valued by consumers, then including these as a product feature will allow a manufacturer or retailer to charge a higher price over identical products without such features. What is important is not what these features cost, but how highly the consumers value them.

Competition

There are few situations where an organization can set its prices without giving some consideration to the activities of its competitors. The pricing decisions of competing organizations will affect the relationship between price and quantity sold for an individual organization: if prices are noticeably out of line, sales will be lost. At the same time, however, it should be recognized that using price as the basis for competition and looking to undercut competitors usually has little to offer as a long-term strategy. In the situation where organizations have broadly similar cost structures, price cutting can be destabilizing and can ultimately lead to damaging price wars. This is not to suggest that price cutting is not an option – it can be a useful tactic to gain short-term advantage – but it will always be difficult to sustain. Exhibit 11.1 presents an example of the use of competitive pricing in a market for a luxury product that has traditionally been characterized by high margins.

Exhibit 11.1   Competitive pricing

Superdrug

Superdrug is the United Kingdom's second largest health and beauty chain, characterized by a heavy marketing emphasis on discounted prices and a value-for-money image. Superdrug is currently causing a furore among the top fragrance houses by its decision to move into selling premium perfumes at heavily discounted prices. The fragrance houses are incensed at the thought of their products being sold at discounts of up to 30 per cent by staff whom they feel are not properly trained and in an environment that does not correspond to the image of the product. Superdrug have defended their moves and point out that they sell premium perfumes from separate counters using specially trained staff. Furthermore, despite the fragrance houses' claim that the high price is an essential part of the brand image, market research suggests that 79 per cent of perfume buyers regard fine fragrances as too expensive and 69 per cent would be prepared to buy more if prices were reduced.

Source: Slingsby (1992).

The distribution network

For consumer and industrial goods the importance of considering distribution channels stems from the fact that many organizations will be involved, not simply in setting a price to their final consumer, but also in setting a price for their goods as they enter a particular distribution channel. Distributors make profits on the basis of volumes and margins, and are often willing to accept low margins for high-volume items and will require high margins for low-volume items. Some awareness of normal or acceptable margins acts as a useful starting point in determining the appropriate price for selling into distribution channels. In addition, an equally important aspect is the nature of discounts offered, which not only affect the price but can often be an important influence on the willingness of the distributor to carry a particular product.

Internal factors

There are a variety of internal factors that affect the pricing process. At the most general level, the nature of internally determined business objectives will affect the level of price. In particular, if market share or sales growth is a prime objective, then it is likely that the price that is set will have to be towards the lower end of the range, while if product profitability is the main requirement, then a rather higher price may be acceptable. In addition to general objectives, the product's stage in its lifecycle will influence pricing, as was illustrated in chapter 9. Equally important as an influence is the way in which the product has been positioned. In particular, if the product is to be positioned as a quality or prestige product, then that image must be supported by a high price – *a cheap Porsche isn't a Porsche*. Indeed, this link may be taken a stage further: consumers can encounter difficulties in judging the quality of certain products, particularly when specialist knowledge or information is required. Examples of such products might include vintage wines, designer clothes and many consumer durables. While in some instances, brand names can be used to provide the consumer with information regarding quality, another option is to use price to signal quality. A high price is often taken as an indicator of a high quality. Thus, for example, the recent advertising campaign for Stella Artois lager uses the idea that the lager is expensive to reassure the customer that it is of a high quality. The use of price as a signal for quality is perhaps most common in services, since the consumer cannot form a judgement of the quality of the service until it has been purchased, and in the absence of information from others who have previously used that service, the price is perhaps one of the best indicators to the consumers. However, a word of warning is appropriate: price can be used to signal quality, but if the quality is not in evidence, the organization is unlikely to be able to sustain a quality premium in the longer term.

When we talk about internal influences on pricing, however, the most widely recognized influence is cost. Although price must be determined in relation to the level of demand and the willingness of consumers to pay, costs cannot be ignored. Costs are typically categorized under two headings – fixed and variable. Fixed costs refer to those costs that are incurred irrespective of the level of sales for a product, while variable costs refer to those costs that relate directly to the number of units sold. To identify the cost of a particular product requires that its share of fixed costs is identified along with the variable cost on a per-unit basis. The price that is set should cover variable costs and make a contribution to fixed costs, though this will depend on the level of sales. We will return to the issue of costs later in this section.

Environmental factors

A final set of influences on pricing can be generally grouped under the heading of environmental factors. This category covers factors that will affect the pricing decisions of all organizations and are largely outside the control of those organizations. In particular it covers legislative and fiscal developments.

The pricing of certain products is affected by specific legislation. Perhaps one of the most obvious forms of legislation is that governing the pricing of 'sale' goods. Equally relevant is legislation regarding the price of credit and agreements which control prices, such as the Net Book Agreement. In addition to legislation, changes in taxation can have a major impact on pricing decisions. Changes in excise duties, VAT, etc., generally affect all firms in the industry, meaning that no individual business is necessarily disadvantaged. Many organizations, however, have been caught out by sudden and unpredictable changes in taxation. Few businesses can have anticipated the increase in VAT to 17.5 per cent in the 1991 budget. Many simply passed on the increase in prices to their customers, but for some organizations, the tax change provided a useful opportunity. By absorbing the VAT increase internally, they were able to gain a short-term competitive advantage over their competitors.

Government-sponsored tax and legislation changes are not the only environmental influence on price. The impact of other macro-economic variables such as exchange rates, commodity prices and energy prices can be equally important. Again, in the short term, a business can gain a competitive advantage by absorbing increases, rather than passing them on to consumers, but if such changes appear to be permanent, pricing policies will need to be re-evaluated.

Approaches to pricing

A business can adopt a number of different approaches to pricing. While recognizing the importance of not setting prices solely on the basis of costs, it is nevertheless important to recognize that costs are an important starting point in any pricing decision. There are two basic approaches to using costs in pricing decisions.

Full cost pricing
Costs are determined in relation to a normal or anticipated level of output. Fixed and variable costs are added together to give total costs and the unit cost is calculated by dividing this by the chosen level of output. A percentage mark-up is added to cover profits and this gives a basic price. This method can be varied according to the treatment of variable costs and the way in which the mark-up is determined. However, the basic principle is that for each item sold, the price should cover the costs of production. Low levels of sales will provide an indication of whether the price is too high, in which case the firm can readjust or move away from that particular market. It is much more difficult to identify whether the price is too low.

Marginal cost pricing
The price is based on the additional costs of producing the product, i.e. on the variable costs of production. This approach does not explicitly allow for overhead costs and so should be used with care. Strictly speaking, it is only appropriate when fixed costs and overheads are covered and variable costs represent the true costs of production. For example, the local bakery decides to add a range of sandwiches to the products it sells. These sandwiches are made on the premises by existing staff. The bakery might well chose to opt for a marginal cost pricing approach, with price based only on the costs of the ingredients. This would be realistic given that no additional overheads are being incurred. If the same bakery, however, decided to offer microwaved hot snacks to its customers, then it would be

inappropriate to price just on the basis of the cost of the ingredients since no allowance is being made for the costs of the microwave itself or the electricity it uses.

Costs are undoubtedly important, but from a marketing perspective it would be unwise simply to base prices on costs in a mechanistic fashion. After all, consumers are not particularly interested in costs, they are interested in price and whether the purchase represents value for money. Costs and other market factors can be combined in the pricing decision, as is illustrated in figure 11.1.

With basic cost information, the business can identify its average variable costs. We can see this as the minimum price at which the business would wish to sell its output. The addition of a mark-up to cover fixed costs and one to cover the desired profit margin will give what we might regard as a 'normal' selling price, in the sense that it covers all costs and provides the normal level of profit that the business would expect to earn. It is quite possible, however, that this price could be too low given market conditions, and we must therefore acknowledge that a higher price might be appropriate, which could be anything up to some theoretical 'maximum' price.

There is, then, a possible range for prices either side of the 'normal' price and the actual price which prevails will depend upon market conditions. When the market is strong and demand is buoyant prices may operate in the range between 'normal' and 'maximum'; when the market is weak and

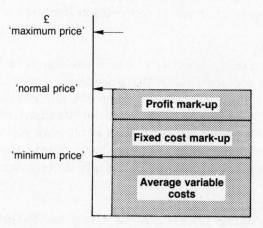

Figure 11.1 Costs and prices

demand is slack, the range between 'normal' and 'minimum' may be more appropriate.

We can consider these variations in a slightly more systematic way by examining the different pricing policies which a business may choose to adopt. A number of the most common approaches are considered below and a more comprehensive review of pricing strategies is given by Tellis (1986).

Competitive pricing
The price setting approach is based on the organization's competitive position in its market. At one extreme, the firm may consider penetration pricing, which involves pricing at a comparatively low level to gain maximum market share. This type of pricing is appropriate when there are significant cost savings as a result of producing on a larger scale (economies of scale), when consumers are price sensitive and in markets where there is a high level of competition. Thus, for example, Proton cars have used a penetration pricing strategy to gain market share following their entry to the UK market. An alternative is to pursue a price skimming strategy where the product is deliberately priced at a high level to gain the maximum benefit in terms of margins. This approach can be justified when there are few cost savings from expanding output (no economies of scale) and when consumers are not particularly price sensitive. It is often used for new products in the early stages of their lifecycle because it allows some of the development costs to be recovered before competitors are able to present their version of the product to the markets. The objective of this approach is to sell initially to the consumers who are not particularly price sensitive, while recognizing that the existing high level of price will need to be reduced in the longer term as competition increases.

Differential pricing
The differential pricing approach entails the use of different prices to different market segments, with the price being varied according to the differing degrees of price sensitivity. There are numerous examples of this type of pricing. Charging a high price for standard rail fares at peak periods and a lower price for saver fares at off-peak periods is a standard example of differential pricing. Volume discounts are another example, as are variations in prices across geographically different markets.

Product line pricing
This involves making price decisions based on the interdependencies between related products. Price bundling involves charging specific prices

for individual items and a lower price to consumers who buy the bundle. For example, a retail outlet may price a television and videorecorder individually and offer a slightly lower price to the consumer who buys the two items together. Complementary pricing aims to exploit the relationship between products and accessories. To attract consumers, the product is priced at a relatively low level, while the necessary accessories are priced relatively high. Typical examples include computer hardware and software. This is often referred to as captive pricing because the consumer is effectively 'captured' by the low price of the product. A particular variant of complementary pricing is loss leadership pricing, which is often practised by retailers. A product is priced to sell at a loss; this low price attracts consumers into the shop and hopefully this will encourage purchases of other more profitable products.

Tactical pricing

This is concerned primarily with short-term pricing decisions where price is almost being used as a promotional device to stimulate an increase in demand. It must be stressed that this is only a short-term policy, but nevertheless it may be useful in producing temporary gains in market share. This incorporates the variety of short-term special offers that are common in the retail sector, as well as decisions to absorb VAT and other tax increases.

For each of these approaches costs are seen as a useful basic input to the pricing decision, in that they give an indication of what the 'normal' price might be and what the minimum price should be. However, that should not be taken to imply that costs should drive the pricing decision. An effective pricing strategy can only be formulated with reference to patterns of competition, the characteristics of distribution channels and the nature of consumer demand, and these features should drive the pricing decision, with costs information providing a broad set of boundaries within which price should be set.

Conclusions

Price cannot be determined without some reference to the cost of providing a product, because unless costs are covered, no price can be sustained on a long-term basis. Costs should not, however, be the overriding consideration. In the short term, coverage of variable costs may be sufficient, though in the longer term, a contribution to fixed costs is essential. The need to cover costs should be viewed as a constraint or a starting point for pricing decisions. The nature and size of the mark-up on costs will be determined in relation to market conditions, consumer and distributor expectations, and the level of competition.

CASE STUDY

Pricing

Jackson's Medical Limited

Jackson's Medical Limited, a Nottingham-based company established in 1931, manufactures a wide range of medical instruments for professional use. In recent years the company has also been involved in manufacturing a limited range of products for use in the home. This range includes scissors, tweezers and thermometers. The best-selling items have traditionally been thermometers, and Jackson's has a 20 per cent share of the market for conventional glass thermometers. These are sold direct to consumers, through major multiple chemists outlets and pharmacies. Currently the company is considering the development of a digital thermometer to be added to the existing range of products marketed in the United Kingdom.

A digital thermometer is not new in the UK market. Last year Jackson's competitors sold in total some 600,000 digital thermometers. The advantage of the digital thermometer over the more conventional glass product is that it offers an easy-to-read digital display. In addition it can be made from durable unbreakable plastic and no longer depends upon mercury, which is widely considered to be toxic. Three main companies manufacture digital thermometers: Fisons Instruments has approximately 30 per cent of the UK market; Brown and Lookman have 25 per cent; and Cambridge Instruments account for a further 20 per cent. The remaining sales come from some small UK manufacturers and from a small volume of imports. Current estimates suggest that the market will expand by about 10 per cent in the coming year.

Prior to the launch of this new product Jackson's undertook a limited degree of market research. This suggested that currently, of the 21 million households in the United Kingdom, only some 5 million actually owned a thermometer, and 75 per cent of these were of the conventional glass type. A further 5 million households appeared to be potential consumers in that they expressed some feelings of guilt about non-ownership. In general, mothers and particularly those in social classes A, B and C1 were more likely to recognize the need for a thermometer. However, they were less than satisfied with the traditional glass product because it was easy to break, potentially dangerous and because the mercury inside was toxic. The digital thermometer, and in particular the variant to be marketed by Jackson's, overcomes many of these problems.

Jackson's product is ready to be test marketed and it seems likely that the test marketing will occur in the East Midlands and East Anglia. One key decision yet to be taken concerns pricing. The preliminary analysis suggests that the costs of production will vary according to the volume sold. Up to 50,000 and unit costs are likely to be £5.10. For volumes between 50,000 and 100,000 the unit costs fall to £4.80 and for production above 100,000 unit costs fall to £4.50 per thermometer. In considering this pricing decision, Jackson's must recognize that it has to consider not only the final retail price but also the price at which the thermometers will be sold into wholesale outlets. Current estimates suggest that buyers on behalf of multiple chemists and pharmacies will expect a mark-up of at least 40 per cent on their buying in price. Competitor's products, which have been on the market for some 18 months, are priced in the region of £7.95 and £11.95.

Source: Adapted from Lancaster and Massingham (1990).

Questions

1. What factors must Jackson's take into account in determining the price for their new thermometer?
2. What pricing policy would you recommend to the company?

12 Promotion decisions

Introduction

The term 'promotion' refers to the range of methods used by an organization in order to communicate with its customers, both actual and potential, and includes advertising, publicity, personal selling and sales promotion. Promotion also covers the various methods that an organization uses to communicate with employees and other interest groups since effective marketing is crucially dependent on the establishment of a marketing orientation throughout the organization as a whole. Promotion is probably the most visible element of the marketing mix to most people and is often seen as one of the more glamorous marketing functions. Promotional activities can, and do, have a significant impact on demand for a particular product or service. Without understating its importance, however, promotion is only one element of the overall marketing mix, and its impact on demand will only be short term if the product is not of the necessary quality, available in the appropriate outlets and acceptably priced. This chapter begins with brief overview of the communications process and then examines the stages in promotional planning and the different elements of the promotional mix.

The communications process

The term 'communications' in a marketing context is used in a way that would be familiar to most people. In very simple terms it is concerned with deciding who says what, how and where they say it, who they say it to and the effects of saying it. From a marketing perspective, the communications process is most commonly thought to be concerned with telling consumers about the features, benefits and availability of a particular product and attempting to persuade them to make a purchase. Increasingly, however, it is being recognized that communication has a rather broader role to play. In addition to stimulating consumer interest in a product, the communications process is also concerned with the way in which an organization projects itself and the image and identity it seeks to create with various interest groups and stakeholders.

The communications process is outlined in figure 12.1, using the example of a television commercial from Heinz. The main components of this process are as follows:

- *Source* The party sending the message, which will typically be the organization itself or representatives of the organization such as the salesforce. If publicity or public relations is the chosen form of communication, then the source may be presented as a quasi-independent body giving 'objective' support to the particular product or service. In our example, the manufacturer, Heinz, is the source of the message.
- *Coded message* The idea that the organization wishes to convey through the communications process must then be coded, either

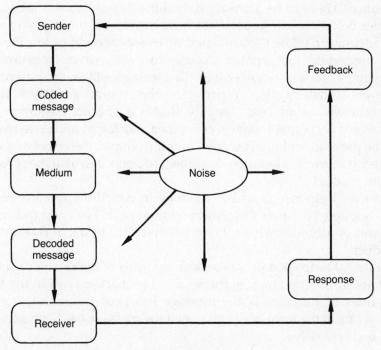

Figure 12.1 The communications process

verbally or in symbols, in a form that is understandable to the target audience. In this example, the sender wishes to convey the idea that Heinz Baked Beans are a popular food, eaten by all types of people and are the only type of beans that the consumer should buy. The coded message takes the form of symbols (various types of people eating Heinz Baked Beans) and words (Beanz Meanz Heinz).

- *Medium* The medium describes the particular channel through which the message is transmitted and may be either personal (sales staff) or non-personal (advertising, publicity or sales promotion). The selection of an appropriate medium is crucial to ensure that the message reaches the target audience. For a fast-moving consumer good such as baked beans, television is probably an appropriate medium for reaching a large and diverse target audience. In the case of products such as luxury cars or designer clothes, for which the target audience is smaller and more narrowly defined, specialist magazines may be a more appropriate medium for communication.

- *Decoded message* As the message is transmitted, the receiver interprets and assigns some meanings to the words and symbols that comprise that message. The sender hopes to encode the message in a way that results in the consumer interpreting the message in the way that was intended. This can be a particularly difficult task since it relies on the sender being able to understand how consumers are likely to see the world. Interpretation is often based on experience and unless the sender can appreciate the type of experiences with which consumers are familiar, there is the danger that the message will be misinterpreted.

- *Receiver* The receiver represents the target audience for the communications process. Usually this is a specific customer group, but where corporate image is concerned, the target audience may well be the general public as a whole. In our example, the target audience is largely housewives but includes other shoppers and also the consumers of the product.

- *Response* Response describes the way in which the receiver reacts to the message, based on their interpretation of it. Typically this refers to the sort of attitudes which the target audience forms in relation to the product.

- *Feedback* Feedback represents those elements of the receiver's response that are transmitted back to the sender. Feedback may be in the form of enquiries or purchase if the message has been successful, but could equally be in the form of complaints if the message has been a failure or has been offensive.

- *Noise* Any unplanned interference with the communications process that distorts the message is described as noise. The presence of noise in any communications process is unavoidable. There will be few messages that are not distorted in some way; the target audience may receive only part of the message being communicated, they may interpret it in accordance with their own preconceptions and they may recall only parts of the message. Effective communications will aim to minimize distortions of this nature by keeping messages brief, distinctive, relevant to the target audience and unambiguous.

Effective communication with customers, interest groups and employees is an important component of any marketing strategy. A well-developed and well-targeted range of products will have little market impact if groups inside and outside the organization have limited awareness of those products. At the same time, it is also important to remember that the communications process described above is subject to problems of misinterpretation and noise. Therefore, effective communication requires careful thought and planing to ensure that the organization has a clear and coherent message to present. Furthermore, that message must be conveyed concisely and unambiguously and it must be credible. Finally, of course, it is important that any promotional activity does not promise something that the organization cannot deliver. Apart from any legal implications that this might have from the point of view of advertising standards, etc., promising what cannot be supplied will lead to consumer dissatisfaction with the purchase and the potential loss of future consumers.

Planning a promotional campaign

The process of planning the promotional effort involves developing an integrated and consistent approach to communicating with consumers, employees and other interest groups. Undoubtedly, advertising is one important component of this process, but it is not the only one. The promotional campaign also includes the use of publicity, personal communications and sales promotions. The stages of promotional planning are outlined in figure 12.2.

Objectives

It is quite common to assume that the purpose of a promotional campaign is to stimulate an increase in sales. However, this is by no means the only

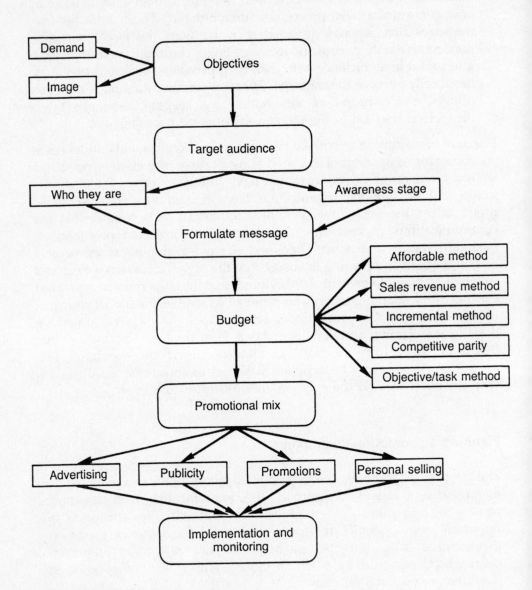

Figure 12.2 Promotional planning

objective that can be specified. As we indicated in chapter 1, marketing is not just about increasing demand but also about managing demand, and the same principle applies to promotional activity. Furthermore, a significant volume of promotional activity is increasingly concerned with the process of building and maintaining an appropriate corporate image. This suggests two broad types of objective which may underpin any promotional campaign:

- *Influence demand* Promotions may be directed explicitly towards influencing the level of demand for an organization's products. Normally, this would imply increasing the level of demand through attracting new customers away from competitors, increasing usage by existing customers and encouraging non-users of the product to use.
- *Corporate image* Many promotional campaigns are directed towards creating and maintaining a particular corporate image. The ability of an organization to create a clear and favourable image for itself with the general public, and particularly with its own customers, is increasingly seen as a valuable way of establishing some form of customer loyalty and as providing the basis for building long-term relationships with customers and other interested parties.

In addition to these two objectives, a third promotional objective is often specified in the context of industrial markets, namely the provision of sales support. Promotion in this sense is not focused on influencing demand or creating and maintaining an image for the organization as such. Rather, it is simply concerned with reminding potential buyers of the organization's operations in a particular market and therefore providing back-up to sales staff who will undertake the bulk of the detailed promotional work.

Any promotional campaign must begin with a clear statement of its objectives and, where possible, these should be quantified. If the objectives are concerned with stimulating demand for a certain product or product group, they can simply be presented in terms of target increases in sales or awareness of the products. If the objectives are concerned with image, quantification may involve specifying targets that refer to the general public's awareness of the organization.

Target audience

The next stage in promotional planning requires the identification of which groups are to be the target of the promotional activity – i.e. which groups are to receive the message. In the case of influencing demand for a particular type of product, this may simply require a statement of which segments of the market the product is targeted towards. By contrast, for image-based promotion, the target audience may easily constitute the 'general public'. This may be a slightly naive approach to adopt, however, since in defining a target audience, it is also necessary to refer back to, and give some consideration to, the nature of the buying process.

It is important to establish the nature and extent of the consumer's knowledge and attitudes towards the organization and its products since this will condition the subsequent formulation and presentation of the message. One simple and widely used approach to this is the AIDA model, which suggests that consumers pass through four stages – from Awareness to Interest to Desire and finally to Action. A promotional message concerned with creating awareness of, or interest in, a product is likely to differ from one that is trying to create a desire to purchase or stimulate an actual purchase. It is equally important to identify the decision makers in the purchase process to ensure that promotion is targeted at the appropriate group.

Formulate message

Having identified the group or groups on which the promotional campaign is to focus, the next stage is to establish what form the message will take. This stage incorporates many of the creative aspects of promotion which are typically undertaken by external specialists, though the marketing groups within an organization inevitably have a substantial input to this process. It is they who know who the customers are and what features of the product or the organization are to be emphasized. Any message can be divided into two key components: the message content and the message form. The message content relates to the basic ideas and information that the sender wishes to convey to the receiver. The message content should make clear why the product is different, what benefits it offers and why the consumer should buy this product rather than one of the available alternatives. This process is often described as identifying the product's (or organization's) unique selling proposition (USP). The USP should attempt to encapsulate one unique feature that is of benefit and which this product (organization) can offer and others cannot.

Once the basic content of the message has been established, the next stage is to consider the form this message should take. It is at this point that the creative input from outside organizations such as advertising agencies becomes important. This process involves finding the most appropriate combination of verbal, audio and visual signals that will present the content of the message in a form which is most suitable for the target audience. This means that great care must be taken to avoid ambiguity, which could lead to misinterpretation At the same time, the information must be presented in a form that will attract attention and maintain sufficient interest in an advertisement or a leaflet to enable the potential consumer to absorb the information being conveyed. Sometimes this may involve using humorous sketches, indirect comparisons with competitors or it may simply focus on the product or the organization itself, using particular lifestyle images, moods or fantasies.

Budget

A budget must be established for the promotional exercise as a whole, and, at a later stage, for the individual components of the promotional mix. There are no hard and fast rules for determining the size of the promotional budget and even within the same broad market, organizations will vary enormously in terms of promotional expenditure. There are a number of different approaches to the formulation of promotional budgets, including:

The affordable method

This simply suggests that the organization's expenditure on promotion is determined according to what the overall corporate budget indicates is available. A target level of expenditure is thus determined without reference to the needs of the campaign, and the marketing department must tailor its activities to that budget. This approach is common among smaller organizations with limited resources.

Sales revenue method

The promotional budget is set as some percentage of sales revenue. By implication this means that sales 'lead' promotion rather promotion leading sales, which is what might be expected. Although this approach does at least establish a link between the success of the product and the level of promotional expenditure, it may present difficulties when budgeting promotional campaigns for new products, and it also tends to limit the opportunity for increased promotional expenditure in periods when demand seems weak.

The incremental method
The budget is set as an increment on the previous year's expenditure. Although this is often used by smaller firms, this method offers no real link between the market and promotional expenditure and does not allow promotional or marketing objectives to guide the level of expenditure.

The competitive parity approach
This approach focuses on the importance of promotion as a competitive tool and entails setting budgets to match those of competitors. It is a rather more market-orientated approach but one which ties the firm to following its competitors and ignores possible fundamental differences between different organizations in the same broad markets.

The objective/task method
This is probably the most rational approach to the establishment of promotional budgets, but perhaps also the most difficult to implement. It requires specific objectives for promotion in terms of the numbers of customers to be reached (exposed to a message), means of reaching them (advertising, direct mail, etc.), the frequency of the message (number of adverts, mail shots, leaflets) and, of course, the precise costs associated with each stage. On this basis, a budget can be established that should enable the organization to achieve its specified promotional objectives and, furthermore, it gives the marketing department a systematic basis on which to evaluate the merits of alternative promotional strategies.

Promotional mix

Having determined the appropriate level of promotional expenditure, this must be allocated between the various promotional tools available to the organization, namely advertising, publicity, sales promotions and personal selling. This mix will vary across organizations and these variations may not obviously be explicable in terms of market/product characteristics. In general, though, we might expect high-value goods, industrial goods and durable goods to be characterized by a significant emphasis on personal selling, while lower-value products would be typified by more emphasis on advertising. Furthermore, in some instances, legal restrictions may affect the composition of the promotional mix as exhibit 12.1 shows.

Nevertheless, there are considerable variations within product classes – for example, most cosmetic firms rely primarily on advertising but one firm

---

Exhibit 12.1 Promoting Marlboro

Philip Morris

The European Community (EC) is moving closer to an outright ban on tobacco advertising in all media. In a highly competitive market, this ban poses a major problem for companies who have relied heavily on promotion to maintain or expand shares in a declining market. The promotional back-up for Marlboro cigarettes has, until now, been heavily dependent on the Marlboro cowboy, who was seen to symbolize the brand's values of freedom and self-expression. With an advertising ban, the Marlboro cowboy will disappear and the most likely replacement in promotional terms is the colour red. The summer of 1991 saw a promotional campaign in Germany built around the theme 'Marlboro is Red, Red is Marlboro'. This campaign included red nights at various night clubs, the extensive use of red on posters and the red people – individuals dressed entirely in red who strolled around cities with the sole aim of drawing attention to themselves. Although the campaign is currently described as a short-term promotional exercise by spokesmen for Philip Morris, many observers see it as part of a longer-term strategy to build a strong association between the Marlboro brand and the colour red. If and when all tobacco advertising is banned, Philip Morris will still be able to use the colour red to keep the Marlboro brand in the customers mind.

Source: Morelli (1991).

(Avon) relies almost exclusively on personal selling. These, and many other differences, reflect the high degree of substitutability between promotional tools and suggest that the firm must consider the relative merits/costs of each tool and select the most appropriate combination for the particular product and target audience. The individual components of the promotional mix will be examined in more detail in the next section.

Implementation and monitoring

As with any plan, the final stage concerns the process of implementation and monitoring. Implementation concerns itself with the allocation of tasks and the specification of time scales. Monitoring focuses on the regular evaluation of the progress of the promotional campaign and the identification of any areas where changes may be necessary. The problem that faces many organizations is the difficulty of measuring the effectiveness of promotional activities; pre-testing attempts to predict the likely effectiveness of a campaign and eliminate weak spots; commercial market research is widely used to determine levels of recall and comprehension; while econometric analysis is often used to assess the impact of advertising on the level of sales.

General techniques of this nature are often unsatisfactory. Pre-testing does not guarantee effectiveness and many successful advertisements have failed pre-tests. Commercial recall and comprehension surveys can indicate whether the basic message has been conveyed to the target audience, but are less suitable for assessing how effective a campaign has been in terms of encouraging purchase. Simply because people indicate that they have recalled an advertisement or are aware of or interested in a product does not mean they intend to buy it. Equally, econometric and other techniques, which entail some element of comparison of sales on a 'before and after' basis, will be able to identify correlations but not necessarily indicate whether advertising has actually 'caused' an increase in sales. Ideally, the evaluation of any promotional activity should be organization/product-specific, with clearly defined objectives and statements of what is to be measured and how. In practice, the costs of this approach often lead to a reliance on general, commercial studies and an acceptance of some loss of detail and relevance in the evaluation.

Promotional tools

As was indicated above, a number of different promotional tools can be used individually or, more usually, in conjunction with each other. As indicated above, developing an appropriate mix of promotional tools is a complex exercise. Product and market characteristics, lifecycle stage, consumer awareness stage, legal restrictions and the nature of the overall marketing mix will all have a bearing on how the promotional mix is formulated. Each of the promotional tools and their particular strengths and weaknesses are outlined in greater detail in the following sections.

Advertising

Advertising is a form of promotion based on mass communication. The term is used to describe any paid, non-personal presentation of goods/ ideas, and as such it covers television and press advertising along with other approaches such as direct mail and direct-response advertising. Advertising is usually classified as being of two types: above-the-line and below-the-line.

Above-the-line

Above-the-line advertising refers to all forms of advertising where a fee is payable to an advertising agency and includes press, television, radio, cinema and poster advertising. Table 12.1 gives some indication of the pattern of above-the-line advertising expenditure across different media, while table 12.2 shows the pattern of advertising expenditure (quarterly) by sector for 1991.

The major advantage of above-the-line advertising is that it enables an organization to reach a large and diverse audience at a low cost per person. A further strength is that the sponsor (i.e. the organization) retains a good degree of control over the message content, its presentation and timing. A potential disadvantage is that advertising messages are highly standardized and as such advertising can be an inflexible promotional tool. It is possibly also wasteful in that it reaches a large number of individuals who are not potential consumers.

Below-the-line

Below-the-line advertising describes forms of advertising for which no commission fee is payable to an advertising agency and includes direct mail, direct-response advertising, exhibitions and point-of-sale material. In comparison with the types of media advertising described above, these methods tend to be much more focused – they reach a smaller number of people at a higher cost per person – but this is often counterbalanced by the higher degree of accuracy associated with such methods.

As well as being categorized according to type, advertising can also be classified according to the role it is required to play in the promotional campaign. In particular, it is useful to distinguish between three forms of advertising:

Table 12.1 Advertising expenditure (excluding direct mail)

	£m at constant 1985 price					
	1986	1987	1988	1989	1990	1991
National newspapers	816	890	973	1003	890	794
	(15.9)	(15.8)	(15.6)	(15.6)	(15.1)	(14.8)
Regional newspapers	1064	1188	1366	1401	1286	1153
	(20.7)	(21.1)	(21.9)	(21.8)	(21.7)	(21.5)
Consumer magazines	338	351	389	396	360	310
	(6.6)	(6.2)	(6.2)	(6.2)	(6.1)	(5.8)
Business and profession	489	559	622	688	592	501
	(9.5)	(9.9)	(10.0)	(10.7)	(10.0)	(9.3)
Other press	526	571	639	679	678	652
	(10.2)	(10.1)	(10.3)	(10.6)	(11.4)	(12.2)
Total press	3234	3559	3989	4168	3807	3412
	(62.9)	(63.3)	(64.0)	(64.9)	(64.4)	(63.6)
Television	1618	1738	1883	1877	1744	1632
	(31.5)	(30.9)	(30.2)	(29.2)	(29.5)	(30.4)
Poster/radio/cinema	292	323	363	382	362	325
	(5.7)	(5.8)	(5.9)	(5.9)	(6.2)	(6.1)
Total	5145	5622	6235	6426	5914	5368

Numbers in parentheses are percentages.
Source: Advertising Association (1992f).

Table 12.2 Advertising expenditure by sector, 1991 (£m)

	Q1	*Q2*	*Q3*	*Q4*
Retail	92.2	104.6	102.1	160.6
Industrial	46.7	59.4	39.2	76.8
Financial	75.2	90.6	67.8	79.0
Government	36.0	26.6	22.3	25.4
Services	101.9	105.9	82.4	92.0
Durables	137.3	169.4	134.9	230.1
Consumables	259.5	307.7	308.8	388.4
Total	748.7	864.1	757.4	1052.3

Source: Advertising Association (1992f).

Table 12.3 Distribution of advertising expenditure in Europe, 1990
(per cent)

	Newspapers	*Magazines*	*Television*	*Radio*	*Cinema*	*Outdoor*
Belgium	35.3	20.5	27.5	1.2	1.4	14.2
Denmark	76.1	11.8	9.6	0.8	0.4	1.3
France	28.6	27.5	24.8	6.6	0.8	11.7
Germany (West)	46.0	27.9	15.8	5.1	1.2	3.9
Greece	26.0	28.2	35.3	5.7	NA	4.8
Ireland	63.7	5.4	19.6	6.2	NA	5.1
Italy	27.8	24.0	43.2	1.4	NA	3.6
Netherlands	50.4	27.8	9.0	2.2	0.3	10.4
Norway	77.2	15.8	2.5	1.0	1.2	2.2
Spain	37.6	15.4	31.3	10.3	0.8	4.7
Sweden	78.6	14.3	2.2	NA	0.6	4.3
UK	44.1	19.3	30.5	2.2	0.5	3.4

NA, not applicable. Figures include agency commission and press classified advertising but exclude production costs.
Source: Advertising Association (1992e).

- *Informative* Advertising that is concerned primarily with conveying information and raising consumer awareness of the product or the organization. This form of advertising is common when a product is in the early stages of its lifecycle, or if it has been modified in some significant way.
- *Persuasive* This type of advertising is much more concerned with creating a desire for the product and stimulating actual purchase. It will tend to be more common for well-established products, often in the growth/maturity stages of the product lifecycle. This is probably the most competitive form of advertising.
- *Reminding* This approach is also often used for well-established products and it is concerned with reminding consumers about the product or organization, reinforcing the knowledge held by potential consumers and reminding existing consumers of the benefits they are receiving from their purchase of a particular good.

The choice of the most appropriate media for advertising will depend upon the nature of the target market and the complexity of the message. Even when target markets are apparently quite similar, the types of advertising media used can vary considerably. For example, in European markets, which might be regarded as broadly similar in terms of levels of development, there is a considerable variation in the distribution of advertising expenditure across media types as table 12.3 shows, and this is reflects different institutional structures and traditions in the relevant markets. While recognizing the persistence of such variations, the choice of media type can still be guided by some consideration of the attributes of particular media against the following criteria:

- *Cost* (in total and per number of consumers reached) Television commercials, for example, are expensive in total, but the cost per consumer reached is typically low. By contrast, direct mail may be low in total cost but high per person contacted.
- *Waste* (portion of the audience served who are not in the target market) Television will tend to be characterized by a high degree of wastage, while magazine and direct mail can be more accurately targeted and thus are characterized by less wastage.
- *Reach* (the total number of people exposed to the advert) Television and advertizements in the national press will tend to have a high reach, while magazines and direct mail tend to have a lower reach. Figures for the reach of magazines and newspapers can be obtained from the National Readership Survey (JICNARS).
- *Regularity* (how often a medium can be used) Daily papers have a high degree of regularity since advertisements can be placed and changed daily. Outdoor advertising, by contrast, is characterized by low regularity since advertisements can only be placed and changed infrequently.
- *Permanence* (number of exposures generated and length of time the message remains with the consumer) Television commercials tend to have a low degree of permanence since the consumer is only exposed to the advertisement while it lasts. Although videoing television programmes is thought to increase the permanence of commercials, the impact of this may be limited as it is estimated that over 25 per cent of viewers skip commercials when watching videos. Magazine advertisements, by contrast, tend to be more permanent because the consumer is exposed on a regular basis while they retain that publication.
- *Persuasive impact* (the ability of the medium to stimulate the consumer) Television typically has the highest persuasive impact because of the combination of audio and visual images. Magazines and radio advertising are often rather less persuasive because they are restricted to verbal or visual images only. Well-designed direct mail can

have a significant persuasive impact because of the benefits of personalization.

- *Clutter* (the number of adverts presented together)   High clutter will tend to distract attention from any individual advert. Television again tends to be characterized by a high degree of clutter since advertisements are grouped during short intermissions. A further problem that can arise concerns the scheduling of advertisements to avoid confusion with other related products. This is particularly important as the volume of television advertising increases.
- *Lead time* (period from the placement of an advert to its display)   This tends to be high for most television advertisements and is becoming increasingly so with the difficulties of getting access to the peak-time slots when the advertisements might be expected to have maximum impact. Newspapers tend to have a much smaller lead time since the main constraint is the actual printing process.

The process of media selection is concerned with trying to achieve the desired number of exposures to the target audience in the most cost effective fashion. The target number of exposures is normally based on past experience and is an estimate of the number of exposures to the target audience that will be required to create a particular level of awareness or encourage a particular rate of product trial. In this situation, the trade-off between reach and frequency becomes an important consideration. Reach, as we have already explained, refers to the number of people exposed to the particular medium through which the message is presented. Frequency refers to the number of exposures to the target audience within a specified time period. The cost-effectiveness of different media can be calculated based on the relative reach and frequency, though in doing this it remains important to give full consideration to the criteria outlined above, all of which affect the quality of the message that is finally delivered.

Direct marketing is one of the fastest growing elements in the promotional mix. The most commonly used forms of direct-marketing are direct mail and direct response advertising. The former, though expensive, is arguably one of the most accurate and cost-effective methods of advertising products. Table 12.4 gives some indication of the growth in direct mail over the last decade. The effectiveness of direct mail is dependent on the availability of suitable databases. With the development of increasingly comprehensive computer databases, an organization can identify precisely the group to which it wishes to direct its campaign and can convey a relatively large volume of detailed information to prospective consumers. In some instances, such databases can be developed 'in house',

Table 12.4 Direct mail volumes (million items)

	Total	Mail order	Other
1980	985	251	734
1981	1034	294	740
1982	1102	333	769
1983	1084	264	820
1984	1262	276	986
1985	1303	330	973
1986	1401	348	1053
1987	1626	393	1233
1988	1766	441	1325
1989	2117	520	1597
1990	2372	612	1760
1991	2122	521	1601

Source: Advertising Association (1992e).

but typically this will relate only to existing customers. The alternative is to use a specialist list broker or direct marketing agency which has access to suitable mailing lists.

The general problem with direct mail is that it is typically seen as 'junk mail', despite the increasingly sophisticated systems that are used to prepare such material. Within the direct mail industry considerable efforts are being made to improve this image, and in some sectors there has been an improvement. For example, customers appear to take direct mail from their bank rather more seriously than direct mail from other organizations. In industrial markets direct mail is widely recognized as an important mechanism for retaining contact with existing buyers and attracting interest from new buyers. Even the Church of England has actively started to consider the potential for using direct mail as exhibit 12.2 shows.

Alternatives to direct mail include direct-response advertising, leaflets, inserts, television and radio. Direct-response advertising tends to be most effective for fairly standardized products where the volume of information required is relatively small. Inserts are often employed for rather more complex products where they typically operate to gain interest rather than directly sell the product. Television and radio are rather less well used for direct marketing at present, primarily because of their cost, though the increased popularity of satellite television may change this.

Exhibit 12.2 Media advertising or direct mail?

The Church of England

Following the 1990 Broadcasting Act, the ban on television and radio advertising for religious organizations was lifted. However, the Church of England had traditionally distanced itself from such promotional tools, at least in part because of the difficulty of defining the product they offered. A poster campaign for US evangelist Billy Graham achieved an 85 per cent awareness rating for meetings organized in London in 1989, while a pre-Christmas campaign run in the Diocese of Oxford in 1991 resulted in a 17–25 per cent increase in church attendance. Consequently, with congregations falling, the Church of England set up a working party to consider national advertising. However, many marketing professionals believe that national advertising does not provide the best way forward. With a diversity of theological beliefs, finding a cohesive image for the Church of England to present in a national advertising campaign would be impossible: a localized approach may have more to offer. Indeed, the Bishop of Durham is currently investigating the potential for an integrated database marketing strategy to link local churches and their parishioners through direct mail. This provides the basis for the church to build up longer-term relationships with existing and potential churchgoers and is seen by many as potentially far more effective than above-the-line expenditure on national advertising, which may not be able to convey the church's message effectively.

Source: Martin (1992).

Finally, as a form of advertising, we should mention exhibitions. Exhibitions tend to be forgotten about in many marketing books and yet they have very significant advantages, the most obvious being the opportunity actually to explain and demonstrate the product on a face-to-face basis with the customer. Exhibitions also have the advantage of allowing the consumer to draw direct comparisons with competing products and provide the supplier with access to a much larger potential market than might be the case with other promotional techniques. Exhibitions are often attractive to final consumers (e.g. the Ideal Home Exhibition), but they are most prominent in business markets where they are probably one of the most important advertising media. Currently, there are around forty-five major exhibition venues in the United Kingdom and some 640 exhibitions are held annually.

Publicity

Publicity is normally defined as being any form of non-paid, non-personal communication, and, like advertising, it involves dealing with a mass audience. For the purpose of the current discussion, we broaden the concept of publicity to include an additional element, namely public relations. By contrast with publicity, this is 'paid for', but it is included under this heading because it is concerned more generally with building and maintaining an understanding between the organization and the general public.

Publicity offers a number of benefits to the organization. It has no major time costs, it provides access to a large audience and the message is considered to have a high degree of credibility. The information is seen as coming from an independent or quasi-independent source rather than from the organization itself. However, it is also one of the more difficult forms of promotion to implement and to control since the final presentation and timing of information about the organization will usually be edited by the relevant media such as television and newspapers.

Traditionally, publicity and public relations were seen as being centred around producing regular, informative press releases and building up good contacts with journalists. As a consequence, its importance has often been underestimated. With increasing pressure on advertising space and costs, however, the importance of publicity seems likely to increase. Two areas merit particular attention, namely the creation of a corporate image and sponsorship.

The development of a suitable corporate image is an aspect of public relations that has been increasing in importance for many organizations. It is unusual for a consumer to purchase a product without giving some consideration to the reputation or image of the supplier. The consumer's concern may also be broader than a simple concern with the organization's reputation for quality and reliability. The decision process, at the margin may be influenced by the organization's performance and reputation in relation to environmental factors, community policy, staff policy, etc. Increasingly, businesses are recognizing that it is not just products that are important: it is the organization itself.

The factors that contribute to the creation of a favourable image are many and varied. A clear corporate identity is important to give the organization a coherent face in its dealings with consumers and make it instantly recognizable. An organization's corporate identity can be represented by a variety of visual symbols associated with promotional material, retail or wholesale outlets, product design, packaging and staff appearance. Esso, for example, attach considerable importance to the design and appearance of petrol station forecourts; a common, easily recognizable design and colour scheme are seen as key factors in building up a relationship with their customers. In the financial services sector, corporate image is often seen as one of the most important forms of branding that is available to an organization. A large volume of financial services advertising has been concerned with imagery rather than specific products. It is important to remember, however, that simply advertising and preparing corporate logos will not be sufficient to create and maintain a desirable corporate image. It is essential to ensure that this image permeates the organization and is then reflected in aspects of the service presented to consumers.

One increasingly important aspect of public relations and the creation of a desirable corporate image has been the growth in sponsorship. The extent to which this method of communication is used varies considerably across companies, but with increased competition for advertising slots on television and rising media costs in general, sponsorship is seen as an important and effective way of projecting the image of the organization. There can be few households that are not aware of the Barclays Football League, the Rumbelows Cup or the Embassy International Snooker. Sponsorship is not confined to sport but has spread to many cultural activities as well, with National Westminster Bank involved recently in providing sponsorship for the Hallé Orchestra and Royal Insurance offering sponsorship to the Royal Shakespeare Company. For corporate customers, the sponsorship of local business seminars is also a widely used technique. The advantage of sponsorship, apart from its cost-effectiveness, tends to be that it is viewed less cynically by the consumer than more orthodox forms of advertising. A possible problem with sponsorship is that the organization's name becomes associated with the event only and not its own products. Organizations engaging in sponsorship should be aware that it can only effectively promote a name rather than a specific image and that there is always the danger that, as with Gillette and its sponsorship of one-day cricket, the organization becomes better known for its sponsorship than for its products.

Sales promotions

Sales promotions are generally either final consumer demand-pull methods of promotion or distributor-oriented supply-push promotions. Demand-pull promotions are specifically concerned with providing consumers with a direct incentive to try and buy a product, while supply-push promotions are designed to encourage middlemen to stock and sell particular products. Sales promotions are considered to be particularly appropriate in the early stages of a product's lifecycle, though they can be equally useful in the later, declining stages of the lifecycle when they can be used to attract custom from competing brands. The use of sales promotions as part of a marketing campaign has increased considerably in recent years, as has been evidenced by the rapid growth in the volume of business conducted by specialist sales promotion agencies.

Although sales promotion is typically concerned with influencing the level of demand for a product, it can also fulfil a number of more specific objectives:

- induce trial purchase;
- build brand loyalty;
- speed up the movement of stock;
- counteract the activities of competitors;
- attract the undecided or marginal buyer.

Any of these, singly or in combination, may be specified as the objectives of a sales promotion plan. There are a variety of techniques available, though the following are probably the most popular:

Free mail-in
This is probably the most popular method of sales promotion in the United Kingdom. By sending in to the promoter some proof of purchase, the customer receives premium merchandise in return. The customer is therefore gaining a very tangible and direct additional benefit from purchasing the promoted product. However, this technique is also costly and these costs can be very unpredictable because of the difficulties associated with determining redemption rates.

Reduced price
This constitutes the most direct method of sales promotion in that it simply involves offering the product to the consumer at a reduced price, and this reduced price would normally be managed to encourage the customer to

buy more of the product. There are some legal difficulties associated with price promotions, including the need to prove that a price reduction is indeed a price reduction. In addition to the simple price reduction there are a number of related techniques including bonus packs (25 per cent extra free), coupons (10p off next purchase) or fixed price packs (50 g for £1.50)

Competitions

Competitions are a popular and easy to manage form of promotion. Costs are generally fixed and predictable at the beginning of the promotion and the exercise is relatively easy to manage. The choice of prizes and the variety of prizes offered must be determined in relation to the needs and expectations of the target market. For example, is it preferable to have a larger number of small prizes or a smaller number of larger prizes? Although the chances of success should ideally be linked to the volume of purchases made, it may not always be possible to restrict entry to the competition. The legal requirements for competitions and related promotional techniques such as lotteries and prize draws are outlined in the Lotteries and Amusements Act 1976.

Couponing

Couponing is probably the technique most commonly associated with sales promotions. The technique is popular because it is easy to manage and readily understood by consumers. Offering coupons is useful as a way of encouraging product trial and building up product loyalty. There are, however, problems associated with mal-redemption by retailers, which often breaks the link between the cost saving and the promoted product.

Although sales promotions in the form of a communication from the manufacturer to the consumer are undoubtedly highly visible, a substantial amount of sales promotion occurs between the manufacturer and the distribution network. Promoting to the distribution network is of considerable importance in ensuring that the product is carried to outlets where final consumers can make purchases. Indeed, as well as using sales promotions directly to influence distributors, many manufacturers will also tailor their final consumer promotions to fit the needs and requirements of the distributor.

Personal selling

This is probably one of the most expensive form of promotion in terms of cost per person contacted. The extent to which sales staff are used varies with different products and different markets, but there are few occasions when some element of personal selling is not needed. The use of personal selling is probably most extensive in industrial markets where the number of buyers is small, the value of the account potentially large and there is often a demand for a specialized or customized product. A particular advantage of personal selling is that communication can occur in both directions and sales staff can respond immediately to specific customer queries and questions.

Although there is often a tendency to think of sales people as pursuing a hard sell and pressurizing clients to buy, it should be remembered that the objectives of sales staff can vary quite considerably. In addition to actually making a sale, the role of sales staff will also include:

- *Prospecting and information provision* This refers to the process of making contact with potential customers and providing them with information for current or future use.
- *After-sales service* For many products and services, sales staff have an important role to play in providing advice to consumers on the use of the product and organizing after-sales service and maintenance.
- *Information gathering* In many markets, sales staff represent an important source of information on customer needs and competitor activities.

Compared with other forms of promotion, the main advantage which personal selling possesses is that it is a two-way form of communication which gives the customer the opportunity to query aspects of the product and the sales staff the opportunity to deal with the specific needs of each customer. As a result, the message itself becomes much more flexible and service provision can more easily be tailored to the needs of the consumer. As a consequence, however, it is rather more expensive and requires a high degree of expertise, both among the management who coordinate and motivate sales staff, and among the sales staff themselves who require a variety of interpersonal skills combined with in-depth knowledge about the organization's product range.

Although there are always some individuals who are natural communicators and naturally good in the selling function, a number of general principles can be identified that will contribute to the success of personal selling. Given the significance of contact with individual staff, it is clearly important to ensure that sales staff develop good personal relationships with their customers. To alleviate any doubts or risks that the customer may feel requires a professional orientation on the part of sales staff to illustrate the competency and familiarity with all aspects of the relevant products. This in turn requires that the organization ensures good training and motivation for such staff. Finally, the personal selling approach should ensure that the actual purchase decision is made easy and that minimal demands are imposed on the customer.

Conclusions

Promotional strategy deals with all aspects of communication between an organization and its customers, its employees and other interested parties. Four main promotional tools are available to an organization: advertising, publicity, sales promotion and personal selling. The balance between these tools will vary according to the nature of the overall marketing strategy, the characteristics of the product, the resources of the organization and the nature of the target market. Whatever promotional mix is chosen, the effectiveness of the communications process depends on the development of a clear and unambiguous message that is presented to the right target audience, at the right time and through the most appropriate medium.

CASE STUDY

Halifax Building Society

The Halifax Building Society is the largest UK building society and is the third largest finance house behind Barclays and the National Westminster Bank. One in four adults are customers of the Halifax and, on average, a new account is opened every 7 seconds. In spite of the weak housing market, the Society made record pre-tax profits of £533.7m in 1990 and its future sights are set on becoming market leader in the personal finance sector.

The position of all building societies, not just the Halifax, changed dramatically when the Building Societies Act was introduced in 1986. Prior to the passing of this Act the activities of societies had been constrained by the provisions of The Building Societies Act 1962 and competition had been restricted up to the mid-1980s until the ending of the interest rate cartel. The new legislation permitted societies to provide a much wider range of services than hitherto, including full personal banking and money transmission services, unsecured lending, integrated house-buying packages, agency services, and enhancements to the provision of insurance broking services. These services could be provided either by the society itself, through the creation of subsidiaries, or through joint ventures. In effect, the Act meant that societies were able to compete with the banks on equal terms.

The banks had developed their approaches to marketing financial services over a number of years; the building societies, by contrast, had to start from scratch. Their marketing had traditionally focused only on their roles as savings institutions and mortgage providers and advertising campaigns were very similar, emphasizing safeness and reliability, friendliness and comfort. Typical of these campaigns were slogans such as 'Get the Abbey Habit', 'Say the Leeds and you're smiling' and the Halifax's own 'Get a little Xtra help'. This contrasted sharply with the rather more awe-inspiring image of the banks. Unlike the banks, building societies were not only portrayed as being more accessible, they were more accessible. The Halifax, for example, had fewer branches than its main banking competitors, but these branches were well distributed throughout the country and open for longer hours.

As market leader, the Halifax was keen to take advantage of the new opportunities offered by deregulation. This required the development of new products internally and also the establishment of two subsidiary companies. Halifax Property Services is a national chain of estate agents providing the Society with direct access to the market for integrated house-buying services. Halifax Financial Services concentrates on the provision of insurance-based products through a tied agreement with Standard Life. Although both of these operations are run as independent subsidiaries, it is intended that they should be presented to the public as part of an integrated package of personal financial services provided by the Halifax.

Questions

1. What is the basic marketing problem that the Halifax faces?
2. What role should promotion play in developing a new marketing approach?
3. What recommendations would you make regarding future promotional developments?

13 Place decisions

Introduction

The place component of the marketing mix is concerned with bridging various time, place, quantity and variety gaps between the producer and the consumer, thus ensuring that the organization provides the right products, in the right variety at the right time and in the right place. In so doing the place component of the marketing mix adds value to the product, its prime function being to create the opportunity for the consumers actually to make a purchase. There are two key aspects to distribution from a marketing point of view. One concerns the process of designing and managing the channels that are used to get products to the consumer (channel management). The other concerns the processes associated with actually moving products from their place of manufacture to their place of sale and consumption (physical distribution).

The choice of distribution channels is a crucial one for the organization; it can take a long time to build up good distribution channels, and where established channels exist it can be extremely difficult for new manufacturers to get their products into those channels. In many instances, the existing distribution network represents a constraint within which the organization operates. For example, around half of the purchases of food in the United Kingdom are made in stores owned by the top six supermarket chains. Thus any manufacturer wishing to supply food products to the mass market would need to use one or more of these chains. The distribution decision is then not so much concerned with what outlets to use as with how to gain shelf space in one or more of these chains and how to manage the relationship with major supermarket buyers. In this chapter, we review, first, the issues associated with physical distribution, before moving on to examine channel management and the factors that influence the types of distribution channel that an organization will use.

Physical distribution

At the most basic level, distribution is concerned with physically moving a product from where it is produced to where it is sold and consumed. The location of manufacturing plants relative to raw materials and relative to storage and warehousing facilities are all important from a marketing perspective because of their influence on production and distribution costs. Logistics is the area that deals with these issues, that is to say, logistics is concerned with integrating physical distribution management and materials management to focus on the whole range of activities associated with moving raw materials through production facilities and moving finished products out to consumers. Our main concern is with the issues surrounding physical distribution, but in many respects these cannot be separated from materials management activities.

On the physical distribution side there are a number of key decisions which have to be taken. These relate to:

- *Warehousing* According to the size of market served, an organization will need a greater or lesser number of warehouses. This decision is, however, influenced by factors other than just market size. The distribution of warehousing will have important implications for the speed with which orders can be met and the type of transport facilities required.
- *Inventory* Holding stock is a major distribution cost and consequently decisions about quantities and varieties to be held will have important implications for marketing costs. The stocking decision should not be taken solely on a cost basis but should also acknowledge the needs and expectations of consumers. Where immediate delivery is expected, or where it can be used to gain a competitive advantage, the extra costs of stockholding may well be justified.
- *Load size* This refers to the size of the units in which goods are packaged. Large packed units which can be stored on pallets are easier and cheaper to handle, but if customers require smaller volumes, then some consideration has to be given to the costs of breaking down loads.
- *Communications* Efficient order processing and invoicing are increasingly important aspects of customer service. In addition to offering customer benefits, an efficient and effective information system can also help keep stocking costs under control. In some instances, it may be possible to further develop such systems to forecast future consumer requirements and initiate automatic reordering if appropriate.

- *Transport*   At the most basic level, the transport decision is concerned with whether or not the business should own its own transport fleet. Owning a transport fleet can have obvious benefits in promotional terms because the organization's name will be displayed on all vehicles. At the same time, a contract fleet can be cheaper because costs can be spread over a number of customers, but the consequence can be a loss of flexibility. Again, the importance of such flexibility from the perspective of the consumer should be an important factor in governing the decision. The issue of scheduling delivery is also important, and again this decision should be taken in the context of market needs and expectations.

There is inevitably a high degree of interdependency between these various physical distribution decisions and there are a number of cost trade-offs to be considered. It is worth noting, however, that customer service is becoming an increasingly important area of any business. In making decisions about physical distribution systems, it is increasingly important to be able to identify what is expected by customers as a minimum and also whether there are any areas in which the system can be developed to provide a competitive advantage. If 'next day delivery' is standard in a market, then the business must have a physical distribution system that will provide this type of service. If 'next day delivery' is regarded a desirable by consumers but not widely available, then there is potential for the business to offer such a service and gain a competitive advantage by so doing. Exhibit 13.1 presents an example of innovative distribution that has produced a competitive edge for the initiating organization.

Reasons for using intermediaries

Channel management concerns itself with developing, organizing and managing the distribution system. This covers decisions regarding whether to sell direct or to use intermediaries, which intermediaries are to be used, what contractual arrangements should be formed with those intermediaries and what should be expected from them in return. Clearly, the most basic issue is whether or not to use intermediaries.

In some situations organizations will distribute their products direct to their consumers, and this is particularly so in the case of major industrial purchases of items such as machinery. However, in general, a distribution

Exhibit 13.1   Innovation in distribution

First Direct

For any bank, distribution is a key marketing decision because of the importance consumers attach to convenient access in selecting a bank. Traditionally, the British banking system has been highly dependent on the branch network to distribute basic banking services. First Direct, a wholly owned subsidiary of Midland Bank, owes much of its success to a radical departure from this tradition. First Direct, launched by Midland in 1989, offers a 24-hour, person-to-person, telephone banking service. Using a telephone network, First Direct offers its customers cheque accounts, savings and loan products, mortgages, share dealing and travel services. This product range is supported by a highly competitive pricing policy that First Direct are able to sustain because they do not have to bear the huge costs associated with a high street branch network. Although still small, First Direct is probably the fastest growing bank in Britain and currently has over 250,000 customers. At present, the bank is operating largely unchallenged in a niche market (primarily higher-income consumers), but competition seems likely to increase. National Westminster, TSB, Girobank and Bank of Scotland all have remote banking services, though none of these offers the degree of convenience and the personal contact that are available from First Direct.

Source: Slaughter (1992).

system will involve the use of a number of intermediaries. Both buyers and sellers have motivations for the use of intermediaries.

- Intermediaries specialize in distribution activities and by operating on a large scale (i.e. over a variety of products) they can benefit from economies of size and scale. The specialization in distribution channels allows both manufacturer and consumer to benefit from lower per unit transaction costs.
- Producers gain access to wider market coverage by using a distribution network, while the consumer benefits from access to a wide product assortment.

- For the producer, the distribution network constitutes an additional forum for competition, that is to say, as well as competing in product markets, organizations can also compete to get products into the distribution network.
- The buyer can potentially benefit from a range of additional services which the distributor can provide more efficiently than the manufacturer.
- The producer escapes the costs (especially fixed costs) associated with the establishment of a distribution network

These arguments are largely based on the idea that using distribution channels is cost effective in an economic sense, and that manufacturers should concentrate on doing what they are best at, namely manufacturing, and leave the issue of distribution to the companies that are experienced in these areas. In practice, however, the issues surrounding the choice of distribution channels are not always simply a matter of specialization and cost minimization.

Channel functions

Obviously the basic function performed by the distribution network is to handle the physical distribution of the product from the producer to the consumer. This will often cover transport, warehousing and stockholding as well as the provision of capital necessary for purchasing and stockholding. Implicit in this is the notion that the intermediary will also assume some of the risks associated with distribution. For example, the intermediary who buys products from the manufacturer to sell on to the consumer is taking the risk that some of the produce purchased will not be sold. This is a risk that would otherwise have been borne by the manufacturer. The riskiness of products varies and when that risk is high, the intermediary may be unwilling to take ownership of the product and will instead distribute on a commission basis. This system of using an agent is common in the distribution of highly perishable products such as fresh fruit and vegetables. It is also common in new overseas markets where there may be some doubt about the market potential of the product.

Although such physical and financial functions are important, these activities are only performed on the assumption that the consumer already wishes to make the purchase. In this sense, the distribution sector is simply facilitating the transaction. However, its role is wider than that in the sense that the distribution sector can also play an important role in the broader aspects of marketing, including marketing research, promotion, provision of customer service, pricing and packaging.

Obviously not all channels of distribution perform all functions, but most channels perform a large number of such functions. Also, within any channel, different intermediaries will perform different functions. In each case, the intermediary will have the potential advantage of cost savings based on specialization.

Choosing distribution channels

A range of different distribution systems can be used in moving products from producer to consumer. These are outlined schematically in figure 13.1, and range from direct distribution at one extreme to the use of a variety of different intermediaries at the other. Many companies will use more than one system if the market conditions are appropriate.

With direct distribution, the company relies on its own sales staff to take responsibility for contacting customers and making sales, and the product will be delivered direct from manufacturer to the consumer. This type of distribution system is common for many large industrial purchases and is also used extensively in the marketing of pensions and life insurance

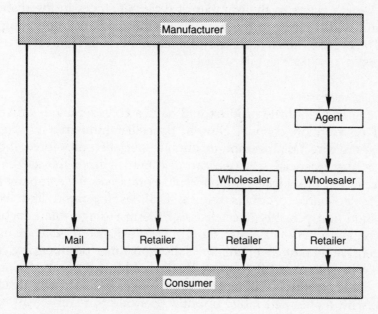

Figure 13.1 Distribution channels

products. A variant on the traditional form of direct distribution through a sales force is to rely on direct distribution through direct mail. This technique was described in the previous section on promotion. It has obvious advantages because of the ability to target customers very accurately and convey a large volume of potentially complex information, which they can absorb in their own time. The disadvantage of this method is still the fact that many consumers have a negative image of direct mail shots.

A third method of reaching consumers is by selling through a retailer. Some companies, such as Boots and Thorntons, have their own retail outlets, but many other manufacturers will simply sell direct to retailers or will sell through a wholesaler. The advantages of using either a wholesaler or an agent and a wholesaler is that these intermediaries will perform many of the functions that would otherwise have to be undertaken by the manufacturer or the retailer. For example, many manufacturers may not sell in the relatively small volumes required by a small local retailer. The wholesaler will normally take on the function of breaking down the bulk orders received by the manufacturer and selling on smaller quantities to the retailer. Agents can potentially perform many similar functions, though as we noted earlier, the agent typically does not take ownership of the products and simply sells on the basis of a fee or commission.

Any marketing channel can be described in terms of its length and width. Length refers to the number of different stages in the distribution chain and width refers to the number of intermediaries operating at any stage. The precise choice of distribution channels is influenced by a variety of factors:

Product characteristics
The characteristics of the product will have a considerable bearing on the type of distribution channel chosen. Specialist industrial products will often require direct distribution through a specialist sales force. Intangible products (e.g. financial services) can also benefit from the use of a sales force because it provides a tangible representation of the company and the product. Perishable products require facilities for rapid and extensive distribution and possibly specialist short-term storage. Manufacturers of such products will typically use short but wide distribution to ensure rapid and extensive market coverage. Specialist consumer products, by contrast, will often be sold in small volumes through a limited number of specialist outlets. These products will tend to use a longer but narrower distribution system, with the limited range of outlets serving to reinforce an image of the exclusive nature of the product.

Characteristics of consumers
Consumer expectations regarding the availability of a particular type of product will have an important bearing on the nature of the chosen distribution system. If consumers are willing to travel to purchase a product or are willing to hold stocks, then the manufacturer can rely on a moderately narrow channel structure. If consumers expect to purchase regularly and in small quantities, then a broader channel structure will be required. Similarly, if the target market consists of a small number of consumers, then relatively narrow distribution channels may be acceptable, but if the target market is large in numbers, then a wide range of outlets is usually necessary.

Characteristics of competitors
As mentioned earlier, distribution channels represent an important arena for competition. If competitors operate an extensive distribution network, then it may be necessary to match this channel structure in order to maintain a competitive position. Conversely, if competitors operate with a narrow channel structure, then it may be possible to a obtain competitive advantage by the use of a wider range of outlets. An example of the importance of competitors and competitor activity in relation to distribution channels is given in exhibit 13.2.

Environmental factors
In addition to consumer and competitor influences on the structure of distribution channels, there are also other more general environmental influences that may be relevant, namely social, legal and technological factors. Changing family structures, increased female participation in the labour force and changing patterns of leisure, for example, have contributed to the growth of out-of-town shopping and the growing popularity of the superstore. The increased use of information technology and computerized stock control has changed attitudes about the availability of products and the speed and reliability of delivery. Finally, legal factors must also be considered, such as formal restrictions on the type of outlet which may be used and any licensing requirements which may exist. Such legal constraints are perhaps most commonly associated with the retailing of products such as alcohol, tobacco and pharmaceuticals, but the impact of legislation can affect other aspects of distribution including store location as exhibit 13.3 shows.

Exhibit 13.2   Rivalry in distribution

Mars and Walls

The launch of ice-cream Mars bars and other related ice-cream products from Mars has been one of the marketing successes of recent years. However, Mars are now encountering some distribution problems. Walls, the dominant force in the UK ice-cream market has put considerable effort into building up its distribution network and in particular has pursued a strategy of loaning freezers to shopkeepers to enable them to sell Walls ice-cream. With increased competition from the Mars products, Walls has reacted to protect its market by advising shopkeepers that they cannot stock Mars products or indeed any other competitors products in freezers owned by Walls. Mars claim that the ruling is in breach of EC competition law, while Walls claims that they are simply protecting their substantial investment in developing an appropriate distribution network.

Source: Marketing Week (1992c).

Strategic factors

The distribution system chosen for a particular product must be consistent with the overall marketing strategy and particularly with the chosen product position; a highly technical product or an exclusive, luxury product will require specialist outlets, while an 'instant access' product needs wide coverage/regular delivery and easy availability. If the product is positioned directly in relation to the competitors, then it will typically require a similar distribution channel, but if it is positioned away from competitors, then the organization has greater scope in terms of selecting the appropriate system of distribution.

Cost factors

The physical costs of distribution through different structures will vary and the relative magnitude of these costs will have an important impact on the system that is finally chosen. The cost issue can also be considered at a broader level, in relation to the overall costs of the marketing campaign. If, for example, marketing budgets are tight and yet the product still has to reach a wide market, it may be more cost effective to achieve this degree of

---

Exhibit 13.3 Legal constraints on distribution

Belgian hypermarkets

Public policy in Belgium has traditionally appeared to favour the small, independent retailer over the larger retailer. Between 1937 and 1961 the so-called Padlock Law effectively prohibited any modernization of Belgian retailing by preventing the opening of large stores. The period after 1961 (when the Padlock Law was no longer in force) saw a substantial increase in the number of supermarkets and hypermarkets. However, this was not to last. 1975 saw the introduction of the Business Premises Act (often described as the second Padlock Law), which once again imposed restrictions on the development of large retail outlets, by enforcing a lengthy evaluation process for proposals to establish new, large stores or extend existing small stores. As a consequence, the development of hypermarkets was almost halted and while the number of supermarkets continued to grow, it was at a much slower rate.

Source: Franois and Leunis (1991)

---

coverage by using a distribution channel that has a wide market coverage rather than relying on limited low-cost television advertising.

These factors together will have a strong influence on the channel structure that is selected for a particular product. In many markets, distribution systems are well established and there may be limited scope to make substantial changes for well-established products, though this does not preclude innovation in distribution as a means for gaining a competitive advantage as the example of First Direct (Exhibit 13.1) showed.

Channel behaviour

Although we have indicated that organizations may not have unlimited scope in determining the structure of distribution for well-established products, this should not be taken to mean that distribution systems are unchangeable. On the contrary, systems of distribution are continually evolving and changing, and an important factor governing this process of change is the nature of the relationship between manufacturers and different intermediaries.

The various intermediaries in any marketing channel are basically dissimilar; the one thing that they have in common is the product that they handle and the desire to profit from that product. The success of any one member of the channel in terms of profitability ultimately depends upon the success of all members of the channel. By implication then, a strategy of cooperation at all levels would appear to be the most sensible route to achieve this goal. In practice, this frequently does not occur. When there are a large number of channel members (because of length or width) then the opportunity to 'free-ride' – i.e. take a more individualistic strategy – increases. The result is channel conflict. This may be of two types.

Vertical conflict
This occurs between intermediaries at different levels in the distribution channel or between the manufacturer and an intermediary. The basis of such conflict will ultimately be profitability, so it may originate in pricing/mark-up decisions. Equally, conflict could relate to broader marketing issues, such as the extent to which particular products are promoted, willingness to hold stocks and the amount of shelf space allocated. A certain degree of conflict/competition may be regarded as desirable in that it will potentially keep market prices down and may produce innovation in distribution. Beyond a certain level, however, vertical conflict can seriously affect the performance of products and the manufacturers overall performance.

Horizontal conflict
This occurs between different intermediaries at the same level in the channel who are effectively competing for sales and thus profit Generally, horizontal conflict is much less of a cause for concern than vertical conflict because it is less likely to be damaging, From the manufacturer's point of view, it is also much less likely to erode profit margins because the intermediaries are competing with each other and not with the manufacturer. In the longer term, however, horizontal conflict can be a cause for concern because it may result in radical changes in the channel structure. In particular it may result in one intermediary taking on a particularly powerful position which could be undesirable from the manufacturer's point of view.

From the perspective of the manufacturer, the effectiveness and efficiency of the distribution channel can be damaged by the presence of particularly vertical, but also horizontal conflict. This conflict may lead to potentially damaging price wars or refusals to stock, adequately display or promote products. The problem is often perceived to arise because channel members are independent or quasi-independent and have conflicting objectives. That is to say, the manufacturer has no real control over the way in which products are distributed. By contrast, if there were a single organization dealing with the various aspects of distribution, then that organization could, in principle, ensure a high degree of cooperation at the various stages of distribution. The organization that integrates forward into the distribution of its products will retain a high degree of control over the way in which those products are presented to consumers; it will retain internally all the profits associated with distribution, but in doing so, it will necessarily incur higher costs. Increasingly this issue of the trade-off between costs and control is becoming a central factor in the choice of distribution channels for many organizations.

Indeed, recent trends have seen many organizations internalizing a variety of elements of distribution, in spite of the economic benefits from using separate channels. Firms have weighed benefits from specialization against risks of conflict and in many cases have opted for a variety of new forms of distribution. These new systems have been chosen with the specific objective of increasing the degree of coordination in distribution and perhaps more importantly increasing control over distribution channels. These new systems are collectively referred to under the heading of vertical marketing systems (VMS). There are a number of basic forms that a vertical marketing system may take:

Corporate VMS
All aspects of the distribution channel are internalized under the ownership and control of a single firm, typically a manufacturer. The manufacturer assumes all the costs and reaps all the profits associated with distribution. An possible example of a corporate VMS would be Boots, who manufacture, wholesale and retail a vast range of products.

Contractual VMS
Rather than formally internalizing the distribution system, the manufacturer forms strong contractual relationships with members of the distribution channel. These contractual arrangements will specify, in varying degrees of detail, the responsibilities of both parties, how

products will be distributed, the financial arrangements associated with distribution and so on. The channel members retain a degree of nominal independence from the manufacturer, so they continue to run their own businesses, but with a clearly defined system for the distribution of a particular product. The contractual VMS includes a variety of franchising and licensing arrangement such as Body Shop, most car dealerships, McDonald's and Pizzaland.

Administered VMS

This is the most informal type of VMS and it operates on the basis of the market power of an individual channel member. That channel member can use its strong position to enforce or ensure strong cooperation between other channel members. The administered VMS gives the weakest form of control but assists in reducing the degree of channel conflict and is a relatively low cost option. A possible example of this type of arrangement would be Marks and Spencers who use their market power and their strength in retailing to build strong working relationships with the manufacturers who supply them.

Some form of vertical relationship between channel members is increasingly common in distribution arrangements. The key issue determining the strength and closeness of these arrangements is the way in which the parties concerned see the trade-off between costs and control. If the loss of control is seen as potentially very damaging, then we might expect a manufacturer to be willing to bear higher costs and seek a more formal structured arrangement. By contrast, if the loss of control is seen as less important, then the manufacturer will be willing to accept a looser and less formal arrangement.

Conclusions

Distribution is used to describe the range of activities which ensures that a product or service is made available to the market in the right quantities, at the right time and in the right place. Distribution creates the opportunity for the consumer finally to make the purchase. From a marketing perspective, distribution decisions typically fall under two headings – those concerned with the physical movement of the product from producer to consumer and those concerned with issues relating to the management of the relationship between different members of the distribution system.

Although there are good economic reasons for using distribution channels composed of a number of different independent intermediaries, an increasing volume of goods and services are distributed through channels that are vertically integrated to some degree. This move towards a greater degree of integration in distribution is based on a growing awareness of the potential benefits to the manufacturer (and in some cases the retailer) of maintaining a degree of control over the ways in which products are made available to the consumer.

CASE STUDY

Distribution

J. C. Bamford Excavators

The Staffordshire-based firm of J. C. Bamford (JCB) is the United Kingdom's largest manufacturer and exporter of earth-moving and materials-handling equipment. It is also a market leader in more than fifty countries worldwide. JCB was traditionally best known for its bright yellow excavators which gave it a strong market position in relation to the construction industry.

When its second leading product, the Loader, was launched, the company experienced some initial consumer resistance. JCB sold a large volume of its output through plant-hire firms and when these firms selected equipment to carry, they tended to look primarily for the best price. They viewed the Loader as rather elaborate and expensive. It was indeed more expensive and more complex than its immediate competitor, the forklift truck, but it was considerably more flexible and versatile. The problem that JCB faced was how to overcome resistance from plant-hire firms. The solution was to approach customers directly. By convincing equipment-hire customers of the benefits of the Loader they were able to encourage plant-hire firms to increase their purchases. The success of this strategy was clear in the jump in sales from 187 machines in 1987 to 2,513 in 1988.

The practice of approaching customers directly was not a new strategy for JCB. Every year it invites thousands of customers to its plant to meet sales and service people and to see how the machines are put together. This is a very deliberate move to encourage sales and create good customer relations. It is, of course, also a very successful one. Indeed much of JCB's success can be attributed to their clear understanding of customer needs and their knowledge of the industry. They recognize that their products are performing a particular function for the customer and that it is important that the products do as much as possible, as well as possible and as quickly as possible. In securing sales, the demonstration of products is an important part of the company's selling technique. If somebody is paying tens of thousands of pounds for a machine it is important that they are satisfied that it will do the job they require of it.

The main competitors facing JCB include the US company Caterpillar, which is nine times the size of the Staffordshire company, and Komatsu, a Japanese company that is six times larger than JCB. Both have the benefits of a much larger home market and the potential to generate economies of scale. Nevertheless JCB competes successfully against these larger firms. Its engineers regularly monitor developments in the industry and keep a close watch on the competition. They will even go so far as to hire competitor's machines and carry out comprehensive checks on these.

An important element in JCB's marketing strategy is its unique distribution system. JCB is unusual in that it sells through dealers on a franchise basis. Their competitors typically prefer to handle their own distribution arrangements rather than employ specialist distributors. The franchise system used by JCB has enabled them to develop the most widespread distribution network of any construction and agricultural manufacturer in the United Kingdom. It has also enabled the firm to maintain a clear corporate identity. All sales staff and mechanics and parts people are trained at JCB's own factory. They are taught the service standards and instilled with a strong sense of corporate identity, though they effectively continue to run their own business through the franchise arrangement.

Questions

1. Why is JCB able to compete effectively against companies much larger than itself?
2. What are the advantages of distribution through a franchise system compared with distribution direct to buyers? To what extent does JCB's unique distribution system provide it with a competitive advantage?

14 Implementing, monitoring and controlling marketing

Introduction

Although the processes for developing marketing strategies and formulating a marketing mix will vary across organizations, the objective of these procedures is essentially the same. The marketing strategy and the marketing mix are concerned with creating a competitive advantage for the organization in relation to its chosen markets, thus enabling that organization to achieve its specified objectives. Specifically, the marketing strategy aims to identify the appropriate position for products in the relevant target markets, while the marketing mix identifies how the various controllable marketing variables should be used to create that position. However, unless the designated marketing activities can be implemented effectively, monitored regularly and controlled where necessary, they will count for nothing. The process of implementation involves turning strategies into actions by deciding who does what, when and where. Monitoring compares the actual outcomes of these actions with specified targets in order to identify any deviations between what is happening and what was intended. As and when such deviations are identified, the control phase must identify the appropriate corrective action, whether in the form of alterations to methods of implementation, alterations to the marketing mix or alterations to the overall marketing strategy. This chapter reviews the key elements associated with effective implementation, monitoring and control of marketing strategies.

Implementing marketing plans

Implementation of marketing and other business activities is the basis of successful performance. The McKinsey consulting group suggest that successful performance in any area of business is dependent on seven elements – the seven Ss framework: strategy, structure, systems, skills, staff, style and shared values. The first three of these, strategy, structure and systems, provide the basic ingredients for successful performance, but without staff with the required skills and without a supportive corporate culture and style of management, this potential for success cannot be realized. Thus, the key to the effective implementation of any marketing strategy will lie with people and their interactions within the organization. Specifically, effective implementation depends on cooperation, coordination, communication and motivation at all levels within the organization. These activities in turn will require the creation or maintenance of an appropriate corporate culture and the operation of a successful internal marketing programme. This framework for implementing marketing strategies is represented diagrammatically in figure 14.1.

Two features of the organization set the context for effective implementation, namely corporate culture and internal marketing.

Corporate culture
Corporate culture is a term used to describe an informal value system which exists within an organization. It is reflected in the way in which decisions are made and communicated, the way in which management behaves, and what is expected of staff. The importance of corporate culture in relation to performance and business success has been stressed by Peters and Waterman (1982). A clear value system within an organization means

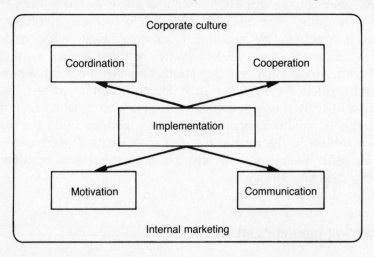

Figure 14.1 Requirements for effective implementation of marketing strategies

that staff at all levels are clearly aware of what they are trying to do, what is important and what is not. Where a strong and clearly recognized corporate culture exists, the processes of ensuring cooperation, coordinating activities and motivating staff are potentially much simpler because the staff themselves will already have a clear idea of what is expected from them and will be aware of the directions in which the organization is developing.

The beneficial impact of corporate culture on strategy implementation is based on the assumption that the strategy itself is consistent with the prevailing organizational culture. Strategies that conflict with corporate culture will almost always be difficult to implement. Thus, for example, the corporate culture at Procter & Gamble is heavily orientated towards quality. A marketing strategy based on a dilution of product quality might be difficult to implement because staff at all levels would find this aim inconsistent with the company's culture.

Internal marketing
Internal marketing deals with the way in which an organization manages the relationship between itself and its employees at all levels. Internal marketing can play an important role in creating and maintaining the organizations corporate culture and is essential if the organization is to ensure a marketing orientation amongst its employees. Jan Carlsson's successful turnaround of SAS (Scandinavian Airline System) in the early 1980s owed much to effective internal marketing. Carlsson recognized the importance of building a customer orientation in all staff to ensure a high level of customer satisfaction. This was achieved through an extensive staff training programme, backed by Carlsson's own commitment and support for a marketing orientation.

There are two basic dimensions to internal marketing. First, the organization will rely on internal marketing to ensure that it is offering the types of jobs and working conditions that will encourage competent and motivated staff to remain in post. Second, internal marketing is necessary to ensure that staff understand the product itself and believe in what the organization is trying to do. If an organization's own employees are not market oriented, if they do not support the overall corporate and marketing strategies, then the chances of successful plan implementation are minimal. Indeed, some authors (see, for example, Morgan, 1991) go so far as to argue that senior managers should view their strategies as products to be marketed to their employees.

Corporate culture and internal marketing create the atmosphere in which the activities required for successful implementation can be managed. Specifically, these activities are as follows:

Coordination

Co-ordinating the activities of those individuals involved in carrying out marketing activities is arguably the first stage in implementing any plan. This requires the identification of tasks to be performed and the allocation of these tasks to the relevant individuals. In addition to coordinating activities within the marketing function it is also necessary to coordinate between functions. Marketing managers need to coordinate with finance departments about resource availability, with engineering and manufacturing about quality and design, with personnel about training and staffing needs, and so on. Furthermore, since many companies will subcontract some of their business to outside agencies, there is also a need to ensure that good links are built and maintained with the relevant contacts. As exhibit 14.1 shows, the development of an organizational structure to encourage greater cooperation in product management has been an

---

Exhibit 14.1   Coordinating the marketing effort

Philips

Dutch electronics giant Philips has been forced to re-evaluate both strategies and methods of implementation in the face of strong Japanese competition. The company found itself losing market share in consumer electronics often because of a failure to get products to the market on time. The problem was, at least in part, attributed to a system of dual management, in which responsibility for each product division was split between a commercial and a technical manager. Differing goals and poor coordination between the two sides often led to an undue emphasis on technical aspects of the product at the expense of timely product launches. Replacing this structure with an interdisciplinary team approach has enabled Philips to adopt a much more proactive stance in the brown goods market.

Source: Whealan (1989).

important component in the development of a stronger marketing orientation at Philips.

Thus, coordination effectively requires the specification of an action plan to identify who does what, when and where, along with an appropriate reporting structure and the identification of who will be responsible for which activities. The action plan must be precise and define exactly what task is to be undertaken, by whom and what the required completion date is. Defining such a timetable and motivating individuals to reach the specified targets is crucial to effective implementation, particularly given the sequential nature of many marketing tasks. Thus, for example, if the individuals responsible for marketing research are not given clear information about completion dates, their report could arrive several weeks later than had been expected by the marketing department. This could, in turn, delay a whole series of subsequent activities such as packaging design, promotional planning, pricing and distribution arrangements. The consequence of these delays could be that the product is late in reaching the market, sales may be lost to the competition and the marketing plan may fail to achieve its specified targets.

Cooperation

No plan can be implemented effectively without the cooperation of staff within the organization. Coordination will assign tasks but the success of the plan as a whole will require the active support of all personnel within the organization. If staff do not believe in the mission and objectives of the organization and the product it is offering to its consumers, then they cannot be expected to market that product effectively. The role of internal marketing is of particular importance in this context, to ensure that a customer orientation prevails at all levels within the organization and that all staff share a commitment to achieving organizational goals.

Motivation

The effectiveness of coordinating and building cooperation will be limited if staff are not motivated. Obviously individuals have different needs and moivations with respect to the work that they do, and money may be only one dimension of individual motivation. To ensure that staff are motivated requires some understanding of their needs and expectations. Management must aim to design reward systems that reflect these needs and expectations. Thus, for example, many sales staff in the financial services sector are employed on the basis of commission only, or basic salary plus commission. The rationale for this is that *payment by results* will motivate people to sell. For the top performing sales staff, however, money alone is often insufficient. Consequently, many organizations have turned to incentive travel and other non-cash benefits as a motivator for their sales forces. The effectiveness of such methods derives not so much from the value of the prize itself, but from the fact that individuals who receive such rewards are being explicitly recognized as *top-performers* within the organization (Kiely, 1990).

In addition to ensuring that reward systems are consistent with the needs and expectations of staff, it is also essential to ensure that they are consistent with organizational objectives. For example, reward systems that are based on the volume of sales achieved for a particular product will be inappropriate if the organization's objectives are profit oriented. It is equally important to recognize the potential trade-offs between short-term and long-term objectives. Reward systems that are built around short-term objectives can seriously hamper the organization's ability to reach its long-term goals.

Communication
Communication is essential if marketing activities are to be fully coordinated and if staff are to be aware of the nature of existing and planned reward systems. All staff within an organization must be aware of the organization's objectives and the means by which it plans to achieve these objectives. Communication with senior management is essential to ensure that marketing activities and objectives are consistent with organizational goals and to ensure that the senior management is aware of the nature and direction of marketing activities. It is equally important to ensure good communication flows between marketing and other functional activities since coordination and cooperation between these different business areas is essential if marketing strategies are to be implemented effectively.

Arguably, implementation is one of the most complex and difficult aspects of marketing and many marketing problems arise because of poor implementation. A poor marketing performance in relation to specified targets may be relatively easy to identify. Establishing the cause of poor performance may be more difficult but is of considerable importance if the appropriate corrective action is to be taken. Bonoma (1984) suggests that there may be three broad causes of poor performance: a poor strategy that is poorly implemented, a good strategy that is poorly implemented, and a poor strategy that is effectively implemented. The last of these three is probably the easiest of the three to identify, but the first two can be difficult to distinguish and the correct diagnosis is essential if the appropriate changes are to be made. When the source of poor performance is unclear, it is generally more sensible to examine implementation issues prior to considering more fundamental adjustments in strategy.

Monitoring and control

As was noted in chapter 2, along with implementation, the process of monitoring and controlling plans is an important aspect of strategic marketing. The impact of marketing activities on the target markets must be monitored on a regular basis to determine whether what was intended corresponds with what is actually happening. Any deviations of actual outcome from target outcomes can then be identified and the appropriate corrective action taken. Figure 14.2 gives a simple outline of the monitoring

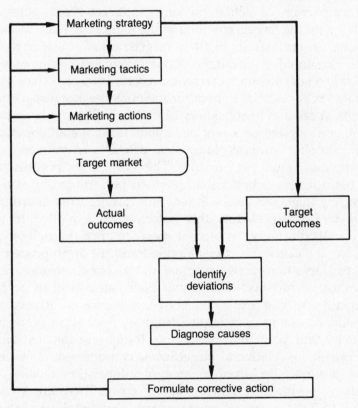

Figure 14.2 The monitoring and control process

and control process. The planning phase results in a marketing strategy and an associated set of tactics. Implementation turns these strategies and tactics into specific actions, which, through their impact on the target market, produce a set of outcomes. A comparison between actual outcomes and desired outcomes will indicate any deviations from plan. Once those deviations have been identified, the control phase requires that the cause of such deviations is diagnosed and the appropriate corrective action identified. Depending on the nature of any problems that exist, corrective action may require adjustments to the implementation processes or adjustments to marketing plans. Adjustments to marketing plans may simply imply changes to marketing tactics or may require more fundamental changes in the overall marketing strategy. The organization that experiences falling sales may need to make modifications to pricing policy if initial prices have been set at too high a level (tactical change) or it may need to look to new markets because of the loss of interest from existing markets (strategic change).

Monitoring will take a variety of forms. At the most basic level it will entail a comparison of actual outcomes (market share, sales volume, profits, etc.) with the targets specified in the marketing plan. Monitoring is not restricted to an analysis of these targets; other subsidiary objectives need to be monitored. For example, an advertising campaign may identify a particular level of consumer awareness as one of its objectives. Following the campaign it is essential to monitor the outcome, because a knowledge of problems in relation to subsidiary objectives will provide an important input to diagnosing the causes of deviations from overall objectives.

The monitoring process identifies deviations between planned performance and actual performance. This may occur in either direction. If actual performance is better than planned performance, it is important that marketing managers establish why this has occurred in order that the conditions which have led to this outcome are exploited to their full potential. Alternatively, if actual performance is below planned performance, the causes must be identified and the appropriate corrective action taken. Deviations between actual and planned performance may be relatively easy to identify; establishing their cause is likely to be rather more difficult. As was explained above, a failure to achieve specified targets could be due to poor implementation, poor strategy, or to both a poor strategy and poor implementation. Initially, a detailed analysis of actual performance relative to target levels can offer some guidelines. In particular, it would be usual to analyse information relating to sales, market share, profitability and marketing costs. There are a number of approaches that the organization can adopt in undertaking such analysis:

Sales analysis

Sales analysis involves using the organization's own sales data to identify possible problems. Two particular dimensions of sales performance can be analysed:

Sales variance

The total value of sales depends on the number of units sold and the price at which they were sold. Thus, deviations from target sales figures may be due to either lower volume or lower prices. A sales variance analysis can help identify the source of deviations and thus guide the diagnosis procedure. Consider for example a situation in which the marketing plan anticipated total sales of £500,000, on the assumption that 2,000 units would be sold at an average price of £250. Actual sales are £408,000, representing 1,700 units at an average price of 240. Total sales variance is defined as the reduction in value as a percentage of target value. In this case, total sales variance is 18.4 per cent (£92,000 shortfall on a target of £500,000). This can be decomposed as shown in table 14.1. While this does not give a definitive explanation for the cause of poor sales performance, it does indicate that attention should be focused on the failure to meet volume targets rather that the failure to obtain the specified price.

Analysis of sales composition (sales mix)

The procedure involves breaking-down total sales according to any of a range of relevant criteria, including customer group/segment, geographical region, product characteristics, retail outlet and sales territory. The precise criteria used will, of course, be market specific. Thus, for example an FMCG manufacturer might analyses sales according to retail outlet, while a manufacturer of industrial components may undertake the analysis according to sales territory. As with the analysis of sales variance, the objective of this procedure is to identify the source of below target figures and specifically to establish whether a poor performance is occurring across all markets or whether it is specific to certain sectors. If a poor performance is in evidence across all markets, then it may be advisable to

Table 14.1 Sales variance

Due to price (£250 − £240) × 1,700	£17,000	18.5%
Due to volume (2,000 − 1,700) × £250	£75,000	91.5%
Total variance	£92,000	100%

look to broad macro-factors for an explanation. By contrast, if low sales are specific to one particular area, then this should be the focus of attention in trying to explain poor performance.

Market share analysis

Poor sales performance may be the consequence of specific failings in the organization's marketing activities, but equally could be the result of a decline in the overall market. An analysis of market share relative to the competition will be the source of additional useful information. The results of this analysis should, however, be interpreted with some care. Other organizations may experience declines in market share as a result of a deliberate policy of increasing profitability and hence the comparison may not be valid. Equally, a decline in market share may simply reflect an increase in competition as a result of new entrants rather than any general weaknesses in the market *per se*.

Profitability analysis

Profitability analysis is concerned with identifying the contribution of different products, sales outlets and customer groups to the organization's overall profit. This process entails breaking up sales into the components of interests and comparing costs and revenues to identify the gross contribution of each component to overall profit. An analysis of this nature can be difficult, particularly given to complexities of assigning costs across different products or outlets. Nevertheless, the importance of this type of analysis should not be understated and indeed many organizations are developing computer-based systems specifically to provide direct estimates of product or outlet profitability. Once again the purpose of this type of analysis is to identify whether specific problem areas exist or whether poor performance is a general feature of the marketing programme as a whole.

Marketing expense analysis

A crude indicator of profitability can be obtained through the monitoring of marketing expenses relative to sales. Although there are no hard and fast rules to indicate what proportion of sales should be accounted for by marketing expenses, the budgeting stage of the marketing plan will indicate what projected expenditure is in relation to target sales. If any aspects of marketing expenditure are out of line, this may indicate a particular problem. Monitoring marketing expenses may be of particular significance in an organization that is heavily dependent on personal selling because such expenses may be more difficult to control.

Customer surveys

Many organizations operate a system of regular market research to monitor customer attitudes to their products and to their advertising, distribution and pricing policies. There are also a number of commercial sources of information on consumption patterns. These systems can provide data on market share as well as offering profiles (by age, gender, class, etc.) of the buyers of particular products or brands. Organizations can use such profiles to identify whether or not it is generating acceptable levels of sales across its range of target markets. Additionally, there are a variety of commercial systems for monitoring the effectiveness of advertising, primarily in relation to levels of recall of the organization or its brand.

Information of this nature should help organizations to identify more precisely the areas in which they are underperforming; it is less suited to explaining why this underperformance has occurred. However, if a particular area of underperformance can be identified, it may be possible to undertake marketing research specifically to examine the causes of that underperformance.

Marketing audit

The marketing audit, as described in chapter 3, represents a comprehensive overview of an organization's marketing activities. This audit can provide valuable input to the monitoring and control process by identifying problem areas that may exist within the organization as well as gathering information on staff views as to the causes of external problems facing the organization.

None of the techniques described above will explain why actual performance is below target performance; what they can do is provide guidance as to the areas that must be investigated specifically in order to diagnose organizational problems.

Once problems have been diagnosed, corrective action must be taken. A key to dealing effectively with poor performance is to ensure that action is taken quickly. This does not mean that the causes of poor performance should not be analysed; what it does mean is that analysis should not be allowed to dominate and delay corrective action. As explained in the introduction, even when problems have been diagnosed it may be difficult to determine whether the true cause of the problem lies with the implementation procedures, with the strategy itself or with both. Given the frequency of implementation problems, it is often advisable to examine implementation first before considering whether tactics or overall strategy should be modified.

Conclusions

Implementation, monitoring and control are essential to the success of any marketing strategy. The implementation phase of planning entails turning marketing recommendations into marketing actions. Effective implementation depends on the existence of an appropriate corporate culture, the development of internal marketing and the design of appropriate systems to ensure coordination, cooperation, communication and motivation. Once marketing activities have been implemented, they must be monitored on a regular basis to ensure that any deviation between planned and actual performance is identified and diagnosed as quickly as possible, in order that the appropriate corrective action can be taken.

Self-test questions

1. What are the roles of corporate culture and internal marketing in guiding the implementation of marketing strategies?
2. How can methods of monitoring actual and target performance be used to aid in the diagnosis of marketing problems?

Further reading

There is a wide range of good marketing textbooks that will deal with many of the topics covered in this book in greater detail. The following are particularly recommended.

Baker, M. 1987: *The Marketing Book*. Oxford: Heinemann.

Boyd, H. W. and Walker, O. C. 1990: *Marketing Management: a strategic approach*. Homewood, Ill.: Richard D. Irwin.

Cowell, D. 1984: *The Marketing of Services*. Oxford: Heinemann.

Dibb, S., Simkin, L., Pride, W. M. and Ferrell, O. C. 1991: *Marketing: concepts and strategies*. Boston, Mass.: Houghton Mifflin.

Engel, J. F., Blackwell, R. D. and Minniard, P. W. 1990: *Consumer Buying Behaviour*. Orlando, Fla.: The Dryden Press.

Ford, D. (ed.) 1990: *Understanding Business Markets*. London: Academic Press.

Hibbert, E. P. 1989: *Marketing Strategy in International Business*. London: McGraw-Hill.

Kotler, P. 1991: *Marketing Management: analysis, planning, implementation and control*, 7th edn. Englewood Cliffs, NJ: Prentice Hall.

MacDonald, M. 1989: *Marketing Plans: how to prepare them, how to use them*. Oxford: Heinemann.

Schnaars, S. 1991: *Marketing Strategy: a customer driven approach*. New York: Free Press.

In addition to these books, there is much useful information in a variety of trade publications including *Marketing* and *Marketing Week*. Academic journals such as *Journal of Marketing Management* and *European Journal of Marketing* are also useful sources of information on the latest developments in marketing thinking.

References

Advertising Association 1992a: *The Regional Marketing Pocket Book*. Henley: The Advertising Association in conjunction with NTC Publications.

Advertising Association 1992b: *The Lifestyle Pocket Book*. Henley: The Advertising Association in conjunction with NTC Publications.

Advertising Association 1992c: *The Media Pocket Book*. Henley: The Advertising Association in conjunction with NTC Publications.

Advertising Association 1992d: *The Marketing Pocket Book*. Henley: The Advertising Association in conjunction with NTC Publications.

Advertising Association 1992e: *The European Marketing Pocket Book*. Henley: The Advertising Association in conjunction with NTC Publications.

Advertising Association 1992f: *Advertising Statistics Yearbook*. Henley: The Advertising Association in conjunction with NTC Publications.

Baker, M. 1987: *The Marketing Book*. Oxford: Heinemann.

Borden, N. 1965: The concept of the marketing mix. In G. Schwartz (ed.), *Science in Marketing*. New York: John Wiley.

Boulding, C. 1992: Rapid fit answer to Ford's prayers. *Marketing Week*, 28 February, p. 17.

Boyd, H. W. and Walker, O. C. 1990: *Marketing Management: a strategic approach*. Homewood, Ill.: Richard D. Irwin.

Chisnall, P. M. 1985: *Strategic Industrial Marketing*. London: Prentice Hall.

Chisnall, P. M. 1991: *The Essence of Marketing Research*. New York: Prentice Hall.

Cook, M. 1991: The DIY market: a case study in competition. *Business Studies*, March, pp. 31–5.

Corstjens, M. 1991: *Marketing Strategy in the Pharmaceutical Industry*. London: Chapman and Hall.

Cowell, D. 1984: *The Marketing of Services*. Oxford: Heinemann.

CSO 1990: *Guide to Official Statistics*. London: HMSO.

De Jonquières, Guy 1992: From bare shelves to blue jeans. *Financial Times*, 10 June, p. 18.

Dhalla, N. K. and Yuspeh, S. 1976: Forget the product life cycle concept. *Harvard Business Review*, January–February, pp. 102–12.

Dobson, Paul and Starkey, Ken 1993: *The Strategic Management Blueprint:* Oxford: Basil Blackwell.

Engel, J. F., Blackwell, R. D. and Minniard, P. W. 1990: *Consumer Buying Behaviour.* Orlando, Fla.: The Dryden Press.

Fern, E. F. and Brown, J. R. 1984: The industrial/consumer marketing dichotomy: a case of insufficient justification. *Journal of Marketing,* 48 (Spring), 68–77.

Ford, D. (ed.) 1990: *Understanding Business Markets.* London: Academic Press.

Foxall, G. R. 1987: Consumer behaviour. In Baker (1987).

Franois, P. and Leunis, J. 1991: Public policy and the establishment of large stores in Belgium. *International Review of Retail Distribution and Consumer Research,* 1(4), 469–86.

Gow, D. 1992: Yoghurt firm creates sour green legacy. *Guardian,* 6 June, p. 37.

Greenley, G. E. 1982: An overview of marketing planning in UK manufacturing companies. *European Journal of Marketing,* 16(7), 3–16.

Greenley, G. E. 1986: *The Strategic and Operational Planning of Marketing.* London: McGraw-Hill.

Greenely, G. E. 1989: An understanding of marketing strategy. *European Journal of Marketing,* 23(8), 45–58.

Haire, M. 1950: Projective techniques in marketing research. *Journal of Marketing,* April, pp. 649–56.

Haley, R. J. 1968: Benefit segmentation: a decision oriented research tool. *Journal of Marketing,* July, pp. 30–5.

Hall, N. 1992: University challenge. *Marketing Week,* 7 February, pp. 26–9.

Hamel, G. and Prahalad C. K. 1991: Corporate imagination and expeditionary marketing. *Harvard Business Review,* July–August, pp. 81–92.

Hill, J. S. and Still, S. R. 1984: Adapting products to LDC tastes. *Harvard Business Review,* March–April.

Jones, H. 1992: Suncares call for a cover up. *Marketing Week,* 15 May, p. 15.

Kiely, J. 1990: Direct distribution. In C. T. Ennew, T. Watkins and M. Wright (eds), *Marketing Financial Services.* Oxford: Heinemann.

Kotler, P. 1973: The major tasks of marketing management. *Journal of Marketing,* October, pp. 42–9.

Kotler, P. 1991: *Marketing Management: analysis, planning, implementation and control,* 7th edn. Englewood Cliffs, NJ.: Prentice Hall.

Levitt, T. 1961: Marketing myopia. *Harvard Business Review,* July–August.

MacDonald, M. 1989: *Marketing Plans: how to prepare them, how to use them.* Oxford: Heinemann.

McMurdo, L. 1992: Every dog will have its day. *Marketing Week,* 10 April, p. 17.

Marketing 1987: Sloane bank. *Marketing,* 29 October, pp. 43–4.

Marketing 1992: Thunderbirds to MD Foods rescue. *Marketing,* 28 May, p. 6.

Marketing Week 1992a: Oranjeboom takes on premiums. *Marketing Week,* 28 February, p. 8.

Marketing Week 1992b: Durex relaunches range and targets women. *Marketing Week,* 20 March, p. 9.

Marketing Week 1992c: Mencap to reposition with harder approach. *Marketing Week*, 13 March, p. 6.

Marketing Week 1992d: Harp lager to go downmarket. *Marketing Week*, 12 June, p. 4.

Marketing Week 1992e: Mars calls in EC as Walls freezes it out. *Marketing Week*, 12 June, p. 4.

Martin, M. 1992: Bishops debate the big question. *Marketing Week*, 20 March, pp. 15–16.

Massingham, L. and Lancaster, G. 1990: *Mini Cases in Marketing*. Oxford: Heinemann.

Mazur, L. 1992: Silent satisfaction. *Marketing Business*, December–January, pp. 24–7.

Meller, P. 1992: Allied: thou shalt have fun. *Marketing*, 27 February, p. 2.

Morelli, R. 1991: Rolling out the red carpet. *Marketing Week*, 26 July, pp. 20–1.

Moutinho, L. and Evans, M. 1992: *Applied Market Research*. Wokingham: Addison Wesley.

Murphy, J. M. 1987: Developing new brand names. In J. M. Murphy (ed.), *Branding: a key marketing tool*. Basingstoke: Macmillan.

Naert, P. 1990: *Strategic Marketing*. Brussels: Video Management.

Norkett, P. 1986: *Guide to Company Information in Great Britain*. Harlow: Longman.

Palmer, A. and Worthington, I. 1992: *The Business and Marketing Environment*. London: McGraw-Hill.

Parasuraman, A. 1991: *Marketing Research*. Reading, Mass.: Addison Wesley.

Parasuraman, A., Zeithaml, V. A. and Berry, L. L. 1985: A conceptual model of service quality and its implications for future research. *Journal of Marketing*, 49(4), 41–50.

Peters, T. J. and Waterman, R. H. 1982: *In Search of Excellence: lessons from America's best run companies*. New York: Harper Row.

Porter, M. 1980: *Competitive Strategy: techniques for analysing industries and competitors*. New York: Free Press.

Porter, M. 1985: *Competitive Advantage: creating and sustaining superior performance* New York: Free Press.

Reese, J. 1992: United States Surgical: getting hot ideas from customers. *Fortune International*, 18 May, pp. 18–19.

Roach, C. 1989: Segmentation of the small business market on the basis of banking requirements. *International Journal of Bank Marketing*, 7(2), 10–16.

Schnaars, S. 1991: *Marketing Strategy: a customer driven approach*. New York: Free Press.

Schypek, J. 1992: Germany on trial over green packaging. *Marketing Week*, 2 July, pp. 14–16.

Shiner, D. V. 1988: Marketing's role in strategic and tactical planning. *European Journal of Marketing*, 22(5), 22–31.

Skelly von Brachel, J. 1992: A high stakes bet that paid off. *Fortune International*, 15 June, pp. 85–6.

Slaughter, J. 1992: Banking at your fingertips. *Observer*, 12 July, p. 33.

Slingsby, H. 1992a: Time to stimulate the feel good factor. *Marketing Week*, 3 April, p. 14.

Slingsby, H. 1992b: Superdrug kicks up a fine stink. *Marketing Week*, 2 May, pp. 15–16.

Tellis, G. J. 1986: Beyond the many faces of price: an integration of pricing strategies. *Journal of Marketing*, 50, 146–60.

Thwaites, D. 1991: Forces at work: the market for personal financial services. *International Journal of Bank Marketing*, 9(6), 30–6.

Watkins, T. 1986: *The Economics of the Brand*. London: McGraw-Hill.

Whelan, S. 1989: The beast bites back. *Marketing Week*, 13 July, pp. 26–7.

Willigan, G. E. 1992: High performance marketing: an interview with Nike's Phil King. *Harvard Business Review*, July–August, pp. 90–101.

Wind, Y. 1978: Issues and advances in segmentation research. *Journal of Marketing Research*, vol. 15, August, pp. 317–37.

Woo, C. Y. and Cooper, A. 1982: The surprising case for low market share. *Harvard Business Review*, November–December, pp. 106–13.

Worcester, R. and Downham, J. 1986: *Consumer Market Research Handbook*. London: McGraw-Hill.

Index